STEPHEN HAGAN is a descendant of the Kullilli people of south-west Queensland. Born in 1959, his early years were spent living in a fringe camp on the outskirts of Cunnamulla. When he was seven, his family moved into a brand new house in town; a defining point in his young life as he became conscious of the huge socio-economic gap between Aboriginal people and the wider community.

Stephen Hagan's achievements in high school saw him attend boarding school in Brisbane where he stood proud as one of only a few Aboriginal students. In 1979, he took up teacher training but disillusioned with being required to teach racist government-approved texts, Hagan made a career move. In between a posting overseas as a diplomatic attaché and business ventures, he worked as a bureaucrat in education and Aboriginal affairs with state and federal institutions in the ACT and Queensland.

In 1996, he joined the State Tripartite Forum (STF), an Indigenous advisory group to Queensland's Minister for Health that went on to form an alliance with the opposition Coalition parties. It was an alliance that was to change the course of government in Queensland and have dire personal consequences.

In recent years, Stephen Hagan has become known as a commentator on race relations and for his relentless legal battle to remove the word 'Nigger' from a sign at a sportsground in the Queensland town of Toowoomba.

He is married with two children and is currently an academic at the University of Southern Queensland, where he is also studying for his PhD.

the N word

one man's stand

STEPHEN HAGAN

MAGABALA BOOKS

First published in 2005 by Magabala Books Aboriginal Corporation, Broome, Western Australia
Website: www.magabala.com   Email: orders@magabala.com

Magabala Books receives financial assistance from the Commonwealth Government through the Australia Council, its arts funding and advisory body, and Aboriginal and Torres Strait Islander Services. The State of Western Australia has made an investment in this project through ArtsWA in association with Lotterywest.

The views expressed in this publication are those of the author and not necessarily those of Magabala Books Aboriginal Corporation. The publisher has made every effort to contact copyright owners for permission to use material reproduced in this book. If your material has been used inadvertently without permission, please contact the publisher.

Copyright © Text Stephen Hagan; © Copyright for photographs and reproduced text belongs with the individual owners.

All rights reserved. Apart from any fair dealing for the purposes of private study, research, criticism or review, as permitted under the Copyright Act, no part of this publication may be reproduced by any process whatsoever without the written permission of the author, the illustrator and the publisher.

Designed by Jo Hunt
Printed by Griffin Press, South Australia

National Library of Australia
Cataloguing-in-Publication data
Hagan, Stephen, 1959- .
The N word.

ISBN 1 875641 98 X.

1. Hagan, Stephen, 1959- . 2. Civil rights workers - Australia - Biography. 3. Aboriginal Australians - Ethnic identity. 4. Aboriginal Australians - Legal status, laws, etc. 5. Race discrimination - Australia. 6. Racism in language. I. Title.

305.89915

*In memory of my mother Jean Hagan (Kooma tribe),
grandfather Albert Hagan (Kullilli tribe),
and my great-grandmother Trella (Kullilli matriarch).*

I search the star-filled sky for signs of life
hoping to catch a smile from my father's wife.
Oh how I miss her dear
but through the pain I feel her near.

*In memory of my mother, Jean, who lost a spirited fight
against a heart condition in December 2000.*

ACKNOWLEDGEMENTS

Special thanks to the Hagan family, principally my father Jim; the Mitchell family; Roger Robinson; Phyllis Marsh; Mary Appo; Jenny Foley; Peter Black; Dr Libby Connors; Ernst Willheim; and David Curtis who tragically died during the writing of this book.

Thanks to Jan Hutchinson and the staff of Magabala Books for their editorial guidance and encouragement.

Particular mention must be made of the invaluable texts I used in my research ... especially those by Hazel McKellar; Henry Reynolds; Dr David Horton; W. Ross Johnston; Janine Roberts; and Dawn May.

Finally this remarkable literary journey would not have been possible without the love, support and patience shown to me by my beautiful family ... Rhonda, Stephen Jnr and Jayde.

Contents

INTRODUCTION

THE HAGAN CLAN 5
1. Fringe Dwellers 7
2. Albert's Legacy 15
3. Ringer Jim and Kooma Jean 21
4. The Yumba 32
5. Uptowners 46
6. Jim's Ascent 59
7. Teenage Years 75

CAREER MOVES 85
8. Enlightenment 87
9. Bombay 21st 93
10. A Foreign Affair 100
11. Charlie's Spell 114

UNCHARTED WATERS 121
12. A Tropical Embrace 123
13. An Unhealthy Alliance 136
14. Political Deceit 148
15. Incarceration 161

A NEW DIRECTION 179
16. Moving South 181
17. Toowoomba's Response 192
18. Legal Foray 201
19. KKK 216
20. An Ernst Approach 233
21. Pinky's Cement Mixer 241
22. United Nations 248
23. Self Belief 261

CONCLUSION

the N word

Introduction

The game started upfront with two large packs of forwards trying to dominate each other. After the initial ten minutes' softening-up period was over, the nimble outside backs started to see more of the ball and were able to create a little bit of their magic out wide. When our team scored first, adjacent to the goal posts, the ground broadcaster's voice came clearly over the public-address system, 'That try scored at the "Nigger" Brown end of the oval takes the score to four points to nil with the kick to come.'

I looked at my wife Rhonda and she frowned in disbelief. In unison, we turned toward the apex of the wooden grandstand to our right and looked at the sign—E.S. 'Nigger' Brown Stand—which the announcer had referred to moments earlier. I glanced around at my relatives before casting a look at other spectators standing close by. There was no discernible reaction from any of them.

Within minutes the broadcaster made another announcement, 'Just a reminder to drinking patrons that the bar is now open in the "Nigger" Brown Stand. Also additional toilets can be located immediately under the "Nigger" Brown Stand.'

Since arriving in Toowoomba a couple of years earlier, Rhonda and I had become increasingly distressed by the word 'nigger' emblazoned on the grandstand's sign.

the N word

We had all been excited at seeing my nephews on the field but now, as on previous occasions, Rhonda and I were struggling to maintain our interest in the game. In hindsight, we should have gathered our young children, Stephen and Jayde, and left the ground. Instead we stayed till the end, feeling more and more frustrated as we endured further references to the 'Nigger' Brown Stand on the public-address sytem.

The game finally finished and our team ran off the ground as victors. Relieved, we grabbed our things and made our way to the car with the children, shaking our heads and wondering whether anyone had ever challenged any authorities about the sign.

In my younger days I had played representative rugby league and had always been an avid supporter but as we left the ground on that wintry June day in 1999, I realised the time had come to make a stand.

This family outing had not turned out as planned and instead it would prove to be a defining moment in our lives.

On 20 March 2002, the Australian Associated Press article published in the *Herald Sun* reported:

> A bid by an Aboriginal activist to remove the word "Nigger" from a football grandstand has been thrown out by the nation's highest court.
> High Court Justice Mary Gaudron said the word "Nigger" on the sign was no more offensive than the word "Pinky" on a cement mixer.
> "Let us assume for a moment that I'm "Pink"—and it's not an unreasonable assumption—and I'm offended by a sign that says "Pinky's Porkies", she told a Brisbane sitting of the High Court.

the N word

> Justice Gaudron rejected Canberra constitutional barrister Ernst Willheim's submission that there was a link between the sign on the grandstand with the word "Nigger" on it and racism.
> The case was brought to court by Stephen Hagan, an ATSIC regional councillor from Toowoomba, west of Brisbane …

I stopped reading for a few seconds to catch my breath, not quite sure what to expect next.

> Outside the court today, Mr Hagan said he was disappointed the High Court had not granted him leave to appeal and would now take his case to the United Nations' Committee on Racial Discrimination (sic) in Geneva.
> "Now it's been formalised that you can have a public sign with the word Nigger on it," he said.
> "Why are they (judges) talking about a pink truck when they are talking about the word Nigger.
> "I'm absolutely astounded that they don't see that Nigger is offensive."
> Costs were also awarded against Mr Hagan, who had no idea how he would have to pay for his legal forays.
> "It could be $100,000, it could be $200,000, it could be $20,000 … but I'm flat out paying my petrol bill back to Toowoomba, so I don't know how I'm going to pay $100,000."

Similar headlines, flashed over national newspapers, television and radio broadcasts, greeted me the day after the ruling. Going to the High Court of Australia had proved to be an unsuccessful attempt to dispose of what I believed to be the only sign bearing the word 'nigger' on any public sports grandstand in the world.

Friends and critics, both privately and publicly, asked why I proposed to take the case to the United Nations. Many said I should abide by the umpire's decision and let it rest. As I pondered these comments I too began to question my motives. What it was that made me want to fight against the odds when all around me were giving up?

the N word

After days of procrastinating as to my next move I recalled the words my father once said to me when I was growing up in Cunnamulla, 'I never called any white person sir or mister because no white person ever called my father sir or mister.' In those words I was at last able to make some sense of the stubborn streak that has been part and parcel of my life. Researching a little deeper into my past, I discovered that I'd inherited that wilfulness.

I was one of the third generation of Hagan men who'd been born on the wrong side of the tracks. The rise from poverty to respectability and distinction by the first two generations was impressive. Beside the achievements of my predecessors, my own journey may not rate. However, I believe my struggle was a journey they too would have undertaken had they been presented with similar circumstances.

That aside, I took on the authorities because I also sought to honour my promise to Rhonda to ensure the sign was removed. I had a vision of my children playing on the oval with children of other races, free in the knowledge that they would not have to confront a relic of a racist past.

The United Nations would be my last legal option. After successfully filing the application to the Committee on the Elimination of Racial Discrimination all I could do was wait. As I waited, I searched the past for answers.

1
The Hagan Clan

the N word

Fringe Dwellers

My home town, Cunnamulla, in south-west Queensland was typical of many rural towns emerging throughout Australia in the early part of the twentieth century. The township, built along the scenic shorelines of the Warrego River on the tribal land of the Kunja people, was also the place many other displaced tribal people decided to call home, including the Kullilli.

My father, his father and grandmother were fiercely proud of their traditional affiliation to the Kullilli tribal lands, 200 kilometres to the south-west of Cunnamulla. They believed their ancestors were formed from the land by the creation spirit (a greater being) at the dawn of time.

The totem of my father's tribe is the red kangaroo (boida) and the Kullilli believe that, watched over by the spirit being Kronkie, the boidas travel over the vast lands between the Wilson and Bulloo rivers. The township of Thargomindah is located at the heart of Kullilli land. In spring, a plethora of wildflowers brightens the arid landscape, a breathtaking sight from ground level and even more spectacular when seen from the air.

The land of the Kullilli was quite substantial—90,000 square kilometres across relatively new precincts of Queensland and New South Wales—and it was a parcel of land that created enormous interest. The Kullilli had spasmodic conflicts with other tribes but on the whole they managed to coexist with their neighbours—the Wankamurra to the west, the Boonthamurra to the north, the Mardjany to the east and the Kunja to the south. All this changed spectacularly with the steady stream of pastoralists into the area.

With the first piercing crack of the stockwhip, followed by the roar of stampeding cattle and the explosion of gunfire from men on horseback, the tranquillity was broken on the land of my forebears. The traditional, aeons-old lifestyle of the Kullilli would disappear soon after the arrival of these strange-looking men and their animals.

The history books heap praise on the early settlers around Cunnamulla, but fail to acknowledge the original owners. Journalist, Thos. J. McMahon, writing for the *Brisbane Courier* under the heading 'A Flourishing Pastoral Town', wrote on 5 January 1924:

> … Cunnamulla in 1883 had several stores, hotels, a church, a hall, a school and many houses. The town was prosperous, capital was flowing into the district for the formation of stations, and Cunnamulla was gradually acquiring much of the big trade that was done with the flourishing business centre of Bourke. Settlement was taking place regardless of dangers and difficulties. The blacks were more or less aggressive and conflicts with them were frequent. There were some serious trouble and one or two tragedies. To-day (sic) few blacks are seen.[1]

The Kullilli, like other tribes, continued to experience the breakdown of their culture that came with forced relocations. Massacres of Aboriginals often accompanied the massive push inland by settlers in search of farming land, with people being indiscriminately slaughtered. Dad's father told him stories of the massacres of hundreds of Kullilli people at Barulyah and Nocaboorara waterholes on Kullilli land.

When I was growing up Dad would often tell me that the European occupation of this country brought hurt and suffering

the N word

to the Aboriginal people. It meant the end of centuries of spiritual affiliation with the land, the trees, the rivers, animals and bird life.

Up until then, Aboriginal people lived in harmony with each other and the environment. Importance was placed on the virtues of a wholesome life and the need for people to embrace one another to ensure the communal spirit was maintained and no one was left wanting. Dad said the survival of his race was reliant on the community caring for and sharing with all its members. It was these essential values that enabled Aboriginal families to survive.

When Dad arrived from Bourke in 1932 with his family there was little evidence of local Kunja people living in Cunnamulla. Most Aboriginals in the town at that time had been displaced from other traditional lands. These new arrivals were forced by the rapid expansion of European settlement out of town onto fringe camps situated on the least desirable parcels of land.

Dad clearly remembers when his family was living on the banks of the Warrego River, about two kilometres upstream from Cunnamulla. He said displaced traditional owners occupied land on both sides of the river. His family lived with descendants of the Bulloo and Paroo rivers on the western side and families who were descendants from the Nebine River area set up camp on the eastern side. The Nebine River fringe dwellers' huts were located adjacent to the rubbish dump; the camp that was later established south of the town was next to the sewage treatment works and separated from the township by the cemetery.

Families on the eastern side of the Warrego had access to town water from a centrally located tap. Members of that community collected water in buckets for washing and household consumption. The families on the western side had to use the dirty river water that

the N word

was available during the good season. During the dry seasons, when the Warrego wasn't running, a well was dug in the riverbed and filled with water. When properly managed, the seepage from the river sand provided the camp with sufficient water, which was boiled over a campfire in large drums to kill harmful bacteria.

Dad's family's dwelling was a construction of kerosene tins and scraps of iron sheeting, gathered from the rubbish tip and fastened with wire onto a bush-timber frame. A hessian bag was used for a doorway and a skillion roof, fashioned out of branches from gum trees tied onto a timber frame, provided shade. Toilet facilities consisted of a hole in the ground with a makeshift cover and seat. Many families used the same toilet, each contributing to the supply of newspapers and magazines that were used as toilet tissues. In emergencies, if the toilet was occupied, there were always plenty of large trees or shrubs close by.

The camping area was located on black-soil country. When the country was dry, any traffic, including horses and horse-driven sulkies, would create dust. It was source of annoyance but something the fringe dwellers learnt to live with. When it rained the area became muddy, too boggy for any form of transport. There was no water drainage or bitumen road to the camp from town and the conditions were generally atrocious. If the river flooded the whole camping area would be underwater.

Those were the years of the Great Depression when many men, black and white, carried their swags from station to station seeking any form of employment at all. Work was hard to find, and families on the western side of the river lived a semi-tribal lifestyle out of necessity, sharing resources with each other, as dictated by tribal and kinship ties.

Though only a child at the time, Dad still recalls the emus that were cooked in a large hole to feed the tribe. The men would prepare the meal by lighting a big fire and carefully placing large rocks in it to heat. They would then put the hot rocks into a deep hole, place the emus on the rocks and cover the hole with green branches from gum trees. Finally a canvas bag would be positioned on top, with soil to hold it firm. If the men had access to bush vegetables or vegetables from the town's general store they would insert them into the cavity of the animal's carcass to add flavour to the meal. Smaller animals such as wallabies and goannas would be thrown onto an open fire to cook.

Two-up, the popular gambling game, was a source of income for those lucky enough to get the ringkeeping. This involved picking up the pennies and calling the results. If there was a run of heads or tails the ringkeeper would get a sling, maybe a shilling or two bob. Dad would help his sister, May and mother, Jessie, with the cooking and serving of meals to their father who often camped at the gambling school all night just to get the ringkeeping.

After a large flood in 1941 wiped out Dad's family's camp on the northern side of town, the local council decided it was time to assist by relocating them across the river to the southern camp. Affectionately called the Yumba, this became the new home for the next two generations of Hagans.

In spite of the 'facilities' Dad believes that, prior to the connection of town water to the Yumba, the dead in Cunnamulla were cared for better than the Aborigines. At the cemetery, which bordered the Yumba, grieving white locals would fill their buckets from one of several taps and water the grass-plot graves of their dearly departed. A second trip to the tap would be necessary to fill the vases containing freshly picked flowers. When the caretaker wasn't on guard, the southern camp Aborigines, without a single tap among them, took advantage of the short walk to the cemetery and filled their kerosene tin containers.

At around the same time, several hundred kilometres west of the Yumba, the Kullilli people were experiencing difficulties of their own with the implementation of Queensland's draconian policy of the forceful relocation of blacks from the pastoral leases.

In the early 1940s a large group of women, children and old people were removed from Nockatunga Station by cattle truck. They were transported the 300 kilometres back to Cunnamulla and taken by goods train to Woorabinda Mission via Rockhampton, over 1500 kilometres north-east of their homeland

The government officials' planning was thorough. They arrived at the Kullilli camp when all the fit, able-bodied men were over fifty kilometres away working cattle in distant parts of the vast Nockatunga property. Years passed before many received word of their families.

The removal of Kullilli people from Nockatunga Station was part of the protectionism approach adopted by the Labor government of the day—ostensibly for their own benefit and safety. In 1939, E.M. Hanlon, the Secretary for Health and Home Affairs, when speaking of the Queensland *Aboriginal Protection and Restriction of the Sale of Opium Bill* had said:

> By this Bill we aim at not only the protection from abuse of the mainland aboriginal but also of the preservation of the remnant of the race. We have realised that it is no good whatever to treat the aboriginal as a kind of museum piece, or, in the way that one writer referred to, as "easing the bumps along the road to the cemetery", but

to endeavour to make him earn his own livelihood and recover a little bit of pride of race and confidence.[2]

There is disturbing irony in this. The Kullilli women, children and elders were in safe hands living with their tribe—and had been for countless generations.

Back on the banks of the Warrego River, before the Second World War, some of the Aboriginal families in the camp at the top end of town decided to leave and pursue employment opportunities in Charleville, two hundred kilometres north-east of Cunnamulla. In the meantime, the Paroo Shire Council knocked down their humpies in the top camp which prevented other families from moving in. Bulldozer tracks could be seen on the walls of new humpies on the Yumba after residents rummaged for building materials from the previous campsite after its demolition.

During the war years Dad's family also moved to Charleville to work on the aerodrome as part of the war effort. On arrival at the Murries' camp on the sandhill on the outskirts of town, Dad's father constructed a makeshift tin hut for his family. Dad went to school in Charleville for two years and to this day he has vivid memories of his teachers conducting air-raid drills with the children. They were required to go into underground bunkers in the event of an attack from the Japanese.

Many American soldiers were based at the aerodrome. The United States military took over the new public hospital building as their command post and there were a lot of black men (African–American) in military uniform about town. Dad reckons they looked very dapper and obviously some of the local women thought so as well. A number of children were fathered out of wedlock.

the N word

Dad's older brother Alf chose a career in the army and saw active duty abroad. He enlisted from Bourke in 1942 and was discharged as a Private in 1946.

From the Yumba, Dave Wharton was one of the first Murries to serve. Dave joined the Second Australian Imperial Forces (AIF) in 1941 and, on his return from active service, like many other Indigenous service men and women, felt the full impact of racism from white leaders in Cunnamulla. When his best mate Billy Ricketts, a non-Indigenous soldier whom he had fought beside in the army, died in a fire at the Kerr's Hotel in town, Dave was distraught. He pleaded unsuccessfully with the local Returned Servicemen's League (RSL) to be a pallbearer at the funeral.

After the war, when big stations were cut into smaller blocks as affordable land for returned war heroes, a large influx of Murries, forced from their traditional land, moved into the Yumba, rapidly increasing the population from about 120 to more than 300. The end of the war ironically signalled a call from pastoralists for more Aboriginal workers to join them on their big sheep and cattle properties. These men and women worked on the stations and around town in a range of jobs—station hands, shearers, boundary riders, drovers and domestic servants.

Meanwhile, families in Cunnamulla continued building their own dwellings from whatever materials they could scavenge from the rubbish tip or find discarded around the perimeter of town. Most of the homes were fashioned from sheets of galvanised iron or old water tanks. Doors were tied together with wire and usually a boughshed was attached to the house for eating or sleeping in during the hotter months. In short, there were no visible signs of progress around Cunnamulla.

the N word

Albert's Legacy

In July 1954, Dad's father, who weighed more than 120 kilograms, had a minor stroke that brought about an honest reassessment of his employment options. Grandfather Hagan, the breadwinner for his family, decided there was a demand for a camp-based grocery store and began the process of establishing one. Although proud of his idea, many Yumba residents doubted his ability to successfully run a general store in their camp.

Grandfather operated his business from home and sold basic everyday grocery items—mostly tinned goods and no food that required refrigeration. There was no electricity on the Yumba and the shire council had no intention of supplying any.

Nonetheless, the business proved to be a financial masterstroke for Grandfather, as the nearest store was several kilometres away in Cunnamulla and he had no competition in the camp.

The family home doubled as the store and it soon became the most frequented place in the Yumba. Commercial salesmen would visit the house to conduct their business. Although reluctant at first to visit the camp, the ongoing trade and the reward of hard currency meant the return trips for the businessmen became more tolerable. The only discomfort was when they drove beyond the cemetery. Here the bitumen road ceased and the potholes in the dirt road began.

the N word

My grandfather had only a basic primary school education but he was highly motivated and intelligent. He never drank liquor or smoked, although he did enjoy card games. His home was always the focal point where people gathered to play cards. Most likely that helped inspire him to establish the Yumba store.

No doubt there would have been an uproar at the town's Chamber of Commerce meeting when it was confirmed that a 'camp black' was successfully competing against the local shopkeepers. However, although they wouldn't have been happy that this niche market had been captured, the town's businessmen would have had to acknowledge Grandfather had independently created and sustained a thriving grocery store. Competition was alive and well in rural Queensland, but in this instance it was coming from an unexpected quarter!

Contrary to the initial doubt of the local Murries, Grandfather operated the store for almost two years until he had his second stroke and became too ill to continue. After he retired it became apparent that no one within the family or the community had the drive or desire to carry on the business. The store closed suddenly and the Yumba people resumed the long trek into town to spend their hard-earned dollars on everyday essential items.

Grandfather could speak several Aboriginal languages and often conversed with those traditional Murries who came with drovers from the northern parts of inland Australia. Some stopped off in town for a bit of recreation after months of isolation, while others visited fellow cattle drovers who hailed from the area.

Most of the visitors could speak English well, but if they felt more comfortable speaking their language they would call at Grandfather's house to chat with him.

the N word

Grandfather's name was Albert Joseph Hagan, his father being an Irishman named Joe Hagan, and his mother Trella, a full-blood Aboriginal woman of the Kullilli tribe. Although I know that Trella was one of the fortunate women who were spared the indignity of being a victim of the 'gin kidnapping' ('gin' being a derogatory term for Aboriginal woman) that occurred throughout the State, I don't know how my great-grandfather came into contact with her as she would have been living on her traditional land among her people.

Despite years of research into Joe Hagan's origins, my family is still no closer to solving the mystery of this adventurous Irishman or of how the two met. Whatever the circumstances, the government at that time frowned on mixed relationships and half-caste children were deemed by officials to have little hope of reaching adulthood.

Albert was born on 25 July 1895 at Yalpunga Tank, a remote community in northern New South Wales, close to the Queensland border near Wompah Gate. He had two sisters, Jean and Elizabeth. The family lived on his mother's land which extended from Mt Margaret Station in the north to Bulloo Downs Station in the south. Nockatunga Station occupied the western parameter and Ardoch Station came within the eastern boundary.

At this time many Europeans treated domestic animals and stock better than they did Aboriginal people. Trella's people did what they could to avoid direct conflict with the settlers and went about their lives as quietly as possible. She managed, through necessity, to assimilate into the new community—a mixture of traditional owners living on the fringe of town alongside farmers, businessmen and government officials.

Hearing stories of massacres would have made the task of providing for her young family extremely difficult. But Trella was, it seems, a resourceful and innovative person. She learnt the ways of the white people, yet her survival skills allowed her to maintain a semi-nomadic lifestyle in the camp.

My grandfather attended the Yalpunga State School and at the age of twelve, started work on Bulloo Downs Station, which covered 405 square kilometres and at its peak ran over 50,000 head of cattle. When work on Bulloo Downs eased up, Albert travelled north to Nockatunga Station. Nockatunga covered over 243 square kilometres and carried a similar number of cattle as Bulloo Downs.

Despite knowing of the atrocities committed against the Kullilli, Albert went about his work without too much complaint. He travelled throughout the cattle country and even ventured into sheep country where he worked on Ardoch Station on the Bulloo River, between the townships of Toompine and Quilpie.

Albert was a determined and adventurous young man, resourceful and capable as well. Life in the far south-western corner of the State would have been extremely taxing, with the hot dry winds forcing the average summer temperature well into the high forties while the winters produced bitterly cold, sub-zero temperatures.

Aboriginal stockmen worked hard, from dawn to dusk, for little more than rations of tobacco, tea and bully beef, although they would occasionally be provided with some pay, jeans and riding boots if the pastoralist was feeling generous at Christmas time. The stockmen were viewed as being inferior and were required to set up camp as far away from the homestead as possible. At meal times they'd often get the worst cuts of meat.

Non-Aboriginal stockmen earned considerably more for doing the same work. And to make matters worse, what little income the Aboriginal stockmen received was not entirely their own. Under Queensland's *Aboriginal Protection and Restriction of the Sale of Opium Act*, pastoralists were required to deduct seventy-five percent from their Indigenous workers' pay and pass it on to the Protector, who was appointed by the government to exercise authority over the Aboriginal people not living on reserves.

the N word

When the Australian Workers Union (AWU) formed in 1894, Aboriginal workers were given the right to join. In spite of this small victory—although few Aboriginals joined the AWU—they were still not permitted to eat with the white drovers and were forbidden to perform their dances, or sing or speak their language. Many ignorant pastoralists resorted to punishing the men with a stockwhip if they were caught carrying out so-called 'pagan rituals'.

Despite these obstacles, young Albert Hagan found time to teach himself to read and write as he carried out the onerous work on the cattle and sheep stations. He had no problem gaining respect from his bosses and even managed to advance himself.

On 22 March 1920, Albert applied for—and received—from the Chief Protector of Aboriginals, a Certificate of Exemption from the Provisions of the *Aboriginal Protection and Restriction of the Sale of Opium Acts of 1897 to 1901*. The exemption certificate stated, 'the applicant is a steady and hard working fellow, can read and write well and capable of managing his own affairs, and is treated like a white on the stations in the Toompine District'.

This meant that Albert could work, collect his wages and be responsible for his income. His hard-earned money would no longer be managed by white bureaucrats with no accountability to him. This independence also made it easier for him to move around the bush, and it was during this time that he met a young lady and made the decision to settle down.

Albert met Sarah Smith while he was working in the Quilpie area. She was a Mardjany woman from the South Comingin area which bordered Kullilli land. Together they had two boys, Alf and Fred. Sarah also had a son by the name of Bobby Bismark before my grandfather met her.

Following Sarah Smith's death, Albert met my grandmother Jessie Lewis. They had four children—May, Albert, Doris and my father, James. Like Albert's first wife, Jessie Lewis was also of the Mardjany tribe, from the Beechal Creek/Humeburn/Mt Alfred area that formed part of the eastern boundary of the Kullilli traditional land.

Although my grandparents lived and worked in the Quilpie area, Dad was born in Bourke in northern New South Wales on 21 April 1932. This was during one of his parents' long trips south to keep their children out of harms way—that is, away from the hands of government officials who were on the lookout for mixed-race children. This was in keeping with the policy of removing these children from their families in the belief that they would better assimilate into the broader community.

Albert was familiar with the country around Bourke from his many droving trips down south and, being a handy, hard-working stockman, managed to secure work whenever the family required any extra cash. Jessie would set up camp at successive locations and wait for Albert to return from his contracted employment.

After living this way for many years, Albert decided he'd had enough of the nomadic lifestyle. He wanted to set up house on a more permanent basis near a large regional centre so his children could have access to better opportunities.

Aware of the decline in the rural sector, Albert knew that if his children were to get a fair chance in life they would need to gain a formal, Western education. He settled for a small community 800 kilometres south-west of Brisbane but only 200 kilometres from the land of his Kullilli ancestors—Cunnamulla.

the N word

Ringer Jim and Kooma Jean

Growing up on the Yumba Dad had many wonderful times. Games such as rounders, similar to baseball, was played with a bat fashioned from a discarded wooden crate or tree trunk. These games had no restrictions on numbers per team and there would always be a big mob of cousins in the outfield, waiting patiently to catch the magic tennis ball. Every game would attract a large audience and older members of the community would sit on a rug under a shady tree in the distance, looking for gullonge (fleas) in the hair of the younger children.

During the nights, especially after the workers had returned from months on the properties with cash to spend, the entertainers with guitars and piano accordions would bring the Yumba community to life. The men would round up as many disused tyres as possible and light a big bonfire on an open clay pan. Rich, black smoke would spiral upwards and residents from over fifty metres away would feel the raging heat. Fleet-footed dancers would join in with the music, tapping their toes on the rock hard earth to the clicking of spoons or animal rib bones.

As in most communities there were exceptions to the rule and some people only associated with their immediate family rather than participating in communal life. Even though at times there were arguments among members of different families, respect was the long-term key to the lifestyle on the camp in order to ensure stability and cohesion among the diverse traditional groups who were not Yumba residents by choice.

Whenever there was a family feud in which conflict between disgruntled men got out of hand, there was a protocol that was adhered to by all. Both men would take along a group of friends to observe the tussle and they'd agree on a neutral referee to ensure there were no illegal blows or unsportsmanlike behaviour. There was no kicking when someone was knocked to the ground and if one of the combatants was clearly outclassed he could save face by calling it quits without further injury. The men would then shake hands and go off and share a drink or a meal together to demonstrate that there were no hard feelings and the families could resume pleasantries again.

In those days the young ones took notice of what their elders told them. Parents always knew where their children were and if kids got involved in mischief their mums were quickly informed by concerned, or perhaps meddlesome, relatives and friends.

When Dad had nearly completed Grade 4 at the Cunnamulla State School, his father wrote to the headmaster seeking permission for him to leave. As he would turn fourteen the following April his father wanted him to go with his uncle to learn to be a stockman.

The headmaster wrote back, approving his request, and also stating, 'I hope he grows up to be the man he gives promise of being as a boy.' Dad kept that letter for many years but regrettably it was lost during the process of moving house.

It was the accepted thing in those days for young boys to go to their mother's brother and be taught all the necessary things to prepare them for employment in the pastoral industry. Under traditional Aboriginal law, Dad's mother could not speak to her brothers or make eye contact with them. If she was in a group and noticed any of her brothers approaching she would immediately withdraw from the vicinity.

Dad was sent to work with his uncle Jim Smith, a boundary rider on Tilbooroo Station, approximately 100 kilometres west of Cunnamulla. Jim taught Dad how to ride a horse, muster sheep and cattle, milk cows, slaughter meat and all the other on-the-job work skills that are considered essential for gaining employment in rural Australia. Dad stayed with his uncle for twelve months, learning all there was to know about life on a station. At the end of that year the station owner offered him a job and he was paid a weekly wage of two pounds.

All workers in rural Australia in those early days knew of the dangers associated with their work, given the extreme conditions and remoteness. Dad had his fair share of physical injuries, the scars of which he still carries with him today.

One day, during those early days of learning the sheep and cattle trade, Dad's uncle Jim told him to saddle up a pony that was not long broken in and they both went off mustering. That evening, not far from their camp, the pony shied and started to buck. Dad was thrown from the cantankerous horse and the consequence was a dislocated shoulder that required a six-week stay in the Cunnamulla Base Hospital.

Another more serious accident occurred not long after Frank Jordon, the station owner, presented Dad the job of station hand. During the dry times mulga foliage was a good source of food for sheep; the trees were burnt and the stock fed off the leaves that were low enough for them to reach if they stood on their hind feet. Branches that were out of reach were knocked down and scattered around for the hungry herd. On this particular day Dad was told to take an axe and lop the branches off those trees that had been burnt a couple of days earlier. He saddled his horse and set off to where the trees were located, about seven kilometres away. Dad tied his horse near the full-bore drain and commenced cutting.

A couple of hours later he suddenly felt a terrible pain in his left eye. He dropped the axe and rushed to the bore drain to wash his eye but unfortunately the water did not relieve the pain. Eventually he rode the horse back to the shearing shed and told his uncle that a small piece of branch must have broken off and struck him.

The next morning a white scum had formed over the eye and his uncle and aunt realised the injury was serious. The boss was notified and that afternoon a station vehicle came out to the camp to take Dad to the homestead. The following day he caught the slow mail truck into town to the Cunnamulla Hospital where the doctor removed a wooden splinter from the pupil of his eye. Dad said he has never endured as much pain as he did in those forty-eight hours after the accident.

Six weeks later when he was released from hospital it was a great relief for Dad to learn that he had not lost the sight in his injured eye. However, twelve months later the visiting optometrist told him that he had indeed lost about sixty percent vision in the eye and he would have to wear spectacles for the rest of his life.

That dramatic event occurred in 1947 when Dad was only fifteen years old. It was his introduction to the workforce. After the accident he resumed work, travelling with cattle droving teams and working in shearing sheds and fencing camps.

Whether he was away for a month or a year working on sheep and cattle stations, Dad would always return home to the Yumba. He often spoke of the tyranny of distance commenting that, such was the vastness of some of the stations, he could be away doing a solo fencing run and not see another person for over a month.

the N word

After Dad finished work on Tilbooroo, his next job was on Tinnenburra Station, a little further west. Here he worked under a very proud Aboriginal head stockman—Toego Robinson. Toego was also from the Yumba and worked on many stations in the far south-west of the state. Dad appreciated Toego's tutelage and the skills he learnt from him stood him in good stead for the future.

After working for some time under Toego's watchful and protective eye, Dad, still only sixteen years old, accepted an offer to go on a long cattle run from Cunnamulla to a property near Collarenebri in New South Wales. He accompanied experienced Aboriginal cattlemen Jackie Young, Chappie Foster, and camp cook Tom Shillingsworth as well as a white droving contractor by the name of McMillan.

Several weeks later the team crossed the New South Wales border at Toulbie Gate. After resting the cattle and hobbling the horses the men ate a hearty meal and rolled out their swags. As was the custom on this trip, the white contractor slept over 100 metres away from his contracted black stockmen.

That night the men slept soundly. Next morning, after they had saddled their horses, McMillan informed them he would ride ahead to chase any station stock out of their path. When their herd of cattle was on its way, the cook, customarily the last to leave camp, overtook the three drovers in his wagonette, gave a wave and was soon out of sight. Shortly after, the trailing team watched in surprise to see the cook racing back towards them, pots and pans clanging in the rear of his wagonette. As he got closer they could hear him shouting, 'He hung himself, the bastard hung himself.'

After Shillingsworth calmed down he described the scene he'd come across. The three startled men rode in a gallop towards the spot and minutes later found the droving contractor, a big man, hanging from a tree branch by a single bridle strap, his feet dangling within half a metre off the ground. Dad felt nauseous at his first ever sighting of a dead body and has told me that to this day he has not seen anything quite so unsettling.

The men hurriedly set off in the direction of Toulbie Station, about five kilometres away, to sound the alarm. After listening to their unbelievable story, the property owner rang the nearby Goodooga Police Station. Within hours the men joined the mystified policeman at the scene of the fatality. But they were in for even more disturbing news when the officer, who didn't touch the body, gave a directive for the stockmen to camp beside the deceased man until the coroner arrived the following morning. They were to stay guard and ward off wild pigs or any other four-legged predators during the night. The policeman assured the men he would make every effort to contact McMillan's next-of-kin so alternative arrangements for the cattle drive could be made.

Anyone who is familiar with the Cunnamulla Aboriginal people knows that they are extremely superstitious and have been known to jump at their own shadows. That night the men agreed to sleep in a circle around the contractor's still dangling body but there wasn't much sleeping going on, just the wind playing havoc with their minds on that breezy, dark night. The noise of dingoes howling in the distance and wild boars grunting only added to their unease. They were in for a long night.

The next morning, as the sun rose above the stand of gum trees, the men, with bloodshot eyes, rose in unison to gather twigs to start a fire. Over a cup of strong, black tea they agreed the night had indeed been long and the entire experience traumatising.

About mid-morning, after the coroner removed the body from its noose, the police introduced the brother of the deceased man to Dad and his work mates. Together they recommenced the contracted cattle run on the long journey to Collarenebri.

Weeks later, when they delivered the large herd of cattle to their destination, Dad learnt a hard lesson. The contractor only paid the stockmen the daily rate from Toulbie Gate where he joined them after taking over his deceased brother's contract. He told the men to speak to the stock agent back in Cunnamulla for the balance owing for the Cunnamulla to Toulbie Gate run. By then the men were too exhausted to quarrel over the unpaid money. Besides, it would have been in vain. The law in those days always sided with a white boss in any dispute with his black workers.

The men were very disheartened. They had put in many long, hard days on the road with feisty cattle. Between them they didn't have enough money to pay their way back to Cunnamulla. But, being resourceful, they managed to make their way home—only to face the disappointment of their families when they discovered the men had returned penniless. Usually after such long trips there would be enough money to pay the bills and shell out for a large feast and entertainment.

Within weeks Dad joined up with a white contractor by the name of Jack O'Shea and his wife, Ivy, to do a cattle drive throughout the west. He stayed with them for a couple of years and saw the birth of their children. Dad describes his relationship with Jack as the turning point in his short droving career. It was to have a profound influence on his life.

When Jack was offered the job as manager on Bulloo Downs Station he immediately offered Dad a full-time job. At last Dad was able to visit the tribal land of his grandmother, Trella. As the years passed, Dad became well acquainted with every square kilometre of that majestic country and often came across sites of spiritual significance during his long hours in the saddle. He found bora rings, cave paintings and artefacts like weapons and cooking utensils. But not once did he reveal their whereabouts to his fellow stockmen or his boss.

As a young man Dad was athletic and blessed with good looks. Now in his early twenties, he began to develop other interests besides mustering. During one of his infrequent trips to Cunnamulla from

Bulloo Downs he became transfixed with a striking young lady from the Kooma tribe who he had previously seen around the Yumba. Through some discreet inquiries, he discovered her name was Jean Mitchell. For the first time in Dad's working life the fascination he had for horses, sheep, cattle and all things rural was to play a secondary role.

Mum was born in Cunnamulla on 7 April 1937 to Jim Mitchell and Kate Whitford. She is a descendant of the Mitchell family from the Kooma tribe on her father's side and the Foster family from the neighbouring Gungarri tribe on her mother's side. As with my father's family, the land barons also displaced my mother's people. In scenes identical to what happened to the Kullilli, Europeans occupied Kooma land with their cattle and sheep, thereby depriving the traditional owners of food. Not surprisingly, violence broke out between the races.

Kooma tribal land was situated between the Nebine and Balonne rivers. In 1855, missionary William Ridley wrote about the dire situation that had developed for those Aboriginals living along the Balonne River:

> Before the occupation of this district by colonists, the aborigines could never have been at a loss for necessaries of life. Except in the lowest part of the river, there is water in the driest seasons; along the banks game abounded; waterfowl, emus, parrot tribes, kangaroos, and other animals might always, or almost always, be found. And if, at any time, these failed to supply food for the human tribe, the fish furnished a sure resource. But when the country was taken up, and herds of cattle introduced, not only did the cattle drive away the kangaroos, but those who had charge of the cattle found it necessary to keep the aborigines away from the river, as their appearance

frightened the cattle in all directions. In fact, it is said that while troops of aborigines roam about the runs, and especially if they go to the cattle camps and watering places, it is impossible to keep a herd together.

After some fatal conflicts, in which some colonists and many aborigines have been slain, the blacks have been awed into submission to the orders which forbid their access to the river. And what is the consequence? Black fellows coming in from the west report that last summer very large numbers, afraid to visit the river, were crowded round a few scanty water holes, within a day's walk of which it was impossible to get sufficient food, ... that owing to these hardships many died.[3]

Against the odds, the Kooma people managed to survive and today their descendants are prominent in many rural towns in south-west Queensland. The Mitchell clan, Mum's people, is one of the largest families in the area. Mum's paternal grandmother, Sarah Andrews, was a full-blood woman of the Kooma tribe. As a teenager, she eloped with an Irishman, Jack Mitchell. Mum said her grandparents lived in and around the Bollon community and raised a family of six girls and five boys.

In 1920 Jack Mitchell bought a block of land on the Nebine River and used that as a base so his children could work on sheep properties in the district. Unfortunately Sarah, known as Granny Mitchell, had to travel to Cunnamulla with her two seriously ill youngest daughters so they could receive medical attention. She was devastated when her daughters died soon after their arrival at the hospital. Refusing to return to her traditional land, Granny Mitchell set up camp on the fringe of town. She sent for her remaining children and they were the first family to live on the southern side of the town cemetery.

Mum's father Jim was the fourth child born to Sarah and Jack Mitchell. Jim had limited formal education and like most Aboriginal

the N word

boys in that era was sent to work to earn his keep at a young age. When he reached the latter part of his teenage years Jim fell in love with Kate Whitford, a woman with an infectious smile from the neighbouring Gungarri tribe. They married and raised a family of nine children.

My grandparents lived on the Yumba with their extended family and Kate Mitchell had a big influence on all her children's lives, as well as those of her many grandchildren.

Granny Kate became fluent in her husband's Kooma language and possessed great knowledge of the traditional ways of her people. She was the elder we all looked up to and sought cultural clarification from, especially in relation to who we could or could not marry. Granny Kate always found the time to tell us kids about the ways of the Moondigudda—the rainbow serpent at the bottom of the Warrego River near Sandy Point—and the legends of all the animals that lived around us.

⁂

Mum was the fourth born in her family of nine children, five boys and four girls. After attending school for six years she was sent off to work as a domestic servant on sheep properties on the land of her traditional people around the Bollon district as well as on properties in northern New South Wales.

By the time the young James Hagan started paying attention to Mum she was seventeen and already working to the east of Cunnamulla at Avondale Station. Despite the distance their jobs put between them and the infrequency of get-togethers, they were able to nurture a strong friendship.

Three years later, on 30 June 1957, before bridesmaid Cathy Brown and best man Doug Orcher, as well as many family members and friends, James Hagan married Jean Mitchell. It was a dim, rain-soaked day in Cunnamulla and the rain was so relentless it was impossible to take photographs and capture one of the happiest moment of their lives, something that saddens Dad to this day.

On 19 October 1957, Pam Elizabeth was born and her arrival brought great joy, especially to Mum who had finished working as a domestic to raise her own family. By now Dad was earning good money as head stockman which allowed Mum to retire from ever again having to wash other people's dirty floors, clothing and pots and pans.

It was customary for new mums to stay close to their mothers so Mum was never short of advice. Whenever Pam ran a fever or had an ear infection or toothache, Granny Kate and Mum's aunties were on hand to offer a traditional bush remedy.

the N word

The Yumba

I was born at the Cunnamulla Base Hospital on 20 December 1959. Mum was twenty-two and Dad twenty-seven. Although I have always spelt my name with a 'ph' instead of a 'v', on my birth certificate, which I first sighted in my teenage years, my name was spelt 'Steven'. When I asked Mum about this she told me it was meant to be spelt with a 'ph' but the nurse wrote my name down incorrectly and Mum dared not contradict an educated white woman.

Soon after I was born Dad packed all the family's worldly possessions into his trusted old Holden utility and we drove 300 kilometres north-west of Cunnamulla over rough terrain to Mt Margaret Station, located on the northernmost tip of the Kullilli boundary and covering 120 square kilometres. Dad had a contract job as a boundary rider managing the dingo fence that passed through the vast property. The dingo fence was the longest continuous fence in the world. Running 5614 kilometres from South Australia through Queensland, its primary purpose was to control dingo numbers in sheep grazing areas.

Our family returned briefly to Cunnamulla for the birth of my brother James Albert, affectionately known as Jimmo. After Mum was well enough to travel Dad secured a job working as a stockman on Yerrel Station, forty kilometres east of Eulo near Humeburn.

the N word

We set up camp at the married couple's quarters, 150 metres from the large homestead.

Every fortnight the station owner invited neighbouring pastoralists and their workers to watch movies—which were delivered by the mailman—at his homestead. The owner was a kind man and allowed Dad to bring us along too. On one of these movie nights our family was lounging on the old canvas seats at the rear when suddenly a flash flood swept through the property, which was located between two channels of the Yerrel Creek. The water rose so quickly it submerged the ground floor of the homestead without warning and the station owner invited our small family and his other guests to spend the night on his first floor verandah.

Dad recalls it was a weird experience sleeping metres from the owner's family. But he was grateful. If we'd been asleep in the married couple's quarters instead of at the movies, our family would have been forced to seek refuge on the roof or in a tall tree. We would not have had time to make it to the homestead, such was the ferocity of the floodwaters.

Earlier that day there had been a storm twelve kilometres to the east although when Dad had started work the sky had been cloudless, with no hint of the activity upstream. He said if he hadn't been so busy and had been paying closer attention, maybe the changes in behaviour of the animals might have given a hint of things to come. The old people always say that they can tell when the rain is coming by the birds screeching and the frogs croaking.

When Dad looked out from the top floor balcony he was amazed at how still and black the night was. He became alarmed when he couldn't see his car parked next to the homestead. Unlike his family who slept soundly huddled together on a thin mattress on the wooden floorboards, Dad didn't sleep well that night. He was thinking about his dependable old car and all night he listened to the roar of the floodwaters and the sound of debris crashing into the old gum trees not far from the homestead.

the N word

The next day, in bright sunshine and with the creek waters gradually receding, Dad's worst nightmare was realised. The distraught young cowboy's beloved car, the family's only form of transport, had been swept away by the floodwaters.

As soon as word got out about Dad's predicament, a small assembly of his work mates volunteered to help in a quick search downriver. After five minutes of walking Dad said he couldn't believe his eyes. There was the car perched precariously between two huge branches of a sturdy gum, three metres above the water.

After Dad and his mates spent a challenging hour manipulating ropes, the car had a dramatic landing as it splashed into the Yerrel Creek. It was then dragged out of the murky water and pushed back to our sleeping quarters. Dad drained all the water from the car and after a quick grease and oil change was thrilled when he heard the familiar sound of his precious vehicle's engine firing on all six cylinders again.

❖

Around this time, Mum decided she'd had enough of adventures in the bush and convinced Dad that we should set up camp permanently at the Yumba. Dad agreed and Mum soon fell into a regular routine of raising us kids alone. Dad would intermittently return home after working many months on the cattle and sheep stations and in the meantime send money via a courier for our upkeep and education.

Two years later, on 30 May 1963, Susan Jean joined our growing family and immediately took pride of place in our parents' bed. Jimmo was now in direct competition with Susan. Although Pam and I had become used to no longer being invited into the big bed, we would still find our place among the clash of bodies on the second-hand mattress whenever we thought we heard ghost noises,

the N word

or the roar of thunder from a threatening rain storm became too frightening for our young ears.

I believe the decision to remain on the Yumba was the beginning of Mum's assertive streak that was to reward the family in years to come. In time, Dad acquired Nat Mitchell's house (Mum's uncle) for the family so Mum could be closer to her mother and father's house, no more than twenty metres away.

* * *

The Yumba was a forty hectare parcel of land with a lofty sandhill to our east and the Warrego River within walking distance to the west. Its location between the sewage treatment plant and the cemetery may not have been the flashest of locations, but as a child growing up all I can remember were happy times of hunting ducks on the sewage works' dam, tracking porcupine after rain on the sandhills and going fishing on the river.

Between the cemetery and the town was a large citrus orchard. Unlike some of the other kids from the Yumba, I didn't have the heart to steal. I wasn't sure if I envied them or was in awe when they returned after their successful raids. The 'fearless ones' didn't seem to worry about stories of the crazed orchard farmer who was rumoured to shoot at trespassers before asking questions.

I was however often in receipt of the 'borrowed goods' and enjoyed the sweet oranges and mandarins that were gathered before they fell to the ground from the row upon row of fruit-laden trees. Mum and Dad would have been horrified if they knew I had participated in such activities—especially when they constantly reminded us kids that there was always enough food in our pantry to satisfy the hunger pains of any growing child.

Our dining table acted as our pantry in those days. The wooden legs were placed in an inch of water in disused golden syrup tins to prevent ants from climbing up and feasting on our limited grocery supplies. Refrigeration was almost non-existent on the Yumba and any perishables had to be consumed on the day of purchase.

There were one or two families who invested in a charcoal cooler but, for most of us, cooked meat and butter were kept in a wet tea towel in a dish. As kids we had the task of keeping the tea towels moist. Tinned meat and canned food were generally the order of the day and Mum would stock up on those items at regular intervals after Dad got paid.

One of my fondest memories is of walking with my cousin Kevin on weekends to the river to check on my Uncle Henry's fishing traps. Uncle Henry had his favourite spot about 100 metres downstream from Sandy Point, a swimming and camping spot popular with Yumba Murries.

On a bad day we would find long-neck turtles that we would free and return to the river; on a good day a large catch of catfish and yellow belly was our bounty. Uncle Henry would allow us to take any excess fish home and he would share the rest with Granny Kate and his family.

The large sandhill that separated the Yumba from town was our backyard—one big playground. We would often see adults wandering off to the edge of the sandhill for their clandestine meetings. Little did they know that nothing was secret on the Yumba!

Our favourite pastime on the sandhill was playing cowboys and Indians, and of course most of the kids wanted to be John Wayne. At times the competition would number twenty warring troops on both sides. We would carry our hand guns that we'd carved out of wood with our pocket knives and hide behind trees or large shrubs. We would wait silently for the enemies to fall into our

the N word

trap before shooting them. The rules were strictly enforced and every fatally wounded fighter had to remain stationary and silent until the contest was over.

Sometimes we would pass the time of day making rolly-pollies by cutting holes in the tops and bottoms of Sunshine powdered milk tins. We'd place wire through the holes, fill the tins with sand and pull them around the camp on long wire leads. The more innovative youngsters made extended rolly-pollies by passing wire through several sand-filled tins, each an equal distance apart behind the lead tin.

In the extreme heat of summer, if we didn't go swimming in the river, we would venture up the hill and dig a deep hole in the moist sand to cool our bodies. I often returned to the hill during my adult years to enjoy a quiet moment's reflection, ankle-deep in the soothing cool sands of the hill.

We learnt from our elders which native plants were edible—blue bellflowers and the sweet honey sap on the gum trees, as well as bush apples and oranges. We always carried a shanghai fashioned from a fork of a tree branch and a piece of old tyre rubber to hunt birds or ducks.

Occasionally, if a feud between us kids got out of hand, we would engage in long-distance battles with shanghai-propelled rocks, although I don't recall any serious injuries. We would always quickly conciliate and walk home to share a golden syrup sandwich or some Arnott's biscuits if we were lucky. Sometimes we'd go behind Mum's back and sneak a suck of her precious tube of condensed milk.

On the occasional Sunday after church the white folk of Cunnamulla would drive to the end of the bitumen road to unload large boxes of clothing and toys. It didn't matter to us kids that they were rejects or outgrown items from their children. After the white folk had climbed back into their cars and headed to the safety of town, there would be a mad rush to see what booty we could claim.

the N word

The only other white person we would see on a regular basis on those narrow unsealed roads, besides the gunjabulls (police), was the fruit vendor, Alan Lipke. Us Murries called him Lulu or Lulu Apple and Oranges. He made a weekly run down to the camp to sell his seconds after he'd sold his quality fruit and vegetables in town. But second best was better than nothing at all, and the women made good use of the over-ripe fruit, cooking up delicious cakes and puddings and biscuits.

One day I was sitting in the shell of an abandoned car pretending to be a racing car driver when I saw the fruit man driving slowly by Granny Kate's house, looking at a group of women playing 100-up (a popular card game) under a large jacaranda tree. Not watching where he was driving, Lulu didn't notice a newly formed hole, the result of torrential rain several days earlier. He carelessly hit the hole with sufficient force to dislodge a big box of bananas.

Before he had time to reverse the car, dozens of kids were running to the scene of the accident. It was much too late for the fruit man to rescue his goods as the kids sprinted off to the safety of the sandhill with their hands, pockets and shirts full of his best-selling items.

Several mums smirked with satisfaction as they resumed their game, content in the knowledge that they wouldn't have to leave the card game early to prepare dinner! After that expensive lesson, the fruit vendor never hit a pothole again on his weekly trek across the dirt road.

※

Once I started going to school it became obvious to me that there was a huge gap between us and the white kids of Cunnamulla—in particular how we arrived at school, what we wore, and the food we ate for lunch. The white kids had the option of being driven to school by their mothers, ride a bike or walk in comfortable shoes with socks.

the N word

Aboriginal kids walked to school and wore no shoes. I certainly noticed the difference in summer when the forty-five degree heat made getting to school without any footwear almost impossible. We managed by stepping on grass and any other green vegetation. But when the south-westerly winds were blowing a gale, the grass would quickly dry and turn prickly, making it tough going, even for the hardened soles of Yumba kids.

The white kids had plastic lunch boxes with meat and salad sandwiches, nuts, a variety of fruits and an iced water bottle. The Aboriginal kids had Vegemite or golden syrup sandwiches folded loosely in a page of a newspaper. Of course there were poor white kids at school too, who didn't have enough food or the clothing that the majority of the white kids took for granted. Most of those kids shared our food and company during recess. But after school the white and black kids walked home in opposite directions.

There were some teachers within the school system with paternalistic attitudes. They broke the heart of many an Aboriginal child who dared to dream of a better life away from Cunnamulla. Comments to the effect that we would never amount to anything of importance were destabilising, to say the least, especially at a time when we felt most in need of reassurance.

Luckily, the good teachers outnumbered the bad at my school. However most didn't have any idea of our living conditions. We had no electricity to study by at night and yet we were given exercises as homework most days. There was one teacher who chastised me because I didn't complete the task of drawing a picture of my bathroom, something non-existent on the Yumba.

Another teacher left me scratching my head in bewilderment when I was asked to draw pictures of ocean creatures. At that point my longest journey in life was from the camp to school and back, a total of three kilometres.

I felt dumb and useless because I had no idea of what the ocean was let alone what animals lived in it. We didn't own any books about

the N word

the ocean and the public library discouraged Yumba kids from taking books out.

Each day as I walked home from school I paid particular attention to how the houses that we lived in differed in design to those of our white classmates. At our place, when the rain came unexpectedly during the night it would blow in through the nail holes in the used galvanised iron sheeting. I would rush around and find discarded newspaper, cardboard or chewing gum to fill the cracks in the roof and walls of our home. I would often lie in the bed that I shared with my brother and any cousins who slept over and visualise all the houses that I passed on the way to and from school. When it rained, did those little white kids who sat at the front of the class have to rush around filling holes with cardboard?

Whenever there was a death on the Yumba parents would withdraw their children from school for the day out of respect for the family of the deceased. I remember walking to the sandhill to be out of the way of the many relatives who would gather at the house of the deceased to grieve before and after the funeral service and burial.

Our elders told us kids that it was bad luck to count the number of cars following the hearse to the cemetery. I remember some of the bigger kids counting the first half of the cars in the procession and then stopping abruptly when it became clear that the line was shortening.

After a funeral, I would help the older children collect dried cow and horse manure to place in a large drum with holes in the side. It was customary for elders to light the dried dung, place green foliage on top, and then walk through the house of the deceased with it. The release of smoke, it was believed, would cleanse the house and make it spiritually safe for the deceased's family to resume occupancy.

the N word

Most Aboriginal people I know are very superstitious and all have a story to tell about seeing a ghost. I saw one when I was about seven years old.

I was sharing a bed with my cousins Kevin and Beverley when I heard an eerie, unfamiliar noise outside, like small wheels rolling on the hard earth. Suddenly there was the deafening sound of something untying the chain on our door. I climbed over the sleeping bodies of my cousins, rolled onto the dirt floor and hid under an adjacent bed. When I peered nervously out, in front of me was the scariest thing I had ever seen. Larger than life, was a dog on a skateboard.

This white dog with black spots steered in the direction of our bed, put one paw up and struck at Beverley, who fortunately didn't budge. It then turned the skateboard around and left the house the way it had entered, taking time to secure the door by fastening the chain. I heard the faint noise of the skateboard's wheels propelling the ghost dog in the direction of the cemetery until they were no longer audible.

I tried to yell out but my mouth wouldn't open; my lips felt like they were fastened with Araldite. As my throat screamed out for water and fear took control, I felt utterly powerless. I was convinced the dog would return and find me cowering under the bed. Too frightened to move, I finally fell asleep on the hard earth.

The next morning I woke to the screeches of corellas, parrots and budgerigars coming from the trees in the general direction of Grandfather Jim Mitchell's caravan. I massaged my neck to rid myself of the stiffness of sleep without a pillow, dusted myself off and slowly rose from the cold, hard ground. To my relief, everyone in the house was still fast asleep.

I tip-toed over to the steel-framed bed to see if Beverley was still alive. As I got closer I heard her softly breathing and then noticed her right hand grasp the end of the blanket. With one thrust she reclaimed her half from Kevin. I was now able to get a clear look at her head and to my astonishment there were scratches on her forehead that hadn't been there the night before. I slid into the single bed beside her and Kevin and went back to sleep.

When we woke I asked Beverley about the scratches as innocently as I could manage. She said she wasn't sure how she got them but thought she must have brushed her forehead against the corrugated iron of the bedroom wall during the night.

Many years later, as I was lying in bed one night, my fear of the supernatural resurfaced when I heard frantic knocking on our door. It was my Uncle Harold Turnbull from Bourke and he was in a very emotional state. I overheard him confess to Dad that he had just seen a recently deceased relative and he wanted advice and reassurance.

Dad always told us kids not to believe any yarns about ghosts but that evening he told my uncle that he too had had a visit from the ghost of the same relative. Dad whispered to Uncle not to be afraid as she was only visiting to make sure everything was going okay and to say her final farewells. Dad's words of comfort calmed Uncle Harold and after a drink of water he left, carrying a kerosene lantern to light his way home.

For many years I thought that I must have been hallucinating when I saw the ghost dog. I'd never told a soul about it, in fear of not being believed, but now here was Dad confirming that ghosts actually existed. With my father's words still echoing in my ear, I tried to get to sleep.

If ghost stories weren't scary enough for us then the four-kilometre return trips from the movies in town ensured our vivid imaginations received their weekly fix. Walking past the cemetery late at night had our small hearts pounding rapidly. Even though we were being escorted home by our mothers, the cemetery always loomed large and terrifying as we hurried by.

Sometimes drunks would attempt to take the most direct route to the camp and detour through the grounds among the gravestones. On one occasion an inebriated Yumba man stumbled into a hole after

the N word

stepping on a loose sheet of tin placed over a grave newly prepared for a funeral the next morning. As us kids walked past the cemetery we heard his piercing screams, 'Help me please, help me please. I'm stuck in the hole and can't get out.'

The commonly-held belief that black people are more athletic than other races may be a fable but that night I witnessed records shattered as we raced back to the men walking a short distance behind. Aboriginal athlete Patrick Johnson, whose time of 9.93 seconds for the 100-metre dash in Mito, Japan in May 2003 made him the fastest of any athlete in the world that year, would have felt the breeze of us Murries racing past him if he'd been with us.

The braver adult members of the Yumba community discovered the offending drunk in the hole in the cemetery and promptly rescued him. Falling into the recently dug grave had no doubt been a terrifying experience and the man made sure he never again took any detours through the resting place of Cunnamulla's beloved.

In spite of this incident, several of the other Yumba men continued to take the short cut through the cemetery after closing time at their favourite pub, having had their fill of 'monkey blood', a potent mixture of Royal Reserve Port topped up with 'white lightning' (methylated spirits).

One brave man, who you couldn't get a word out of when he was sober, didn't make it through the cemetery and after taking a seat on a tombstone slowly eased himself into a horizontal position and fell into a deep sleep. Early the next morning he awoke to see a headstone atop of which was a beautiful white angel with outstretched wings. The man thought he had died and gone to heaven.

I understand he took a sabbatical from the 'monkey blood' for several months and resumed his interest in fishing—much to the consternation of his drinking buddies.

the N word

◈

Still, such scary incidents didn't put us off going to the movies. And neither did the thick ropes across the front and sides of the cinema that marked off where we could and couldn't sit. We didn't dare take ourselves beyond the roped area, or sit on any of the seats, all of which seemed to permanently have a large 'reserved' sign on them. We knew that to do so would mean being barred from ever attending the cinema.

Whatever the weather, however we were treated, nothing was going to keep us from the pictures. All us kids were movie critics par excellence. We would analyse each movie from beginning to end—and just to make sure that our appraisals were precise, we would make the long journey into town a few days later to see the same movie all over again.

After watching many westerns and war movies at the local cinema it became apparent that John Wayne, armed with his trusty six-shooter that was capable of taking out a tribe of treacherous Indians without reloading, could do no wrong. We also loved Audie Murphy who was forever conquering the immaculately-dressed Germans. I thought these strong handsome white men were unbeatable but I also dreamt of the days when I would see a strong, handsome black man in the lead role.

When I was not quite into double figures, however, I became a supporter of the underdog. After the monotony of witnessing defeat after defeat of the villains on the big screen I decided to cast a conscience vote. I shifted camp and commenced barracking for the Indians and the Germans. I felt they deserved at least a win or two.

There was one old fellow from the Yumba who told us kids that there would be no new films made featuring his favourite actor since he had been killed the previous week in a war movie. Being broken-hearted on account of the 'death' on the big screen of

the N word

his popular hero, he kept true to his word and never went to any movies that featured that actor again.

One night, during a western, some of the Murrie kids began shouting out to John Wayne who loomed larger than life on the big screen. 'Watch out behind ya John,' they yelled. 'Them Indians are sneaking up on ya'.

the N word

Uptowners

In 1964, along with several other Murries from the Yumba, Dad began to take an interest in trying to improve the conditions and opportunities for our people at the local level. In other parts of Australia, Aboriginal leaders were lobbying the trade unions and petitioning the government and the British Monarchy with statistics on the appalling neglect of our people by successive governments.

At that time, as is still the case today, Aboriginal people comprised the most disadvantaged and oppressed group in the Australian community. We have the highest birth rate, the highest death rate, the highest incarceration rate, the worst health and housing and the lowest educational, occupational, economic, social and legal status of any identifiable section within the country.

Not only did Dad want to improve the living conditions on the camp, but also people's attitude towards Aboriginals generally. Some racist publicans would not serve Aboriginals in their hotels and many businesses discriminated against them.

Some proprietors were quite open about their desire not to have black customers patronising their premises while others were more subtle but just as effective with their message. At the same time Aboriginal people were experiencing harassment and intimidation from the police.

Dad's quest to improve the living standards of his people saw him become one of the foundation members of the Cunnamulla Australian Native Welfare Association when it was formed in 1964. That small but significant step was the beginning of his journey into the world of Aboriginal affairs.

With boosted self-confidence after the success of joining with other community leaders in establishing several Aboriginal organisations to improve the plight of the Yumba people, Dad sought membership of the local branch of the Australian Labor Party (ALP). This was at a time when Aboriginals were not seen as taking an interest in party politics. It was no easy task for Dad to stand up and speak in front of a group of white strangers, many of whom he knew looked on Aboriginals as nothing more than 'those people who lived down past the cemetery'.

Dad had the desire and the drive to make a difference. The fire was in his belly but he didn't quite know how to set about achieving his goals. He had no mentors, black or white, to give him guidance. All he had was a gut feeling that there was an alternative to Aboriginal people tolerating poverty and discrimination and accepting second-best. Like his father before him, he sought answers to questions that many community members had no response to.

During the 1960s the message penetrated the white Australian consciousness that Aboriginal people could not—and would not—accept assimilation, a social policy which entailed loss of identity with all its richness of culture and timeless wisdom. Dad too did not believe in assimilation. For him it meant giving up the one thing that had been passed onto him over many generations—pride in his Kullilli origin.

Joining the ALP was a defining moment in Dad's fight to improve the living conditions of his people in Cunnamulla and to secure a better quality of life for his family.

the N word

After attending several ALP meetings and gaining a perspective on how white people lived in Cunnamulla from visits to his new friends' homes, Dad felt the time was right for Mum and him to have a serious chat about changing their residential address. This would mean a move from an exclusively black community on the Yumba with a population of several hundred to an almost exclusively white town of a couple of thousand residents. But Dad was on a roll and believed anything was possible with self-belief and hard work.

Mum's initial response was one of trepidation. She queried why a man who had lived much of his life in a fringe-camp humpy would want to live among white people. Most worrying to her was how he thought he could raise the deposit to buy a block of land and convince the bank manager to lend him considerably more money to build their dream house. In her days of working as a domestic Mum had cleaned many fine homes and even though she'd often dreamt of raising a family in one, she knew that home ownership for Yumba Murries was virtually unheard of, in spite of the fact that some Aboriginal families were renting houses from white people in town, a major feat in itself.

Mum was also apprehensive of the move away from her comfort zone of communal caring and sharing, to a life in a strange neighbourhood, in a dwelling with modern conveniences. However, she remained unfaltering in her resolve to support her husband and his dream of a better life for his family.

When Dad became aware of a vacant block, owned by the Land brothers and situated between their own homes, he made an approach to them. They were more than happy to sell to Dad provided he could come up with the asking price of 200 pounds. Dad approached his trusted friend and boss, Jack O'Shea, and explained his plan. Jack was impressed with Dad's ambitious pitch and his desire to advance his position in life.

After talking it over with his wife Ivy, Jack agreed to lend Dad the staggering amount needed to put a deposit on the quarter hectare property at 22 Bedford Street. Such was the respect Jack and Ivy held for Dad, the loan was sealed through a gentleman's handshake. True to his word, Dad worked for Jack on Bulloo Downs Station for two years to pay off the debt. He never once missed a day's work or stalled his loan repayments to his boss.

Throughout his life Dad took great pride in not owing anyone, black or white, anything. He paid his bills promptly and lived within his budget. Because he never had any unpaid debts, he could look people in the eye without guilt. With solid references from Mayor Jack Tonkins and Cunnamulla Native Welfare Association Chairman Scott Doling, Dad met with the local Commonwealth Bank manager and convinced him that, with a good steady income and being of fine character, he would be a worthy recipient of a housing loan.

With bank finance approved, Dad entered into the uncharted waters of agreeing on a design for a three-bedroom wooden house with verandah and laundry attached. He sat down with local builder, Merv O'Brien, and after studying various brochures, identified what he thought would satisfy the needs of his growing family and look good on the block. After discussing it with Mum, Dad signed off on the plans and the building commenced. Every week or two, Dad would drive past the site and smile as he saw the house take shape—from its foundations through to the walls being erected, and finally the roof being securely nailed down.

In 1966 Dad moved the family into our new house. Mum and Dad had the largest room at the end of the house while Pam and Susan shared the room facing the backyard. Jimmo and I occupied the room facing the front and adjacent to the front steps of the verandah.

Off the verandah to the left were twin doors and to the right was a single entrance door. On entering the house visitors were greeted by a spacious lounge that led to a separate dining room. The dining room overlooked a large kitchen and servery that opened out to the back steps, and to the left of the steps was an enclosed laundry with spaced palings for ventilation. From the lounge, visitors could walk down a short hallway, past the boys' room on the right or on to our parent's room straight ahead. If they turned left at the end of the hallway they would arrive, two metres away, at our toilet. To the right of the toilet was the girls' room and to the left was a large bathroom.

The sprawling backyard was soon turned into a playground with swings and several native trees, which we planted in the first week we moved in. A chicken pen measuring twenty by ten metres was built on the left corner of the block. In the centre of the yard was a clothes line that soon had its perfectly parallel-to-the-ground arms bent from us kids using it as a swing—although before long Mum put a stop to the energetic twirls us four errant kids perfected on it.

I guess our place was typical of most houses in the street but to us kids it was like a castle. I'm not sure how many times our parents told us to stop turning the light switches on and off. We were amazed at how much a room could be illuminated by one small light fixed to the ceiling. Down on the Yumba we worried about our kerosene lanterns and were always warned by our elders of unnecessary usage. Open fires were for outdoors and only permitted indoors in extreme cases, for example to provide warmth for a sick child or to dry wet clothes when there was continuous rainfall over consecutive days.

If the lights were enthralling then the beds with springs and thick mattresses were a revelation that took weeks to sink in. We jumped and jumped on our new beds that, to our delight, supported our weight unlike our beds on the Yumba whose timber supports creaked and at times split from the constant pounding.

I felt like a king when Mum told us kids that we could sleep in our own beds. This was truly a remarkable experience. Mind you, it didn't take long for our cousins to invite themselves over and we were soon back to sharing again, fighting over a single blanket. When Mum saved enough money and bought us all sheets, top and bottom, to go with our blanket I felt like a white fella.

Most exciting of all was that I no longer had to wake up early, especially during winter in sub-zero temperatures, to perform my chore of cutting the hardwood into small pieces to light a fire. White man's magic came to the fore and at the flick of a switch Mum was able to cook a meal on one of three cooking plates.

On weekends we didn't have to dig a hole in the ground to cook our Sunday roast; the white fella thought of that as well and built an oven into the stove. The heat was constant and Mum didn't have to remind me to add wood to the fire to maintain the temperature. Just when we thought we could not be surprised any further, we discovered the oven had a built-in timer that would ring like an alarm clock to remind Mum that the meal was ready. Us Murrie kids had exceptional mungas (ears) and could hear that oven bell from 100 metres away.

⁂

One of the first things Mum did after we moved into town was to take us four children to the local photography studio to have our portrait taken (youngest brother Lawrence wasn't yet born). The photographer didn't believe we had just come from the Yumba, but anyone who knew my mother knew that she was strong on the wholesome look and always had us children well-groomed. I'm not sure what he expected us to look like.

In town, I noticed how quiet white people were. They all seemed to go to bed at a respectable time of night and in the morning they ate quietly and went to work without knocking on the door to borrow milk or sugar. I thought that if this kept up Dad would be able to save a lot of money, not having to cater for relatives who were regularly asking for a loan of food and promising to pay us back later. Unfortunately the borrowed items at times didn't always return like boomerangs, but Dad kept lending.

The only noises I heard—and grew to enjoy—on the eerily silent streets in the early hours of the morning in Cunnamulla, were the distinctive sounds of thoroughbred horses' hooves on the road heading for the sandhill, fifty metres past the caravan park. Trevor 'Speck' Miller lived around the corner from our house and was the first trainer to lead his horses to the hill. His horses roamed freely in the compound bordering our backyard. Trevor was a friendly fellow and his manner suited him in his daytime job as a taxi driver.

Half an hour later I'd hear Barry Miller's horses, travelling several blocks further from town, breaking the quiet of the morning again with the rhythm of their hooves against the firm terrain. The sounds of the cantering horses became more pronounced when they crossed the bitumen road on Watson Street at the command of their trainer.

These horse-training brothers had great success on the western racing tracks and their strategy of making use of the sandhill to condition their horses proved a masterstroke. When the brothers felt they were in need of greater challenges in the 'sport of kings' they packed their belongings and prized horses and moved their families closer to the action on the coast.

However the most famous of all horsemen to come from Cunnamulla was Darby McCarthy, an ambitious Aboriginal rider from the Yumba. Darby left school at the age of eight and rode his first winner when he was ten years old. In his celebrated riding career he won many prestigious races including the Newcastle Gold Cup, three Stradbroke Handicaps and the Brisbane Cup.

the N word

⁙

Once we were settled in town, Mum soon discovered that the corner store owner, eager to attract new business, was prepared to give her credit. She enjoyed this luxury, especially as it meant she could avail herself of her only vice—a packet of Viscount cigarettes—every couple of days. If we were good kids during the week Mum would allow us to put a few lollies on the tab as well. But we never exceeded our limit, as she was vigilant with her account.

My fondest memory on first arriving at Bedford Street was being amazed at the sight of white men stopping at our house to deliver the mail and cart the rubbish away. On the Yumba if we wanted to collect our mail we had to walk several kilometres to the post office in town. And if we accumulated rubbish we would merely dig a deep hole away from the residence to dispose of it. Later I found out that the Hagan family wasn't getting any preferential treatment; every rate-paying household received these council services.

Our house was opposite the caravan park and separated from the Yumba by the sandhill which rose to a height of five metres and was in parts 200 metres across. Whenever I got homesick I would walk over the large sandhill to be greeted by friendly faces. There were plenty of return visits too. My relatives and friends seemed as excited as us about the amenities at our new address and were always dropping in.

The biggest advantage for me was living close to the public swimming pool. Many times I remember walking to the pool from the Yumba on towels and any patch of grass, to beat the burning hot summer sand.

Most Aboriginal families couldn't afford shoes although a few had thongs, which were useless anyway as the soles of your feet got burnt when the thongs sunk into the soft sand. Our Bedford Street home was close to the public pool and not a sandhill to climb. We also

the N word

had the luxury of walking along our white neighbours' soft, well-manicured green lawns.

It didn't take Dad long to catch on to the white people's favourite pastime of hand-watering their lawn of an evening. I would often join him in the front yard to yarn while he hosed the already saturated grass. The watering worked. The grass grew greener and longer and before long there was a new chore for us kids—mowing. We couldn't wait for winter to come when the grass wouldn't grow so fast.

Walking soon became a thing of the past when us kids succeeded in our campaign to have Mum and Dad buy us Gold Star speedster bikes. At a steady speed we could comfortably ride across town and back within the hour. When we got older and more daring that time shrunk considerably as we took routes which we knew were off limits.

※

During my first year at Cunnamulla Primary School my teacher recommended to my parents that I be sent away to the Sir Leslie Wilson Home at Margate on the Redcliffe Peninsula. She felt I needed specialist speech therapy to help me pronounce my 'ths' and 'hs'. Apparently I was saying 'dat' instead of 'that' and 'airs' instead of 'hairs'. The speech therapist must have been off her game because I'm still stumbling over like-sounding words on occasions.

For the three months I was at the Home I missed my family so much that I was constantly crying. I was just a kid of six or seven and had no comprehension of why I needed to be 800 kilometres away living with strangers. Sure I got to see the ocean for the first time and enjoyed playing with the multitude of sea creatures darting around the rock pools on the beach beyond the hostel's back steps. I built sandcastles and was fascinated too by the silhouettes of the ships on the horizon way out in the Pacific Ocean. But all this meant a big

the N word

fat nought when I tried to understand why I was there. I asked over and over again as to when I would be permitted to return home. 'Soon' was the recurring response.

The hostel children had to march over a kilometre to school and back everyday—rain, hail or shine. There were almost 100 children, mostly white, who went there for problems with their ears, nose, throat, eyes and speech or some combination of these. But there were also many Aboriginal kids from Cunnamulla and other rural communities who'd been summarily rounded up and sent off to the hostel. Some had fond memories; others like me had no positives to recall, except for the trip home on the train, which proved to be the biggest highlight.

Several years ago I made a journey with Mum, Dad, Rhonda and my son Stephen to the hostel to show them the place where I was sent thirty-six years prior. When we arrived Mum had a perplexed look on her face as she didn't recall ever sending me there. In fact, she did not remember me ever leaving home as a kid until I was in high school and travelled away for sport. I can only surmise that she repressed any memory of those dreadful three months.

In the meantime, life in Cunnamulla began to change for the better with the voluntary relocations of some families from the Yumba to town. Dad, too modest to accept any major credit for this, put it down to opportunities being presented from a number of quarters. But after talking to older Murries who made the early move I believe that Dad was in fact their main inspiration.

Dad was increasingly being viewed by his people as a leader. There was an increase in people traffic to our house at all hours of the day and night with Murries requiring assistance. Housing, health, law, education, finance, alcoholism and domestic violence concerns were

the N word

among their priorities and Dad was available to all who required advice, whether it was a minor or more serious matter. But he stipulated that they didn't present themselves at our doorstep at an unacceptable hour. Mum was an impatient person and a stern word from her was sufficient to ensure there weren't repeat offenders. With her protective eye on us kids and our commitments to school work and need for a good night's sleep, she made it patently clear what were acceptable visiting hours. Otherwise Dad, being more tolerant, would have entertained at all hours of the day and night.

Mum was a very strict person generally. She refused to answer the door if she knew it wasn't an emergency or if the person was drunk. She never drank alcohol herself and no one ever made the same mistake twice of seeking a sympathetic ear at our house when under the influence.

Even her father, Grandfather Jim Mitchell, after a night on the town, wouldn't bother to knock at our door during the evening. He just slept on the grass in the backyard under one of several trees which would shield him from the rays of the early morning sun. When he awoke, he'd come inside for breakfast. After a hearty meal, consumed with minimal table talk, he'd up and leave to walk home to his humpy—an old caravan—on the Yumba.

Not long after we made the move over the sandhill, Lawrence Michael, the last of the five children in our family, was born in June 1967. His arrival into the world came four years after Susan's and rather than move an extra bed into Jimmo's and my shared room, Mum prevented any sibling arguments by placing his cot in her and Dad's room.

Around the same time, the Land brothers sold both their houses and we were blessed with the arrival of new neighbours. On the corner block, a family with an interest in opal mining took up occupancy. They had a son and daughter who were around the ages of Pam and Jimmo. We became good friends and visited each other's houses often.

the N word

On the other side was a family whose head of the house was the imposing figure of Sergeant Nutley, 'boss man of the gunjabulls' as Grandfather Mitchell would affectionately proclaim whenever he visited our house. The Nutleys also had a son and daughter who were the same ages as Lawrence and me respectively.

I don't recall any discrimination ever being displayed towards us from either side of the fence. We all fed the chooks and played with trucks and dolls in and under each other's houses. And whichever parent was about bathed and bandaged the numerous cuts and scratches that resulted from our youthful exuberance. Those were wonderful years.

After Dad honoured his financial commitments to Jack O'Shea he changed careers and took up a labouring position with the Paroo Shire Council in Cunnamulla. Not long afterwards he was promoted to ganger. Dad mixed well with the predominantly white workers on the council and soon developed good working relationships with many of them.

He was invited to attend the Buffalo Lodge Association which was becoming an important social committee for local men. Us kids joked about the association and called the gatherings 'old men's pow-wows'. We were never invited to attend any of their meetings and never asked why.

Merv Kundie, who had recently arrived in Cunnamulla, revived the old Buffalo Lodge in Emma Street. After a short recruitment program the membership—comprising fellow council workers, shearers and businessmen—grew to around forty regular attendees. Dad quickly threw himself into new committees and would get especially excited prior to the fortnightly Lodge meetings. I could sense the pride he took in getting himself prepared with all the colourful gowns and medals. He was particularly pleased when his older brother Albert (Uncle Chum), a respected shearer, got involved in the Lodge as well. It was the only association Dad ever recalls his brother joining.

Dad enjoyed the company of tough, hardworking, honest men such as Merv Kundie, Doug McGregor and Colin Walk who, along with every member of the Lodge, espoused the philosophy of fostering a brotherhood spirit in which all members were treated equally. Tud Murphy also joined Dad and Uncle Chum and together these three men played significant roles in changing attitudes towards Aboriginal people in Cunnamulla.

In the Lodge, Dad rose to the rank of Worthy Primo, which allowed him to induct new members and be involved in decision making. Unfortunately other clubs around Cunnamulla at the same time were holding firm on their unofficial policies of keeping the blacks out. But the Buffalo Lodge allowed Dad and other Aboriginal men to enter into genuine friendships with white men— and in turn their new colleagues got to enjoy strong and lasting friendships with the Aboriginal members.

These relationships flowed onto their children and it didn't take long for us former Yumba kids to be mixing freely after school with the sons and daughters of Buffalo Lodge members. The Christmas period was the most exciting time of all. I got presents from Dad's Paroo Shire Council Christmas party, the Buffalo Lodge Christmas party, my birthday on 20 December and of course on Christmas Day. I enjoyed these celebrations and the numerous parties that concluded the year. I was sure getting used to this way of life and knew my relatives living on the Yumba would enjoy it too if only they had the same opportunities.

the N word

Jim's Ascent

Throughout the early 1960s Aboriginal leaders were continuing their campaigns across Australia in an attempt to gain popular support and embarrass the longstanding Liberal government into addressing critical issues facing Aboriginal people. As a result of the outcry about the appalling conditions Indigenous Australians had to endure, a national referendum was held on 27 May 1967 on whether two sections of the Constitution should be amended.

The first amendment would enable the Federal government to take on more responsibility for Aboriginal people. The second would mean the inclusion of Aborigines in national censuses. Aboriginal leaders and their supporters were overjoyed when 90.77% of the voting age population supported the 'yes' vote.

On 10 August 1967, the government enacted the legislation and made the amendments to the Constitution. However, it wasn't until 1972 that full advantage of the new powers was taken and the newly-elected Whitlam Labor government established the Department of Aboriginal Affairs (DAA). The Department was to make policy recommendations on how to manage the growing social problems of Aboriginal people. Ironically most of the staff employed to make the policy decisions were non-Indigenous.

the N word

Cunnamulla, meanwhile, continued to have its fair share of troubles and one of the most publicised became known as the Nancy Young Affair. In July 1968, Nancy Young's baby daughter Evelyn had become seriously ill and was rushed to the Cunnamulla Hospital in the middle of the night. The duty nurse did not call the doctor on duty and he did not see the baby until the following morning. Evelyn died two days later.

A few months later Nancy was charged with manslaughter. She was found guilty in April 1969 and sentenced to three years' imprisonment. There was an immediate outcry from relatives and friends and although Nancy appealed against the conviction, she was not successful. By now the media had exposed the story and national attention was focused on the case. At a further appeal in November new evidence resulted in Nancy being freed. To this day she has received no compensation for her wrongful imprisonment.

As a result of the publicity of Nancy's case, in August 1968 the Australian Broadcasting Commission's (ABC) *Four Corners* programme screened 'Out of Sight, Out of Mind', a documentary which highlighted the poor living conditions at the camp and the lack of support by authorities. It was a wake-up call for non-Indigenous Australians who until then had not understood the terrible living conditions that many Aboriginal people were forced to endure.

I met Aunty Nancy—in our culture all elders are called 'Uncle' or 'Aunty' out of respect—in Cunnamulla in mid-2003 when I was assisting *Four Corners* on an unrelated documentary. I found her in a frail condition and she said that she wished she was still living down the Yumba. She had no hot water system in her house and had to boil the jug and pour the water into a baby's bathtub for a daily wash.

the N word

As the new decade of the 1970s arrived Dad and other Aboriginal leaders in Cunnamulla continued to agitate for improvements in the living conditions of their people. They demanded access to affordable housing in town and a change in attitude by the local civic leaders towards the Yumba Murries.

The highest profiled Aboriginal in the land at that time was Senator Neville Bonner who, in 1971, became the first Aboriginal person to be elected member to the Federal parliament. Senator Bonner made many memorable speeches on behalf of his people, the most significant being his maiden address which included the following excerpt:

> Those who avoided death, and the subsequent great roundup, and others who had escaped from the missions and reserves, came to the cities and towns, there to be completely shunned by white society and forced to lead the life of pariahs in tin shanties, in bark humpies and in other degrading accommodation, on the banks of creeks, on the outskirts of the towns and, indeed, in any place sufficiently far from the cities and towns so that they would not offend the delicate senses of their so-called superior white masters. These of my race were the fringe dwellers, the legion of the lost, the dirty, ignorant, mentally inferior, 'Abos', 'Boongs', 'Blacks' as you were wont to call us, and treat us accordingly."[4]

The continued barrage of public statements such as Senator Bonner's and the willingness of the media to cover them resulted in the government taking a more direct approach. In 1973 the Labor Government took the radical step of introducing the concept of an elected Aboriginal advisory body to provide policy advice and direction, a role previously held by white public servants, many of whom had no contact with grassroots Aboriginal people. The

the N word

National Aboriginal Consultative Committee (NACC), a separate entity to DAA, was to advise the Government on all matters relating to Aboriginal and Torres Strait Islanders affairs. The Australian Electoral Commission (AEC) was charged with conducting elections for its forty-three members who would represent some 800 Indigenous communities across the country.

Dad was unaware of this momentous decision. However, some of his colleagues in the ALP in Cunnamulla spotted the advertisement in one of the national newspapers and, having seen him grow in confidence over the years as an active member of their party, believed Dad would make an ideal candidate.

With the support of the ALP, Dad received the unbelievable amount of 100 pounds towards his election campaign. He took time off work and travelled with Mum to towns that until then he hadn't heard of, let alone visited. Dad's brother, Uncle Chum and his wife Aunty Joyce looked after us five kids while Mum and Dad were away. Uncle Chum had married Mum's older sister, Joyce, and over the years their children had become like brothers and sisters to us, so the move to their place wasn't very difficult as we were forever staying over at their house and vice versa.

After receiving a detailed briefing from Tom Beresford, local manager of the State's Native Welfare Department, on the best route to undertake on the campaign, Dad and Mum were off on a journey that would change our lives forever. Although somewhat daunted at first, Dad became quite resourceful and innovative as he travelled from town to town, introducing himself and making promises to improve the conditions of the local Indigenous people if they elected him to office.

On arriving at each destination he would visit the local police station, inform them of the nature of his visit and ask if there were any Aboriginal people in the town, and if so, where they resided. If he didn't gain much information from the police he would ask a taxi driver or even drive through town until he saw an Aboriginal.

the N word

Back in those days campaigning by Indigenous people was unheard of within Indigenous communities and Dad got mixed responses ranging from positive 'tea and biscuit' hospitality, to a rude 'don't have time to talk to you, you've come at a bad time, the Aussies are playing the Poms in a test match on television' reaction.

However Dad must have had a good sales pitch because he became the first elected Indigenous representative for the region. The area he represented included the townships from Tin Can Bay on the east coast to Noccundra near the South Australian, Northern Territory and New South Wales borders, a stretch of land about 2000 kilometres long and 500 kilometres wide.

Most towns throughout Australia at that time had fringe camps similar to the Yumba. One of the first things Dad did as the elected member was to encourage communities to become incorporated organisations and apply for State or Federal grants to purchase houses so families could move out of their camp situations. To become incorporated a community needed to recruit twenty-five adult Aboriginals through the process of advertising and conducting an election. In keeping with the community's constitution, the committee would then elect an executive and organise signatories for a bank account.

In 1974 Dad became the foundation Chairman of the Housing Co-operative in Cunnamulla and, along with other leaders, was successful in relocating some families from the Yumba into state houses in town. The State Department for Aboriginal and Islander Affairs had been purchasing homes in Cunnamulla for Yumba Murries and by the mid-1970s owned several homes and flats. In 1975 the Housing Co-operative received a grant from the Commonwealth Government and purchased an additional seven houses.

the N word

The following year was both significant and sad for the Murries in Cunnamulla as the Yumba no longer housed displaced people who had arrived gradually over several decades.

In 1975 Dad also became a member of the south-west Queensland Aboriginal Legal Service (ALS). Aboriginal legal services were being set up all over the country to provide better and more equitable legal representation for Aboriginal people. At that time, many Murries in Queensland were being charged with summary offences, commonly referred to by Aboriginal people as 'the trifecta'—public drunkenness, obscene language and resisting arrest. Young people were also starting to accumulate criminal records and they had little access to adequate legal representation. These minor offences were starting to appear regularly on many people's charge sheets. In later years they would be viewed in a detrimental light when presiding judges assessed their criminal history.

The immediate effect of the ALS was a reduction in the incarceration rate of Aboriginal people. It also altered the way publicans and the police dealt with Aboriginal people in places where racism was a way of life.

The police, however, were not always prepared for the change in their dealings with Murries. They had to be accountable for their actions and although their blatant mistreatment of Aboriginal people eased off in the public domain, more covert operations of intimidation were adopted. In Cunnamulla, where once an offender might have left the watch-house with a black eye and a swollen lip from a beating inside an isolated cell, they could now depart with no obvious facial injuries but with sore, or even broken, ribs. The local police officers were well known for their strong-arm tactics.

The pubs weren't much better. My brother-in-law, Roger Robinson, recalls going to the Cunnamulla Hotel to test out the rumour that the hotel wouldn't serve blacks. Roger was the pin-up boy in Cunnamulla, and the town's most famous sportsperson on account of his many achievements in the boxing ring under trainer

Billy Johnstone. He was also an apprentice mechanic at Bill's Auto and the Johnstone family treated Roger like a son.

At the pub that afternoon the first thing that surprised him was that the white barman was, ironically, the husband of a black lady. Under sufferance, the barman served Roger but signalled for the owner to come to the front bar. He told Roger that the pub didn't serve his type. When Roger asked what he meant the owner told him he knew very well and promptly organised a few bouncers to throw him out.

Weeks later, prior to his first overseas boxing tournament, the Oceania Titles in Tahiti, Billy approached Roger and asked him to attend a function put on by the Lions Club as part of a fundraiser for his international quest. When Roger heard that it was to be at the Cunnamulla Hotel he told his trainer he wouldn't go.

The next day, Bill approached Roger again and asked if he would attend the function for his wife's sake, suggesting that Roger could leave immediately after the formalities were over. Reluctantly Roger agreed and did his best to forget the hotel's appalling reputation, just for one night.

To Roger's surprise the owner greeted him like a long-lost customer. To add insult to injury, Roger was also greeted affectionately by a local detective who had been heavy handed with him in the past. Such was his respect for the Johnstone family that when he was urged to acknowledge the generosity of the Lions Club he chose to be polite and gracious.

In those days the RSL, bowling club and the golf club all had an unwritten rule of not serving Murries. Around the same time as Roger's incident, racism reared its ugly head again when Mrs Eva Manthey (also known as Eve) was refused membership of the Cunnamulla Bowling Club. Aboriginal people were familiar with this type of discrimination, but in this instance Mrs Manthey (a descendent of the Kooma tribe and a relative of my mother) was the wife of a well-known and respected member of the bowling club,

the N word

Mr Frank Manthey. Frank wrote about the event in a chapter he contributed to the publication *Anything's Possible! The Bilby Fence and Beyond:*

> Eve, my wife, was an aboriginal, and one of a family of five girls. She was the second oldest and was extremely well educated. Her mother saw to that.
>
> ... Being of European descent and married to an aboriginal has a lot to offer, but it also has a lot of hardships attached to it. I saw what I never believed I would see. Racism.
>
> ... I was a member of a bowling club and I played a bit of bowls when I was home. Our wives decided they would join the ladies bowling club. My mate wasn't a member but I was. The president's wife nominated both of the ladies, Eva, my wife, and my mate's wife, for membership. The meeting where they accepted nominations was held and it was one of the most tragic and heart-wrenching episodes of our lives. They knocked back my wife for membership, with no grounds; an inconceivable decision!
>
> I played bowls. They all knew me. They all knew our kids went to Catholic schools. My mate wasn't even a member, and yet they accepted his wife and knocked my wife back, solely of the grounds of colour! It was absolutely devastating to her! I resigned from the club.
>
> I had a very good friend who has written numerous songs for Slim Dusty. He wrote "Trumby", and he was staying with us in Cunnamulla. He wrote a poem called the Duller Colour Bowling Club and it referred to the ladies that knocked her back. [5]

I had an experience of that no-go zone myself some years later when I returned home from boarding school at the end of Year 12 and, with several Aboriginal and white friends, tried to gain entry to a New Year's Eve dance. My white friends were allowed in but my Aboriginal friends and I were told we weren't welcome. To make matters worse, the person who refused me, under orders from his manager, was an old friend from Cunnamulla State School. My white

the N word

friends refused to go in without us and instead reported the matter to their parents who were furious and drove to the club to voice their disgust. The old friend from Year 10 resigned from his job that night in protest and joined us at another venue.

※

In July 1977 it became a talking point around town when a steel cage was erected in the public bar at the Kerr's Hotel and the Aboriginal clientele had to be served their drinks under an opening in the grille. The opening was so low that it restricted drinking to stubbies as long neck bottles couldn't fit through.

According to my cousin, John-John Mitchell, there had been a disturbance the previous night, involving several Yumba men. The publican pulled a shotgun and after that incident arranged for the cage to be erected.

The Yumba men weren't allowed in most of the other dozen or so pubs in town and so had little choice but to return to Kerr's. One day, another cousin, Henry Hagan (who later became notorious for his fighting prowess throughout the eastern states), ordered a packet of peanuts from the proprietor. On receiving the nuts he threw them through the cage with the remark of 'catch monkey'. He was banned from the pub for life.

A few days later he staged a fist fight in the public bar and while watching the feuding factions from a safe distance was motioned to the bar. The publican offered to rescind the ban if he stopped the fight. On Henry's signal the fisticuffs were brought to an abrupt end and his short-lived 'lifetime ban' was lifted. City media outlets got news of the steel cage and sent journalists and photographers to Cunnamulla to cover the event. As word reached government sources, the proprietor relented to pressure and at length took the cage down.

Back in Dad's youth such racial discrimination didn't just come from the pubs and clubs however. The attitudes of retailers as well as of public sector agencies would be to give preferential treatment to white queue hoppers. Clothing shops would only allow Aboriginal customers to look at clothes and purchase the item by sight—under no circumstances would they ever allow the Murries to try them on. Some tried to object, but in those days it got them nowhere.

Then there were the unscrupulous contractors who would engage Aboriginal workers as cheap labour and on completion of the job pay them less than what they agreed on and in some cases not at all. Most Aboriginal workers weren't affiliated with any union and couldn't afford to take civil action against the contractor. Those who did retaliate would invariably be seen as the offenders and find the law taking the side of a 'battling' contractor.

Despite the ongoing racial intolerance in Cunnamulla, Dad's rapport with his white colleagues continued. His rapid elevation to the dizzy heights of elected representative for his people on the NACC posed new challenges for him in his hometown and some wondered if he was up to the task.

However Dad was not fazed by the doubters and, realising his standing amongst his peers, enjoyed the new demands on his skills and time. Life was starting to look up for him and, with increased age and wisdom, the challenge of taking on the plight of his people did not appear as insurmountable as it had at first.

In 1976 Dad had registered as a Justice of the Peace for the State of Queensland, becoming the first Aboriginal in Cunnamulla to do so. Nevertheless, after a long period of dedicated work in the town, and having seen many social and physical improvements in the living conditions of the local Aboriginal people, Dad felt he could achieve more for himself and us by selling the family home and moving to Toowoomba. He could still keep a close eye on Cunnamulla, but as he often had to go to Canberra for meetings he was finding it increasingly difficult organising his travel itinerary from Cunnamulla.

After its election in 1975, the Fraser government commissioned a review of the NACC. It was found that the NACC had not been an effective mechanism for providing advice to the Minister and it was replaced by the National Aboriginal Conference (NAC), which differed from the NACC in that its structure included representatives elected to state branches, and from the state branches a ten-member national executive was elected.

In the new NAC elections Dad was again successful and in 1980 was elected Chairman. This position increased his profile significantly. As the most senior elected Indigenous representative in Australia he assumed more responsibilities and, by all accounts, handled the new challenges with distinction, largely through his conciliatory approach. The downside to the elevation was that it meant he was required to be away from home more often and the family now found they were competing for his time with bureaucrats, media representatives and his constituents.

That year also catapulted Dad into the international limelight when he led a four-person delegation to Geneva to address the United Nations on the Noonkanbah dispute. The traditional owners of Noonkanbah Station in the Kimberley Region of Western Australia had approached the NAC when their requests to the Commonwealth Government to stop the State Government's support of a mining company drilling on their sacred site failed. When the Minister for Aboriginal Affairs turned down their request to intervene, Dad felt his elected body had no other option but to put the matter before the United Nations. The NAC was affiliated with the World Council of Indigenous People and had automatic speaker status at Geneva. Presented with that opportunity Dad addressed the 33rd session of the UN Sub-Committee on the Prevention of Discrimination and the Protection of Minorities, becoming the first Indigenous Australian to do so.

Before they left, the NAC Executive Committee accepted an invitation from the Prime Minister, Malcolm Fraser, to meet at Parliament House with senior Cabinet members. The talks were historic as it was the first time Aboriginal representatives had held such discussions in the Cabinet Room. Unfortunately the importance of government initiative was somewhat lost in the blaze of publicity on the Geneva trip, but Dad said the delegation he led to Parliament House did not dismiss the significance of the occasion.

In his speech to the UN, Dad outlined what the NAC was seeking from the Australian government:

- An immediate halt to drilling at Noonkanbah.
- Emergency legislation to prohibit mining on Aboriginal land until proper negotiations between the communities, the companies and the State governments had occurred.
- Legislation to make the NAC a statutory body (as the Haitt committee recommended originally).
- An initial allocation to negotiate a treaty (or makarrata).
- A budget allocation to the NAC that would benefit its status and increase annually by 10% in real terms.
- Funds for a research unit within the NAC to develop the treaty or makarrata proposal and other programs.

Dad's address to the UN was an important step for Aboriginal Australians and his fine articulation of the problems his people were experiencing at home won publicity for their cause throughout the world. Dad was highly aware that he was paving the way for many other Indigenous people to follow. Still, the Australian government did not respond to the NAC's proposals and with the exception of the ABC, the delegation's success at the UN was not widely covered by the Australian media. Many couldn't see the point in covering the outcome of a group of blacks travelling to the UN to criticise the government who paid their wages. Dad was covering completely new territory and the national media had no idea of the ramifications of the outcome.

Dad eloquently put his views on the success of his United Nations campaign when he addressed the Foreign Affairs Association in Canberra on 28 April 1981:

> After all, the problems of the Aboriginal people ... alcohol, unemployment, disease, illiteracy, social unacceptability ... are all problems that stem directly from the white man's invasion of our land. Before you came we did not have such problems, so can you wonder that we seek compensations, that we seek guarantees, and that we will not sit back and merely accept social welfare payments.
> It is another irony that we have had to turn to strangers for solace and understanding and it is the warmth of their response that has made our international venture an avenue of real hope.
> Will we go overseas again? Of course we will. And we will continue to speak with a voice of authority no matter where. No one knows Australia like an Aboriginal ... no one is an Australian as an Aboriginal ... no one can tell us what we want or what we need more than our own people. No one can spread this message further than an Aboriginal.[6]

How prophetic those words were. Twenty-three years later to the month, I would receive a decision from the UN after taking my own campaign overseas.

Months after Dad returned from Geneva, Malcolm Fraser's Liberal Government acknowledged his performance as Chairman of the NAC and his distinguished performance on the international scene. They conferred upon him the award of Member in the General Division of the Order of Australia.

the N word

Dad was not able to attend the Government House presentation in Canberra on 13 June 1981 due to work commitments. However, some time later he escorted Mum and my sister, Pam, to the State Governor's residence in Brisbane and was presented with his award by the Governor of Queensland, Commodore Sir James Ramsay. The ceremony was a very formal affair and it was a day Dad would treasure forever.

Mum accompanied Dad to many official functions during his time in public office, and even met the Queen when she opened the National Art Gallery and the High Court buildings in Canberra. Although Mum was very supportive of Dad's work and enjoyed the benefits that came with the job, she did not enjoy the lonely days and nights when he was away and would have preferred to see him around the house on a more regular basis. Already his journey had far exceeded her expectations from that first venture away from Cunnamulla when she helped him campaign for the NACC elections.

The third NAC election was held on Saturday 17 October 1981. Dad once again nominated but this time was unsuccessful. He viewed this defeat as the end of one chapter and the beginning of another. He successfully applied for a job with the Aboriginal Development Commission (ADC).

After three month's training in Canberra, a short stint managing an ADC-owned property outside Moree and a short-term appointment in Bourke, he was posted to Roma where he established an office and was appointed branch manager. When the Roma office closed in 1985, he transferred to Brisbane and stayed with the ADC through their transition to become the Aboriginal and Torres Strait Islander Commission until he retired in 1997.

Throughout the early 1980s there was growing concern among Aboriginal groups that action on land rights and the need for a treaty was stalling. The government was clearly nervous about the legal implications but during Dad's term as chairman, they did agree to fund the NAC to consult widely on a 'makarrata' or treaty. Dad led the makarrata committee to every state in the country, including the Torres Strait Islands and remote Aboriginal communities, seeking input into the negotiations.

Sadly Mum's father passed away while Dad was consulting in some of the remote Aboriginal communities in northern Australia and Dad could not be contacted. I can clearly remember the night after Mum and her family buried Grandfather Mitchell. Mum was naturally quite distraught and she boiled a pot of water, placed some salt and a lemon in it and held a cloth over her head to take in the steam. I heard her crying for several hours and felt hopeless that I was unable to comfort her.

As expected, from their exhaustive rounds of consultation the NAC gained an overwhelming level of support from the Aboriginal and Torres Strait Islander people to negotiate a treaty with the Commonwealth Government. Unfortunately, after all the money spent in preparing a report on the makarrata, the government did not implement any of the recommendations and allowed the report to sit on the shelves and gather dust.

Dad believed that it was cheaper and easier for the government to spend money on the consultations and let people believe they were serious about a negotiated treaty than to say no in the first instance. Either way the end result would have been the same.

On reflection, Dad says the major achievements in his career in public office include being registered as a Justice of the Peace for the State of Queensland (1976); being the first Indigenous Australian to address the UN General Assembly in Geneva (1980); becoming a Member in the General Division of the Order of Australia (1981); having the Jim Hagan Hostel in Toowoomba named in his honour (1983); and being listed in Who's Who in Australia in the same year.

the N word

There's no doubt in my mind that my father has made a huge difference to the lives of Aboriginal people living in Cunnamulla and throughout the country. Perhaps without realising it, he raised the bar and in so doing sent out a challenge to all of his children—but especially to me, his eldest son.

the N word

Teenage Years

As I entered my teenage years I became more conscious of racial discrimination in Cunnamulla, particularly from the cinema proprietor who appeared to have a huge dislike of his Aboriginal patrons. He was also the Deputy Mayor of the Paroo Shire Council and a respected man within the white community. But the only equality we had with his white patrons was standing in the queue to buy a ticket. Even as a child I knew walking down a damp, poorly-lit laneway with no covering was not a choice thing, especially when we were soaked from a sudden downpour.

At the cinema, Aboriginal patrons had a separate entrance to the white folk, and we used different toilets that were annexed to the side door. White patrons strode to the cinema entrance on plush carpets. Inside the theatre they had the option of sitting upstairs, in grand seating, or to the rear of the cinema in comfortable seating. We were herded towards the front rows of canvas seats in a roped-off area. If any 'cocky black' dared to slip past the rope to the seats with reserve slips, they would be pounced on and given a life ban. We would often leave the cinema with sore necks from viewing the large screen at such an acute angle. When the lights came on at intermission we'd look around and try to spot our white friends from school and give them a little wave of acknowledgement.

the N word

Throughout the screening the proprietor would prowl up and down the aisle. If he caught anyone talking he'd flash a torch on them. It struck me as his way of letting us know that he was keeping a close eye on us and that we were not to even think of sitting outside our allotted area.

His biggest concern however was whether any of the townsfolk's daughters would defy their parents and sit with an Aboriginal, especially one of the opposite sex. Still, I looked forward to the movies and tolerated the draconian rules of conduct, even if I felt humiliated and hopeless at my inability to make things more equal. As it had been when I was younger, going to the movies was the highlight of the week, and critically important for a teenager in a small rural town with limited opportunities for entertainment. There were no other social venues in town where my parents would allow me to go unsupervised, so the pictures was really the only chance to hang out with my friends—black or white.

·:·

It was around this time that I joined the Anglican Church and served as an altar boy. I would wake early on Sunday mornings and arrive at the church in time to put my altar gown on and perform the first twenty rings of the huge church bell to signal to the town's Anglicans that service would commence in half an hour. At ten to nine I would ring the bell ten more times to signal the imminent start of service. I recall that there was more than one Sunday when one of my shoes was in need of a new sole and I would place the good shoe over the top to hide the holes as I knelt towards the altar to ring the gong for communion.

As I'd be walking to church some of my people would be walking home after sleeping at a friend's house, unable to make it home the night before. Although still looking and smelling the worse for their night on the drink, they were polite to me whenever I passed them on the street. Most were familiar with my Sunday routine. Some even made predictions that I would one day leave Cunnamulla to become a priest.

I was confirmed in the St Albans Anglican Church, Cunnamulla, and had the privilege of travelling with the parish priest and other altar boys to serve at St Johns Cathedral in Brisbane at the ordination of new priests. That trip was educational for me as I got to meet a lot of important people in the church and observe their hierarchy. I was intrigued by how the more senior clerics wore richer blue or purple robes and had more distinguished caps.

Growing up in the country as an Aboriginal youth I often felt the negative vibes from older white people, for instance when they saw me talking to white girls after school hours, or doubling on a bike with a white boy. Despite this, I formed good relationships at school with many students. I had little option, especially since once I made it past Year 8 many of my Aboriginal cousins and friends were dropping out of school. Hanging out with my white friends, I now understood the close relationship Dad had with Jack O'Shea many years earlier.

In high school I chose not to do the popular courses that Aboriginal students were expected to undertake if they made it to high school—subjects like woodwork, metalwork and home economics. I chose typing, history, economics, science, maths and geography as they were prerequisites for senior high school. Typing gave me a good start over others my age when the computer era arrived, although at the time it did not seem exciting being one of only two boys in the class.

the N word

My first real fist fight was with a boy one year ahead of me when I was in Year 9. He called me a 'black nigger' in the music room. Instinctively I struck him in the face and to my surprise he didn't retaliate. But he then continued with his vitriol. 'You're blacker than the ace of spades,' he said.

Throughout high school I excelled in sport and broke most short distance sprint events as well as the long jump and triple jump at our school's annual sports carnival. I played the occasional game of tennis and entered swimming competitions, both without much success. I was not a long distance runner and would always be one of the last in my age group over the line in the cross-country event, a gruelling race around the perimeter of town.

I enjoyed playing cricket in summer. A highlight of 1974 was when Eddie Mitchell and I were selected to attend the renowned Sam Trimble coaching clinic at the Gabba Cricket Ground in Brisbane. I was a fast bowler and an average middle order batsman while Eddie was an all-rounder. We were billeted with cricket officials opposite the Gabba and the experience and tutorship received during our short stay proved invaluable for both of us.

My life was almost turned upside down on the first day of Year 10 when I had an altercation with my new teacher. As we lined up to enter the classroom, my teacher commented in front of the class, that she had heard bad reports about me from the Year 9 teacher and would not put up with any of my antics. I replied that I had heard that she had a history of not treating her black students well.

I was immediately marched off to the principal's office and after giving me a lecture about how lucky I was to have made it to Year 10 he asked me to put out my right hand. After the first stroke of his cane I felt I was being unfairly dealt with. On the second thrust I grasped the cane as it struck my palm and broke it. I told the principal he could shove his school and gathered my gear and walked off the school grounds. I was quite a big kid for my age, in fact quite a bit taller than the principal, and I could tell by the anxious look

the N word

in his eyes that he had not experienced such insubordination from a student before.

As I walked home it dawned on me that it could well be my last day of school. I felt overwhelmed at being a loser. I thought of all the insensitive comments I'd received from the occasional narrow-minded teacher, mostly along the lines that us black students should not set our expectations too high but instead focus on skills that would secure us jobs in the rural industry, in other words labouring.

I told Dad and Mum that I was leaving school and would go cotton chipping with my Uncle Wally in Toowoomba. Dad briskly reminded me that he had not worked all his years to put me through school only to see me end up on the long rows of a cotton field, earning one dollar an hour over a ten-hour day. The next day he met with the principal and after a lengthy discussion I was allowed to return to my Year 10 class.

Cunnamulla State School only offered classes up to Year 10, so I had little option but to travel away to complete Years 11 and 12. I was successful with an application to attend a private boarding school in Brisbane, 800 kilometres east of Cunnamulla. Marist College Ashgrove was to be my home for the next two years. Although I had no idea how I would fit in, I viewed the move in a positive light and figured if I could manage the transition over the sandhill from the Yumba I could handle just about anything.

Even though my upbringing had been Anglican, I opted for Marist College Ashgrove, a Catholic school, because of its academic and sporting reputation. A few white boys from my year also chose Ashgrove but I was one of the first Aboriginal students to enrol at the picturesque school on the hill.

the N word

I soon made friends with the sons of middle and upper class families who came from vast properties in the west, from colonial outposts such as Papua New Guinea (PNG), as well as from the more desirable suburbs in Brisbane. In spite of their arrival at school in expensive European cars I never felt intimidated by my more affluent classmates, many of whom remain friends.

In Year 11, I shared a dormitory with over fifty boys and had to adhere to the regimental lifestyle imposed by our dorm master. I did what I had to do and tried not to draw special attention to myself. I wanted to prove to my parents that I could stay out of mischief and complete matriculation. The experience of my poor start to Year 10 was foremost in my thoughts whenever I felt the urge to stray.

Although I was an average student academically I did enjoy the discipline of set study time for boarding students. At night, dormitory masters would pace up and down the aisles to ensure we were doing our homework, and on Sundays we were allocated time to write letters to our parents and friends. We also had to make our beds, clean our personal spaces, be neat and tidy at all times and complete cleaning duties on weekends to keep the school immaculately presented. Teachers would periodically walk past and check our hair length and those of us with an advanced stage of facial hair would be reminded to shave and trim our sideys.

I was popular with the PNG boys primarily because the majority were black and also a long way from home. However, my closest friend for the two years was Merek Smyth, a white PNG student from Boroko. He was a compassionate and thoughtful person who I enjoyed being around. One Monday morning after returning from weekend leave I noticed bruising on the faces of a couple of the PNG boys. I discovered the culprits were a group of Year 11 boys and went in search of them. When I found them loitering under a large tree in the schoolyard, I identified the leader and asked him why they had assaulted the boys. 'What's it to you, nigger?' he retorted.

the N word

Without hesitating, I struck him as the others watched in horror. Not one of the bullyboys attempted to intervene for their mate and I left them, moderately happy at accomplishing my goal of defending my friends. I don't know what possessed me. I had gone through school in Cunnamulla with just a single altercation with another student and within weeks of starting at this school I found myself brawling. The principal summoned me to his office and asked if I knew the name of the train that went to Cunnamulla. I replied that I did. He didn't want to hear my version of events but let me know in no uncertain terms that if I repeated such a vicious attack at his school, I would be on the next Westlander out of Brisbane.

The incident didn't impact on my friendship with other students and if anything it assisted me. Despite a minor tussle with another boarder over a racist slur in the school gymnasium, I was never harassed about my race.

It wasn't until I entered Year 12 that life in general started to blossom for me. As one of the privileged few who made the first XV rugby side, life was always going to be exciting. On match days we ate in the teachers' dining room and had the most delicious steak and vegetables. We were even allowed to indulge in seconds and helped ourselves to a much wider range of desserts than offered to our classmates in the downstairs dining room.

As the pride of the school we got to travel in our special bus and were greeted with applause when we arrived for the game. There was a lot of pressure placed on us to win. It was expected that Ashgrove would take out the competition every year but unfortunately that year we failed at the last hurdle when we lost to St Columban's by a single point. However, I had a good game and the write-up in the 1977 Marist magazine, the *Blue & Gold*, read:

> The best try of the season was that eventually scored by Steve Hagan against Columban's after the major part of the lead-up work was done by Ozzie (Peter Osborne).[7]

the N word

That night, hours after the game, many of the players were inconsolable at losing. On the other hand I was quite relaxed, happy to have been part of the build-up and pleased to have made a contribution. I tried not to take life too seriously having made a point not to get upset with losses on the sporting field. This attitude stemmed from my desire to correct some very bad sportsmanship during my primary school and junior high days when I had an unhealthy competitive streak in me and a real aversion to losing.

Apart from rugby, I also represented the school at basketball and athletics. The highlight of my athletic career was in 1977, running before the Queen at a State Championship when she opened the Queen Elizabeth II Jubilee Sports Centre in readiness for the Brisbane Commonwealth Games in 1982. Mum and Dad sat on the hill that day, along with 30,000 other spectators, in pouring rain.

I still enjoyed playing cricket but wasn't quite at the level to make it into the first XI side although I managed to make the second XI. I enjoyed the camaraderie of the boys in that squad and we went through the season undefeated. I was used primarily as a bowler and batted down the order.

But of all the sports, nothing rated with making the first XV rugby union side. It certainly helped me through school, particularly in terms of social interaction and acceptance by my peers. I was popular with younger students who sought my number—eleven—in the weekly sweep of tickets for the first try scorer.

While I enjoyed being looked up to by the rest of the rugby-mad school population, I did not enjoy the barbs of racism that came my way from other students in our away games. One weekend we were playing against a big Catholic college when some of the older boys sitting on the sideline started calling out, 'Hit the nigger with the boomerang' and 'Tackle that abo'. But their racist outbursts only spurred me on to one of my finest games in the blue and gold.

At half-time, my coach, ex-international Barry Honan, said that I was killing them with my pace in attack and front-on aggression in

the N word

defence. I seldom got a big head but on that day those words were special. The jeering from the rednecks on the hill shifted to a slight applause as I determinedly raced towards the try line to extend our winning margin. Sport consumed me in Year 12 and for a while I didn't experience the same level of homesickness as I had in Year 11. Entries in the *Blue & Gold* probably added to my sense of well-being.

> Steven Hagan. One of the team's most improved players. Steven proved himself to be the best attacking winger in Brisbane with eight competition tries to his credit. Steve made memorable dashes throughout the season but that 80 metre try against Villanova was one of the season's highlights. He may not be the fastest schoolboy in Brisbane but he certainly is the fastest footballer.
> St. Columban's batted first and their openers gave them an excellent start by compiling 53 runs for the opening partnership. Stephen Hagan dismissed both openers and then continued to give his finest bowling display for the season finishing with 6 wickets for 26 runs … Stephen Hagan completed a fine double by making 27 runs not out …[8]

Despite my popularity as a sportsman I still found it difficult when students asked me to visit their homes on school breaks on the proviso that I introduce myself to their parents as being of Indian or Fijian descent. I'd promptly reply that I was a proud Aboriginal and would decline their offers.

Attending school formals with sister girl schools in Brisbane proved awkward too at times. While I wasn't exactly bashful, I would probably have felt more at ease in the company of Indigenous girls. Unfortunately, time and again I'd be let down. After putting a lot of effort into trying to make myself look cool for the big night out, I'd enter the brightly decorated hall and cast my eyes about, only to find there was not an Indigenous girl in sight.

2

Career Moves

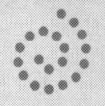

the *N* word

Enlightenment

After completing my studies at Marist College Ashgrove I took time off before beginning a Diploma of Teaching at the Townsville College of Advanced Education (now James Cook University). During this break I was invited to attend a Leadership Development Training course run by the Moral Re-Armament (MRA) group.

I had just started in a part-time position with the Foundation for Aboriginal and Islander Research Action (FAIRA) in George Street, Brisbane, where the new Magistrate Courthouse now stands. Hiram Ryan, an exquisitely dressed and extroverted Aboriginal leader, was the CEO of FAIRA and had received an offer to attend the MRA training course in Melbourne. He called me into his office and explained that he was unable to take up the invitation and asked if I I would like to go in his place.

Moral Re-Armament had been founded by American Frank Buchman forty years earlier. He felt the world needed a wave of change set in motion by individuals with personal experience of moral and spiritual renewal. 'Whatever our background, our talents (imagined or otherwise), our colour, our experience, each of us has a part to play,' he said.

The philosophy of MRA revolves around the principles of absolute love, unselfishness, honesty, purity and restoring for past mistakes.

Its program aimed at drawing together—across social, economic, religious and ethnic divides—people who do not usually work together. The purpose of the training was to introduce participants to successful people in politics and business life as well as ordinary folk who had made a success of their lives by adopting the principles of the MRA.

Since its inception MRA has brought together people of diverse backgrounds and faiths and provided a rallying point for individuals and groups to work for justice, healing and human development. Now, with decades of collective experience, MRA has developed many 'initiatives of change' around the world.

Hiram's offer took me by surprise and after some prompting, I agreed to take up the offer, telling Hiram if I didn't like it I would return home on the next flight. When I arrived at Tullamarine Airport in Melbourne I was warmly greeted by MRA officials. Being the only black person getting off the plane made it easy for them to pick me out in the crowd.

We chatted about our backgrounds as we drove along the freeway through the city, until we took the exit to leafy Kooyong Road, Toorak, where the MRA had its headquarters. I thought the car trip would never end. Perhaps we should have caught another plane to get there, I thought.

I was gob-smacked by the million-dollar mansions; Kooyong Road being one of the most affluent streets in Australia. The MRA headquarters stood out, even among the other houses, with its imposing white brick fence, swimming pool and tennis court.

The interior of the mansion had several libraries and lounges, a ballroom, many bedrooms and a commercial-size kitchen. There was another large residence at the rear of the grounds with its own side street entrance. But as hard as I looked I couldn't find a corner store or pub in Toorak. Worse, I couldn't spot any second-hand cars, which in Cunnamulla were regarded by locals as 'brand new used cars'. I was more used to seeing old Valiants, utes and the odd horse competing for space on the streets. What did strike me was the number of people walking the spotless footpaths with their small but very clean dogs.

After a short time at the MRA headquarters the participants travelled to Canberra. The idea was for us to meet politicians to better understand their responsibilities as elected leaders. The delegates were from a range of countries including the Philippines, Vietnam, Papua New Guinea, Malaysia, New Zealand, Japan, Laos, New Caledonia, Fiji, Taiwan and Korea as well as several Australians, including Ron Lawler, a good friend of mine.

Being in Canberra meant I could meet up with my parents for the inauguration of the National Aboriginal Conference on 3 April 1978. I have fond memories of meeting prominent Indigenous leaders who I had read about and tried to emulate—Senator Neville Bonner, Mick Miller, Charles Perkins and his nephew Neville Perkins (former Northern Territory Member of Parliament at the age of twenty-one and Deputy Leader of the Labor Party at the same age) to mention just a few.

I sat with Mum in the Parkroyal International Hotel Conference Room, feeling privileged to be able to share this special moment with her and Dad. I was in awe of my father as he took his seat, as Deputy Chairman, on the front table with then NAC Chairperson, Lowitja (Lois) O'Donoghue, Leader of the Opposition, Bill Hayden, and Minister for Aboriginal Affairs, Ian Viner, as they listened to Prime Minister, Malcolm Fraser, officially open the conference.

After the formalities I felt like a boy with a pocket full of coins in a games arcade, not quite sure which game to play first. I was mesmerised as I stood in the room filled with national Indigenous leaders I had read so much about. I didn't know who I wanted to meet first.

But Dad saved the day, casually introducing me to his colleagues and associates over a cup of tea. To cap off that historic occasion, Dad asked me to join Mum, NAC representative Ted Loban from the

the *N* word

Torres Strait and his wife, Sadie, in a feast at a Chinese restaurant in downtown Canberra.

The following night I encouraged Dad and his fellow NAC representatives to address a dinner meeting with the MRA leadership group. The young leaders were transfixed as Dad, Cedric Jacob, Frank Roberts and Bill Bird shared their experiences. As I sat listening it dawned on me how much respect Dad commanded. For years I had heard of his political prowess but until that night I had never seen him in action.

Several eventful and highly educational months later, including visits to most capital cities in the country, I packed my bags and headed back to Queensland. I was off to Townsville to commence the tertiary studies that hopefully would lead to a fulfilling career as a primary school teacher.

On my first night in the Halls of Residence at the Townsville College of Advanced Education, my sleep was broken by the eerie noise of the curlew bird. It sounded like the high-pitched cry of a woman in distress. Growing up in Cunnamulla the sound of a curlew, rare out west, was seen by Murries as a message of death. It frightened my people who thought it meant that someone close to them, but far away, had passed on. It was a sound I had to get used to as those pesky birds were on song most days of the year.

The sight of Indigenous people going about their business in Townsville was reassuring to me. In the couple of years I'd lived in Brisbane I had often travelled from one side of town to the other to represent Ashgrove, without seeing a single black face. In this new environment I was able to study and socialise with other Indigenous students, a combination of school leavers and mature age students.

I most admired Ray Warner, who had started his working life as a fettler on the railway in south-west Queensland and decided he could achieve more in life by going back to study. Ray graduated as a teacher and later successfully pursued a medical degree at Newcastle University. Dad always said that everyone has ability, regardless of race, and it is just a matter of how far an individual is prepared to go to take advantage of opportunities. Ray grabbed his opportunities with both hands.

∴

After settling into the daily grind of studies I became good friends with many students of Torres Strait Islander (TSI) descent. Townsville had a large TSI population, many of whom were the sons and daughters of workers brought to the mainland to build the vast network of railway lines that travel the length and breadth of the State.

Like the South Sea Islanders who were blackbirded to Australia from the Solomon Islands in the Pacific to do the menial work in the cane fields of Queensland, the TSI people, although not blackbirded, were also seen as hard workers who could be relied upon to work under difficult conditions in the State's hot interior.

I was conscious that white people in Townsville spoke about the Islanders as being more assimilated than the Aboriginals. Over the years missionaries and white employers may have reinforced that belief. I heard several lecturers say how they were more advanced in their stage of mental evolution than Aboriginals for a range of reasons including their habit of living in houses in settled communities, their agricultural skills, construction and navigation of canoes, and use of the bow and arrow. I certainly didn't believe the rhetoric. To me we were equals—both in the lecture theatre and socially—and it didn't take long before I became close friends with many of the TSI students including Eddie Mabo.

Better known by his people as Koiki, Eddie Mabo was highly regarded for his work in establishing the first independently-run black school in Townsville, indeed in Australia. At times I didn't know where he found all his energy as he was trying to balance his studies with a dozen or so Indigenous organisations that required his time on a voluntary basis. But the workload never fazed Eddie. He was always on the move and constantly challenging himself and those around him.

Eddie and I would often chat, in the corridors before class or outside the cafeteria on the grass, about political events as they related to Indigenous issues. He was quick-witted, widely read and fiercely proud of his homeland of Murray Island (also known as Mer).

It did not surprise me when I learnt many years later that Eddie Mabo, along with David Passi and James Rice, had asserted to the High Court of Australia that since time immemorial the Meriam people had continuously occupied and enjoyed Murray Island and had established settled communities with a social and political organisation of their own.

As a result of Eddie's efforts, the Mabo decision, as it came to be known, was handed down by the full bench of the High Court in June 1992. As Chief Justice Gerard Brennan put it, 'The fiction by which the rights and interests of indigenous inhabitants in the land were treated as non-existent was justified by a policy which has no place in the contemporary law of this country.'

I followed the case for many years and was saddened when Eddie, at fifty-six years of age, died of cancer just a few months before the historic ruling. But the Mabo decision launched the struggle for native title in Australia and put an end to successive governments' claim that Australia was 'terra nullius', a Latin term that meant 'no one's land'.

the N word

Bombay 21st

During my final year of teacher training I received an invitation to give an address at an international MRA conference titled 'Dialogue on Development' at Panchgani, 100 kilometres south of Bombay (Mumbai). In India I was struck by the facial similarities of the Indian population and Aboriginal Australians. The Bombay journalist Rupa Chinai portrayed this in more dramatic fashion in the *Sunday Standard Magazine* of 8 March 1981:

> A little boy came up to Steve Hagan, an Australian Aboriginal, on his very first day in India, and asked him if he was a well-known Hindi film star who normally plays the role of a villain! Steve or his older friend Reg Blow could easily pass for a Tamilian or a Keralite. Anthropologists believe that the Aboriginal people of Australia originated from Southern India and made their way to Australia when the two continents were part of one land mass. Another theory is that the Aboriginal came out from Australia and settled in south India—hence the remarkable similarity in features. The Aboriginal people themselves, according to Reg and Steve, believe they "came from the land" and have occupied the Australian continent for around 40,000 years, long before the coming of the white man only 200 years ago.

the N word

Designed and built by Gordon Brown (a Professor at the School of Architecture at the University of South Australia and father of former South Australian Premier Dean Brown), the conference facilities at Panchgani were situated on top of a majestic mountain. After I unpacked my bags I sat on my bed and fell into a state of fretfulness. At the time I put it down to being abroad for the first time and in a totally foreign environment. I could keep up a façade of appearing to be in control and self-assured among the international delegates but in truth it felt odd for a boy from a fringe camp to be in a strange country while some of my old Murrie schoolmates were back in Cunnamulla and well into the advanced stages of alcoholism.

As I was assessing my new surrounds, I heard the familiar sounds of country and western singer, Don Williams' song 'I believe in you' filtering through the thin high-altitude air. I approached the door of the second-floor room where the music was being played, at volume, paused and then gave a firm knock. Immediately a distinctively Canadian voice answered. The door opened and there, standing before me, was the imposing frame of Ed Burnstick, a Sarcee Indian. We introduced ourselves and from that moment on we became close friends.

The next day I shared the platform with Ed and other leaders from many parts of the globe when I gave my paper titled 'Educational Empowerment'. It was well received by both delegates and the media and included an historical perspective of black–white relations in Australia from first contact to the present day.

I touched on the need for Indigenous Australians to move forward with a positive attitude and articulated my belief that the road for a brighter future lay with Indigenous people empowering themselves through education. I emphasised that we needed to shed our dependency on white people and come up with answers of our own so we could address the high level of social and political disadvantage within our communities.

the N word

Over the next few days I made invaluable contacts with people from all around the world including the politician, Rajomohan Gandhi, grandson of the late Mahatma Gandhi. Rajomohan was an inspirational speaker and I learnt much from him; not only about poise and presentation but also about making personal commitments to socially just causes.

After the conference I undertook speaking engagements in Bombay, New Delhi and Calcutta with Reg Blow and Ron Lawler. We were introduced to trade unionists and civic leaders and spoke at several universities but none struck me more than the university in Calcutta which was exclusively for women. I was very ignorant and, thinking perhaps there was some religious reason for their absence, I asked the professor why there weren't any men on campus that day.

Some time was spent working with various welfare organisations. The most memorable of these experiences was working alongside Mother Teresa at her Sisters of Mercy Mission in Calcutta. Mothers who were experiencing difficult times were encouraged to leave their children to the care and safety of the Mission staff. Three months later they would return to be reunited with their well-nourished offspring, provided they could match their wristbands. My role was to place a wristband on the arm of each mother and an identical wristband on her child.

I'll never forget the moment I met and first spoke to Mother Teresa. She was a frail old lady who appeared to be either constantly walking or sitting in a slouched position. She didn't show any discomfort and responded in a cheerful manner when I introduced myself as an Aboriginal Australian. The first thing that came to my mind to say was a reference to the Sisters of Mercy working on the outskirts of Bourke in northern NSW. Mother Teresa told me she was familiar with their work and often prayed for the success of their vocation among my people.

the N word

Reg Blow and I were determined to check out the local entertainment and decided on a visit to a nightclub. Once again I was surprised as Indian culture forbids direct interaction between the sexes at such venues. I'd never seen so many men dancing with one another before. There was a section of the club for married people and sections for single men and women. I looked at Reg and shook my head. How could you hope to meet a future bride at a segregated nightclub?

On one occasion in Bombay I boldly asked a young Indian woman, who I'd met at the Panchgani conference, to accompany me to the movies. She told me that in order for her to gain permission her parents would have to call a special meeting of all the family, including extended family members. They would discuss the request, but even then there were no guarantees of a favourable response.

A week later, after much deliberation, they sanctioned the arrangement provided the young woman's brother and two uncles accompanied us. I agreed and although I thought the conditions were quite bizarre, I respected her culture. The only time I got to speak with her alone was when I gave our chaperones several rupees to spend at the canteen. That gained me a maximum of ten minutes to chat, quite extraordinary in the rarefied atmosphere of that Bombay theatre where intimacy of any description was frowned on.

Back in Calcutta, Reg and I found ourselves in another predicament when we came across a group of disabled street kids, the oldest girl being about nine years of age. She said that her mother was in need of medication and Reg, filled with compassion after a lengthy period away from his family, reached into his pockets and gave her several rupee notes. The next morning we were greeted by dozens more kids. Word had got around about these two big Aboriginals from the land down-under who were sympathetic to a sad story.

… the N word

The remainder of our stay was based on meticulous planning so we could leave and return to the hotel without being detected. If the kids confronted us on the street we would enter one of the many up-market restaurants or shops in the district and depart via a side door.

After that experience, whenever we encountered beggars we would offer them food such as a piece of fruit or a sandwich—never money. We later discovered the children were working for an unscrupulous merchant who would blend in with the crowd and pounce on them for his majority stack as soon as they received cash from unsuspecting tourists.

One day, back in New Delhi after a memorable visit to the Taj Mahal at Agra, I was in need of a visit to the toilet and asked for directions to a public restroom. I soon found myself standing with five others at a urinal with no walls. I had little choice, even though throngs of people were passing by just a metre away.

During my final year at school in Brisbane I had attended several gatherings of the local 'Black Panther' movement. I enjoyed listening to the philosophical debates that activists Pastor Don Brady, Dennis Walker, Cheryl Buchanan and Sam Watson Jnr engaged in. Those proud Indigenous people with their leanings toward proactive social justice were among my early role models.

Around this time I was also reading and re-reading the biography of Malcolm X. I had thought no race on earth was as badly off as my people but my pent-up anger temporarily abated during my travels around India. In Calcutta, I saw workers picking up the dead bodies of those who didn't make it through the night, for transportation to pits where crows and other vultures would dispose of the human flesh.

Several weeks after the culture shock of Calcutta I arrived back in Bombay where, on 20 December 1980, I stood at the front door of a Hindu friend's house to welcome guests to my twenty-first birthday party. To mark my coming of age, Mum had offered to pay for a party

the N word

in Toowoomba and as I celebrated on this cool Bombay evening, I had visions of a backyard party in southern Queensland with cold beer and wine, good food and beautiful women.

At this party I was blessed with good food and beautiful women, although they were covered from head to toe in their traditional saris. The only exception was an unexpected guest, Marilyn Beazley (sister of Federal Labor Party leader, Kim Beazley Jnr), who was doing her doctoral studies on the socialist movement in India. She arrived in a dress that turned quite a few Indian heads.

On 14 March 1981, after arriving back in Australia, Neil Naessens from the *Townsville Bulletin* wrote an article under the heading 'Indian trip was a real eye-opener for Steve':

> To Steve, the conference was like a mini-United Nations and, emulating his father's performance in Geneva last year, he fired off his first major speech, addressing the conference on the history and future of Aborigines in Australia.
>
> During his stay in India he met people from all walks of life, including trade unionists, government ministers, teachers, politicians and businessmen.
>
> He and the other two members of the small Australian delegation, Ron Lawler and Reg Blow, also met Sister (sic) Teresa in Calcutta, and India's former ambassador in Washington and High Commissioner in London, Mr B.K. Nehru ...
>
> "I used to say that I didn't want to get into politics, the way my father has, but I am now beginning to change my mind," (Steve said.)

During my final year of teacher training I started to lose interest in the profession and thought more about how I could bring about practical changes to improve the living standards of my people. The straw that broke the camel's back was when I was doing my teaching practice at a Townsville primary school and sought permission to teach my social studies class from books I thought were more relevant than the set texts. I was offended that the set text contained inappropriate, demeaning references to Aboriginal people. My supervising teacher told me that as the text was government-approved, it would be used in the teaching of that subject. My assessment from that school was not glowing, to say the least.

There is a saying that goes; 'If you're white you're right, if you're brown stick around and if you're black stay back'. As I began to read more extensively I discovered that many of the school textbooks contained derogatory remarks about my race. This was at a time when some fair-skinned Aboriginal people avoided any association that would link them to their Indigenous ancestors. They tried to pass themselves off as Gypsy, Maori, Indian, Asian—anything to avoid being seen as an Aboriginal.

Sadly many such references are still in school texts, for junior and senior studies, throughout Australia and exert a significant influence on people who continue to deny their Aboriginal ancestry. Fortunately I never once had a problem with my Aboriginality and, thanks to my parents, was proud of my Kullilli culture and all that it stood for.

Meanwhile, my dire experiences in the classroom influenced my aspirations. I now had an urgent desire to make a career change and I decided on a move to Canberra, the national capital. A big part of the attraction was the yearning to work under the charismatic and controversial Aboriginal leader, Charles Perkins, affectionately known as Charlie.

the N word

A Foreign Affair

For many people, both black and white, Charlie Perkins will always be remembered as the man who had the vision and drive to coordinate the US-inspired 'Freedom Ride' in an attempt to raise awareness of racial discrimination against Aboriginal people.

Charlie led the group of about thirty Sydney University students who, in February 1965, undertook a 3200-kilometre bus tour of northern NSW towns. (To celebrate its 40th anniversary, a re-tracing of the 'Freedom Ride' route took place in February 2005).

The rural centres of Walgett and Moree in particular achieved notoriety as clashes between the students and townspeople attracted national media coverage. The locals didn't take too kindly to being told by a radical black and his 'do-gooder' friends that they should share their public facilities, including the municipal swimming pool, with Aboriginals.

That single event made the rest of Australia take notice of the discriminatory policies and high levels of intolerance and bigotry that existed throughout the country. For the rest of his distinguished career no one ever doubted or questioned Charlie's ability to roll up his sleeves and go into battle for better and just conditions for his people.

the N word

In 1972 Charlie became chief departmental adviser to the new Minister for Aboriginal Affairs, Gordon Bryant, in the setting up of the NACC and in 1981 he was appointed chairperson of the newly created Aboriginal Development Commission (ADC). By March 1984 he was the Department of Aboriginal Affair's first Aboriginal secretary.

I arrived in Canberra in early 1981 and commenced work as a training officer with the Aboriginal Development Commission. Early in my professional career I had a meeting with Charlie Perkins. Being aware of the work and social performances of all his young charges, he called me to his office. 'You have a lot of potential Stephen,' he said to me, 'but you must never allow your social life to be an impediment to your long term professional aspirations.'

This get-together occurred in my second week in Canberra but little did Charlie know that my initiation into the capital's bureaucracy had occurred on my first day at work. Two senior non-Aboriginal bureaucrats invited me to lunch at the Woden Valley Leagues Club, not far from the ADC office in Phillip.

There were five men including myself in our lunch group and one volunteered to buy the first round of drinks. Unlike drinking etiquette in Queensland where the majority of drinkers consume middies (ten ounce glasses) the drinkers in the Australian Capital Territory drank schooners (fifteen ounce glasses). With one swallow the four men had downed their drink and another was at the bar ordering another round. After my third drink I started to feel a little light-headed and asked the group if they were going to order a meal. 'Soon' I kept hearing from my work colleagues over the next ten quickly-consumed schooners.

Before I knew it, not having ordered any food, the self-appointed spokesperson of the group signalled to our noisy table that it was time to gather our loose change and head back to work. By this stage my head was starting to spin and as I passed the doorway I grasped the handrail. Walking down those twenty steps to exit the small sportsclub seemed like making the steep descent from Mt Everest. As we walked towards our office, less than one hundred metres away, I tried valiantly to walk as straight a line as possible, desperate to appear in step with the four culprits who didn't appear in the slightest affected by their liquid lunch. All afternoon, as I tried unsuccessfully to focus on the task at hand, I could hear my older work colleagues gloating that they had netted another novice.

※

During 1982 Alan Griffith, a personal acquaintance and senior public servant with the powerful Department of Prime Minister and Cabinet, asked me if I was interested in joining the Department of Foreign Affairs. I'd met Alan years previously through his connection with Moral Re-Armament.

When I told Charlie about the offer he reluctantly endorsed my move but made sure it was on a secondment basis only. Always one for a challenge I agreed and thus began my life as a public servant in the imposing surrounds of the Department of Foreign Affairs and Trade. For a start, there were security officers at all the entrances and staff generally drove a wider variety of European cars into the carpark. My Mazda RX7 may have looked impressive parked at the office of the Aboriginal Development Commission but it hardly turned eyes when I pulled up beside my new work colleagues in their vehicles.

It was apparent from the outset that these public servants thought themselves a level above the run-of-the-mill workers in the many fine establishments dotting the landscape of the national capital. But all pretence went out the window on pay nights when most departmental staff adjourned to the basement social club for drinks. I tried to encourage my Indigenous buddies from other departments to attend these gatherings but they usually chose not to hang out with 'stuffy elitists'.

the N word

One good friend in Canberra, Ralph Richardson, a hostel yardman, was a large Aboriginal man, over six feet tall. He was born in Brewarrina, left school at a young age to do a range of labouring jobs throughout New South Wales, and reminded me of my relatives in Cunnamulla who had no pretence in their make-up whatsoever. Ralph insisted on coming along with me to one of the many dinners I was invited to by diplomatic acquaintances from the embassies and high commissions who I'd met in the course of my work. These dinners generally took place on a Friday or Saturday evening.

After one late Saturday session at the popular Statesman Hotel, I agreed to take him along to a dinner the following Friday. As we alighted from my car on an arctic winter's night in mid-July, I reminded Ralph to follow my lead and not mix his drinks.

The beautiful hostess from the Embassy, in her formal attire, welcomed Ralph and myself and introduced us to the other guests. Pre-dinner drinks went well and Ralph slowly eased himself into the conversation telling stories about life in a small country town. He talked about hunting kangaroos, porcupines and emus—all of which was riveting for our diplomatic friends. As Ralph helped himself to the avocado and prawn dip and the chicken liver paté, I started to question my initial apprehension about inviting my knock-around buddy to meet with people he wouldn't come across at the corner pub.

By the time the host clanged a piece of silver cutlery against a glass to signal that dinner was about to be served in the dining room, we had already consumed several bottles of imported beer. Ralph followed a guest from Sweden and sat beside her until the host brought to his attention that his place at the table, marked with his name card, was several seats to his right. The entrée was a fennel, asparagus and pea soup and when I asked Ralph later why he'd been stirring it so much he replied that he'd been searching for meat.

As I predicted, Ralph accepted every one of the wide selection of wines that were on offer. During the main course the conversation strayed into unfamiliar territory as the other guests discussed what their favourite childhood toys had been. Some mentioned ponies to ride whilst others volunteered motorised toy cars or boats bought for them by wealthy parents in Europe.

When they focused their eyes on Ralph, I too wondered what he had played with as a Murrie kid growing up in Brewarrina. Witty and confident as ever, Ralph told them, 'When I was young my parents were so poor that if I didn't wake up in the morning with an erection I had nothing to play with for the rest of the day.'

There was a slight pause and then the uncontrollable laughter commenced. Ralph was now centre stage and his new friends wanted more. They were mesmerised by his wicked sense of humour, which for many was like a breath of fresh air. I sat back, knowing they couldn't stop him once he got into the zone.

By dessert Ralph was on fire and had the diplomats eating out of his hands. As he moved from Johnny Walker Black Label to Armagnac and with several liqueurs yet to sample, I knew we were in for a long night. Days later when Ralph surfaced, he asked me when the next diplomatic dinner was taking place. I told him that I would get back to him soon.

Everyone at times needs a mentor working within the top level of Canberra's bureaucracy and I was fortunate in having Alan Griffith as my senior adviser. I would often call around to his house for a meal or attempt to make an appointment at his office. The latter was near impossible as he had the ear of the Prime Minister and other Cabinet

the N word

Ministers daily, so I didn't bother, unless it was critical, to call him during working hours.

On a semi-professional basis, inside the highbrow confines of the Department, I also enjoyed the company of Gordon Matthews, who later became a high profile career diplomat. Gordon arrived several months after I started and was a university graduate, one of the 'shiny new recruits' as some envious administrative staff from the Department preferred to tag them.

The first day I met Gordon I was impressed. This handsome man identified himself as an Aboriginal and was keen when I offered to introduce him to the Canberra Aboriginal community. Gordon was adopted and decided to identify as an Aboriginal during his university years after wrestling with the idea that, since he most definitely wasn't like all the other white kids, in all probability he must be Aboriginal on account of his complexion. He embraced his new identity and became well known within parliamentary and diplomatic circles. He was a talented diplomat and became an important role model for many Indigenous people, particularly those in the public sector.

Throughout his distinguished career he constantly searched for his father, wanting answers and seeking confirmation of his Aboriginality. In 1987 Gordon was in for the shock of his life when he came face to face with his father in Iowa, United States, and discovered that he was not of Aboriginal descent but Sri Lankan. I had tears in my eyes as I read his autobiography, *An Australian Son*[9], which details his journey. As I watched him on television during the week of the book launch, I thought how brave he was exposing his past. No doubt Gordon figured the best way to inform his scores of friends and colleagues was to put pen to paper and write his fascinating story.

the N word

During my time at Foreign Affairs, I was seconded as a protocol officer with the Hospitality Section of the Prime Minister and Cabinet Department (PM&C). My first job with the PM&C was as a Royal Visits Officer during the Commonwealth Games held in Brisbane in October 1982. In addition I looked after the Minister of Sport from the Bahamas, Senator Kendall Nottage.

My first experience of seeing international black pride exhibited publicly was when I attended the Prime Minister's reception at the Queen Street Lennon Plaza Hotel. As we arrived at the hotel I noticed a rather large gathering at the entrance. Initially I thought there was a long queue of invitees waiting their turn to ascend the escalators to the function room. As we crawled our way to the red carpet area behind several slowly moving limousines, it became apparent that those not dressed in formal attire were protesters.

I tried to look inconspicuous as I opened the door for the debonair Minister of Sport and advanced slowly along the carpet trying not to crowd the guest ahead of us. I felt I was blending in quite well and trusted that I looked no different from any of the younger VIP staffers or security entourage. Halfway along the carpet one of the protestors caught my eye. She pointed to her tee-shirt and gave me the thumbs-up.

I nodded to her and it dawned on me that she must have spotted the striking colours of the Aboriginal badge on my suit lapel. She was wearing a sarong and an ochre-coloured tee-shirt with the words 'Aborigines discovered Cook' emblazoned across it. I recognised the wording as I owned an identical tee-shirt during my student days in Townsville. I felt like rushing back into the crowd to tell her that I supported their protest action against the Liberal Party Government and its abysmal handling of Indigenous affairs and the environment. However, as a dedicated staffer I stayed glued to my charge, although the thought did occur to me that maybe I was getting too comfortable with the perks associated with the ceremonial and hospitality work of officers from the Department.

As I waited to introduce the Sports Minister to Prime Minister Malcolm Fraser and his wife Tammy, and the Queensland Premier Joh Bjelke-Petersen and his wife Flo, I noticed the Nigerian athletes standing in line before us. When the Prime Minister and Premier extended their hands in friendship the tall, black Nigerians looked down in an aloof manner and refused to shake them. I'd be second guessing if I tried to explain why as I was also snubbed when I tried to enter into casual conversation with them during the evening.

Later, during the Games, I had one of my colleagues on the Royal Visits team cover for me as I took unauthorised time off to join the large Aboriginal protest march from King George Square to Musgrave Park. On television that night I watched police using excessive force to break up Aboriginal protestors and their supporters outside the QEII Jubilee Sports Centre, the same stadium where I had represented my school on the day it had been opened by the Queen back in 1977. This was the era when the National Party government ruthlessly controlled Queensland and gained the name the 'police state'. Protestors and activists at this march were brutally treated by police, in particular the tactical response squad, and there were many arrests. Men and women were thrown into waiting paddy wagons to be taken to the city police stations.

In February 1983, on completion of my training at Foreign Affairs, I became one of the first Aboriginals to join the diplomatic ranks when I was posted to Colombo, Sri Lanka, as the Administrative Attaché. My new life in Colombo was to present me with a situation I never envisaged—having domestic staff. I lived, as a single man, in a two-storey, five-bedroom house with servants and a twenty-four hour sentry at the front gate. Under the headline 'Aboriginal diplomat to fight bad publicity', Marsali Mackinnon wrote in the *Weekend Australian* of 5–6 February 1983, 'The jump from the dusty little outback town of Cunnamulla, 960 km south-west of Brisbane (and famed for its lizard championship race) to a diplomatic posting in Colombo is a long one.'

Like most Australians, I was not accustomed to servants waking me in the morning by bringing a pot of hot Ceylon tea to my bedside and running a lukewarm bath. Walking down a flight of stairs to the oak dining table, I was then attended by other servants who offered me an extensive breakfast menu. After breakfast my chauffeur would pick me up at the doorstep in Gregory Road, Colombo 7 and deliver me to the High Commission office only a few blocks away. At first I decided that I was going to do away with the servants and do things myself. However, it soon dawned on me that it would mean all my staff would be without a job. In real terms it cost me little more than thirty dollars a week to maintain their services such was the favourable exchange rate.

Two events that stood out for me during my time in Colombo were the coordination of the first Australian test cricket match at the Asgiriya Stadium in Kandi from 22–26 April, and coordinating the naval visit for HMAS *Canberra*. Part of my role as the attaché was to make sure the Australian cricketers and their support team were looked after. This included approaching all the available single women—diplomats, businesswomen, nurses, aid workers, doctors and teachers, for example—to accompany the cricketers at various VIP functions, although it was often the Sri Lankan women who received the most attention.

I was glad to be involved behind the scenes in this historic five-day test match between Australia and Sri Lanka. Australia won by an innings and 38 runs, and Keppler Wessels was named man of the match. I also attended the one-day match in Colombo and had the pleasure of sitting in the players' box. But when the Australians started losing I managed to mingle with the locals since I was often mistaken for one. My Sri Lankan friends found this all very amusing.

The navy visit was a little more intense as I was involved in organising a cricket match for the sailors and formal functions for the officers. I also had to delicately arrange the release of several sailors from jail, after they'd become involved in a drink-driving accident. On release, the drunken sailors tried to unlock the cells and free all the local prisoners.

My senior diplomatic colleagues briefed me that I had to organise appropriate security to accompany me to and from the bank when I took delivery of the sailors' recreational leave pays. I put in an order for low-profile and experienced police officers, but when they arrived to escort me I almost died. There before me were two of the biggest officers in the entire Colombo police force.

As discreet as I tried to be with the large briefcases of money, my uniformed officers, walking shoulder to shoulder and armed with automatic weapons, caused quite a scene in the normally subdued part of the business sector of town. It would have been apparent to anyone inside the bank that I was in possession of some very serious loot. I was more than a bit nervous as I walked the short distance to our vehicle and had thoughts of a sniper from an adjacent rooftop taking out the two officers and me being set upon by accomplices.

When I finally reached the HMAS *Canberra* I was rushed aboard and directed to the officers' mess, where I sorted out the paperwork and converted their pays into rupee notes. It seemed like an eternity counting every rupee—the exchange rate was twenty Sri Lankan rupees to one Australian dollar. As I was being escorted off the ship I knew I would have my hands full for the duration of the sailors' rest and recreation leave in Sri Lanka. During the next couple of days, I enjoyed a number of social functions on the ship and at the High Commission for the officers. The sailors weren't invited to these VIP

the N word

functions but then again, after months at sea, I think they had better things to do than to hang out with their superiors.

❖

My time in Sri Lanka reminded me of when I'd been in India a few years earlier. Class was the ticket into the casino, the swimming club, the yacht club, the golf club and the better restaurants in Colombo. The locals could immediately pick someone who didn't belong and when faced with an impostor, made it clear they weren't welcome.

I always had difficulty gaining entry into any of these places for local staff members from the Australian High Commission who I wanted to entertain after hours. I made a big mistake one night when I naively decided to invite a senior staff member to the Casino. He received the usual disapproving stares but was allowed in because he was with me. I gave him some money to play blackjack and with a bit of tutoring from me he won the equivalent of a year's pay. Unfortunately he went missing from work and couldn't be contacted. My do-good attitude had backfired, and I immediately eased back on trying to solve the inequality within Sri Lankan society.

On another occasion I invited a taxi driver into my home for a drink and a bit of a yarn. He seemed to have a wealth of knowledge and I wanted to ask him about events of significance that I should be aware of on the Sri Lankan cultural calendar. As soon as I entered the house one of the servants came forward to ask me if I wanted anything to eat. I told her I would like some finger food with a couple of light drinks and she immediately gave me an anxious look. The taxi driver rescued her by saying he didn't feel hungry. At first I was unaware of what was transpiring and insisted that he join me in a snack. It then dawned on me and I told the servant that I would organise the food and drinks myself and that I would catch her nice and early for breakfast.

I was truly having difficulty with this class thing and I didn't know who I should blame or what I could do to change things. I came to the conclusion that there wasn't anything that I could do in my short time in Sri Lanka but whenever a situation presented itself I would try to demonstrate a more caring and compassionate way of expressing my gratitude to workers and friends.

A couple of weeks before the end of my term I took several staff for a weekend at the High Commission's secluded beach house, two hours drive up the coast from Colombo. The cottage, used by Australian diplomatic staff on a roster system, was located on a beautiful, white sandy beach among soaring palm trees.

Before we arrived at the spectacular weekender I decided to call into the residence of one of my staff to say hello to his family. When I knocked on the door of his house in one of the outer suburbs of Colombo, I was greeted by the smiling faces of his children and extended family members. They looked surprised that I would take the time to visit them in their home and even more startled that I was black and not a white colonial diplomat as they had expected.

After we bid the family farewell we set off on the long but enjoyable trip to the beach house. I suggested to the staff that they play some local Singhalese music instead of the Western tunes they had to put up with every time they got into a diplomatic vehicle. I could tell they were uncomfortable with the request but after a couple of tunes they knew I was happy listening to their music.

When we arrived, I told them and the servants who tended to the cottage that over the weekend we were on the same footing and would share the cooking and cleaning. Although the old habits were hard to break, I believe the experiment provided at least a few light moments of role reversal that I'm sure they remembered long after I left their country.

the N word

❂

Besides the obvious privileges that came with being the holder of a diplomatic passport, I was amazed when I first arrived in Sri Lanka to be told that I had to keep one bedroom vacant for the storage of alcohol. Every month, we were given access to storage space on an Australian cargo ship to transport a pallet of beer and spirits. I didn't know what a pallet was but when it arrived I directed dozens of cartons of beer and an assortment of spirits into my top floor room. I was flabbergasted, to say the least, but equally impressed with how cheaply alcohol and other luxury items could be purchased by diplomats. I soon found out that when you entertain as a diplomat you have to provide, free of charge, for every thirsty and hungry VIP on your invitation list. At last I understood why people tried so hard to be placed on these lists.

One day I was summoned to the High Commissioner's office and asked why a certain suspect businessman and his partner were on my list. Apparently he had been trying for years to be seen at these events and because of his questionable background was always crossed off. I took the advice from my boss and that was the last I saw of the suspect businessman.

I received a lot of media interest in Sri Lanka. In *The Island* of 8 April 1983, Christine Nadarajah wrote under the headline 'Youthful Ambassador Extraordinary':

> During the past six weeks here, Steve has had a packed schedule. When he first arrived, they were involved in drafting estimates for the new financial year. Then came the Australian elections and this took up quite a lot of time. The elections were followed by a visit from HMS Canberra of the Australian Navy.
> "The work here was demanding but I think I'm fortunate to get so much experience in such a short span of time", said Steve relaxing in the cool comfort of his office in the Australian High Commission.

Although he is here as Administrative Attaché, twenty-three year old Steve says he has had a look at everything ....

Having seen a bit of Sri Lanka during his stay here, Steve found the close similarity between our people and his, overwhelming!

"The language, their features ... I am convinced there is some connection", stated this man who generally does not believe in theories ....

He hopes to visit our Veddah's (sic) of whom he has read and heard much and compile some sort of report to take back with him.

This, he feels, will arouse a lot of interest in his people back home.

With his charming manners, pleasant and forthright speech, this handsome young man has a bright career in politics.

He is an ambassador in his own way, for the down-trodden, and an inspiration to all young people, both in his land and ours.

My posting to Colombo was an eye-opener both personally and professionally. It was made even more enjoyable by the supportive diplomatic staff headed by High Commissioner David Rutter, but as I flew back to Australia I had a feeling that I would not be going abroad again with Foreign Affairs to represent my country. I felt there was more to be done by working for and with my people. All I needed to do was find the right career path to achieve that aim.

the N word

Charlie's Spell

I left the Department of Foreign Affairs after my return from Sri Lanka. I wasn't keen on accepting a three-year posting to a country abroad and my short stint in Colombo had made me realise how much I took for granted my contact with family and Aboriginal people in Australia. At times I had been extremely homesick and wanted nothing more than to forego another round of cocktails and formal dinners to be at home enjoying my family's laughter and home cooking. I missed the little things—like going down to the pub for a game of pool with my mates or buying the *Rugby League Week*.

I said my farewells and took up a position as the CEO with the Aboriginal Education Consultative Group (AECG) in Canberra, where I worked from 1983 to 1987. I admit I had an ulterior motive. I wanted to pursue my tertiary studies in the field of education. When I left Townsville I did so without gaining my teaching diploma, even though I'd successfully completed all the academic requirements. The only thing I didn't finish, by choice, was my final teaching practice in a primary school.

Now I wanted desperately to achieve my long-term goal of gaining a tertiary qualification. On 9 May 1986 I finally realised that dream and graduated with a Bachelor of Arts in Further Education from the Canberra College of Advanced Education. Taking pride of place in the packed auditorium were the two people who had made it all possible, my proud parents Jim and Jean Hagan. I was overjoyed that they had made the long trip from Toowoomba to Canberra to share the occasion with me. I was the first in my immediate family to gain a tertiary qualification but today I'm delighted to say that I'm not the last.

During my time with the AECG, members of the Jewish movement in Sydney who were affiliated with the ALP invited me to attend the inaugural International Youth Conference and World Youth Festival of Arts in Kingston, Jamaica in April 1985. I didn't need to be asked twice and graciously accepted the generous invitation.

They asked me to invite three other Indigenous representatives so I contacted a friend from Townsville, Aboriginal academic and activist Grace Smallwood, for her views on who might benefit from the experience. Grace nominated Tanja Akee, Trevor Pierce and Grace Savage and as soon as our passports were processed and bags packed we flew off to Jamaica via Los Angeles and Miami.

They were exciting times for the large Australian delegation which travelled as three groups. Peter McGauran, Member for Gippsland, Michael Danby and I led the Liberal/National Coalition, Labor and Indigenous delegations respectively.

My paper was on the treatment of Aboriginal people in Australia and included some suggestions for the future. After delivering it, I was overwhelmed with the positive responses I received from the other representatives and the international media covering the conference. But the Australian representatives received my speech coolly and I believe my paper may have been circulated for comment around the power brokers in the PM&C back in Canberra.

the N word

I awoke late on the morning of my departure. As my Air Jamaica flight flew over Cuba on its descent into Miami, my mind flashed back to the days when I was sent away as a kid to the Sir Lesley Wilson home in Redcliffe to correct my speech. Now I was on a plane returning from a conference where I'd addressed future leaders from all over the world and not a 'h' or 'th' out of place. Perhaps the speech therapist did a good job after all.

Later in Los Angeles, I was surrounded by armed airport security officers as I made my way down the escalators to the baggage carousel. They stood a safe distance behind me until I took delivery of my bag and then directed me into a room adjacent to the ticket sales office.

I tried to remain calm although I felt a little anxious with a sniffer dog growling nearby. When I asked the burly officers what the commotion was about they simply asked me to open my luggage and then rummaged through my clothes, many of which hadn't been washed since I arrived in Jamaica. After a few minutes they announced I was free to leave, reluctantly adding that it was just a random drug inspection. If I had gotten out of bed a little earlier and shaved, perhaps I wouldn't have looked so much like a drug courier.

⁂

After I returned from Jamaica I happily went back to my job with the AECG. Towards the end of 1987 I was approached by Charlie Perkins to have a coffee and a talk about work. Charlie was several years into his appointment as the first Indigenous Secretary of the DAA and was in the process of engaging in extensive consultation to amalgamate the Aboriginal Development Commission with the DAA. I didn't need to be asked twice and joined the DAA as a senior project officer in the Aboriginal Employment Development

the N word

Policy area where I had a great boss in Terry Kapeen, who became a close friend and remains so today.

Charlie had a vision of developing an economic base for Indigenous people in Canberra and offered me a position, along with several other prominent Aboriginals—Andrew Jackomos, Ruth Miller, and Toni Alderman (now Peachey)—as one of the Directors of the Woden Town Club (WTC) which was situated in the basement of the offices of the ADC. Aptly named Bonner Tavern, it was the first Indigenous owned-and-operated licensed club with poker machines and a restaurant in Australia.

It was a momentous occasion for the local Indigenous community of Canberra when we had the official opening of the WTC, with Indigenous identities arriving from around the country to join in the celebrations. Charlie's biggest problem was policing the dress code. It appeared that everyone who wasn't suitably attired was threatening staff that they would go over their heads and contact Charlie if they weren't allowed inside the premises. Several national leaders fell into that category.

The WTC was the place to be for Indigenous public servants and visiting leaders. Unfortunately, at around the same time as the club was being established, Gerry Hand, the Minister for Aboriginal Affairs and Charlie were going through some prickly times over the future direction of the Department. Minutes of a meeting of the club proved to be the catalyst that brought about Charlie's demise from public office. It was believed that he should have excused himself from decision making when the WTC funding application to the ADC was under discussion.

Charlie rang me from Prime Minister Bob Hawke's office, asking me to convene a meeting of the board of directors of the WTC to discuss whether he had breached a conflict of interest policy in gaining further funding from the ADC to upgrade the premises. Before I could organise the meeting, I was summoned along with most staff of DAA, to the executive floor to hear Charlie announce he

the N word

was taking leave. We were told that the government was going to conduct an investigation into his handling of the matter and his alleged approval of taxi fares for protestors to attend a protest against racist remarks made by the President of the RSL. I have always maintained that the government of the day was out to get Charlie. It would not have mattered if it had been over the theft of an office pencil. In my view he was a marked man with a limited career as Secretary of DAA.

In late 1988 Gerry Hand doggedly claimed that he could no longer work with Charlie. A complex series of events made Charlie's position as Secretary untenable and he decided to resign from the public service in 1989. I recall senior black and white staff whispering in the corridors at DAA that they had enough dirt on Charlie to sink him for good, but I believe they were the whispers of jealous men with suspect motives.

They were distressing times. That year, I had walked beside Charlie when he led a large Aboriginal march from Parliament House to the RSL Headquarters, a distance of five kilometres, to protest over a resolution passed at the RSL national congress that week. Brigadier Alf Garland had said the Federal government should check on the genealogy of people who said they were Aboriginals and claimed government benefits.

I was extremely happy for Charlie when the exhaustive Federal police investigation found that there were no wrongdoings in his affairs. The government had no choice but to exonerate him and tried to make some recompense. Unfortunately, the strain of the accusation was too much and Charlie left Canberra in 1991 and returned home to Alice Springs. In the town of his birth he took up a position as Chairperson of the Arrente Council of Central Australia.

By this stage, many of the Indigenous people who had made the decision to pursue a career in Aboriginal Affairs under Charlie's charismatic leadership had become disillusioned with the direction of government policy and started to drift home themselves.

the N word

For me, at that time, Charlie Perkins was the second most influential person after my father, in shaping my future. I aspired to the same goals and admired Charlie's integrity as much as his ability to reach out and work with the grassroots members of the Indigenous community. He never forgot where he came from but at the same time he had no hang-ups about living in the more affluent parts of town, owning a Mercedes Benz and socialising with the leaders of the ethnic and business communities.

Charlie also had an incredible memory for names and was the only person I was aware of who personally knew the heads of the major families of every Aboriginal community in Australia. Travelling around the country with Charlie was like being a minder for a movie star. Everyone, black and white, recognised him and wanted to shake his hand.

With Charlie's departure from the national capital I also reviewed my tenure in that challenging, and at times, lonely city. I decided I had achieved over and above what I had set out to and it was now the right time for me to move on.

Top: Albert (Chum) Hagan, Roy Shillingsworth, Jim Pegler. Bottom: Jim Collins, Dad aged 5, Wally Pegler—Top Camp 1937.

Ringer Jim Hagan, aged 17.

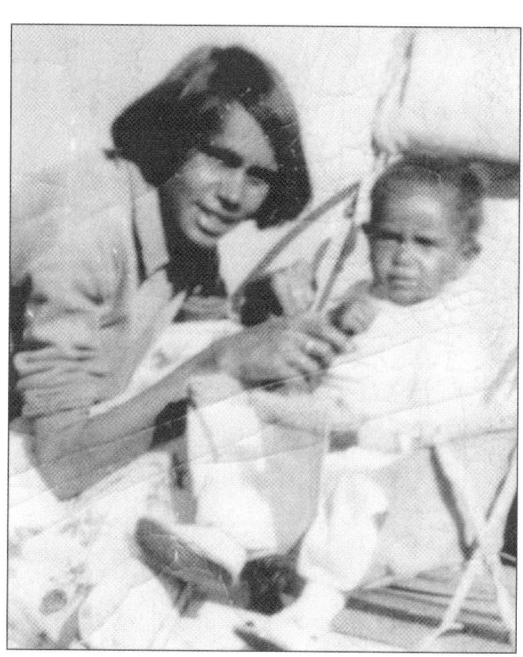

Mum and Pam at the Yumba, 1958.

Studio shot taken not long after the move into Cunnamulla from the Yumba, 1966—Pam, James (Jimmo), Susan and Stephen.

The Hagan's family home—22 Bedford Street, Cunnamulla, 1966.

Standing in the Bedford Street front yard opposite the sandhill that separates the Yumba from town, 1974.

First XV, Marist College Ashgrove, 1977.

Willy Martin, Jim Hagan, Governor General Sir Zelman Cohen, Lowitja (Lois) O'Donoghue—Government House, Canberra 1978.

Jim Hagan at the United Nations Geneva 1980.

In Panchganie with Rajmohan Gandhi, Mrs Nehru, B.K. Nehru and Reg Blow—1981.

With Visiea Sanjo (Nagaland, India), Huns Ragnar Mathisen (Sweden), Ed Burnstick (Canada) and Reg Blow—India 1981.

Student days in Townsville, early 1980s.

First day at Foreign Affairs with fellow diplomatic recruit, Ross Jirra Moore, Senator Neville Bonner and Minister for Foreign Affairs, Tony Street—Canberra 1982.

With Dennis Lillee and Sir Garfield Sobers (Sri Lankan coach) at High Commissioner's reception for the Australian cricketers—Colombo 1983.

With parents, Jean and Jim Hagan, at his Bachelor of Arts graduation ceremony—Canberra College of Advanced Education, 1986.

Rhonda and Stephen's wedding—Cairns 1991.

Stephen with Rhonda, Stephen Jnr and Jayde, 2003.

A publicity shot with the Gulbari Wata dancers on the Rainbow Serpent Cruiser, 1996.

With Mike Horan (Health Minister), Mick Miller (Chairman STF), Rob Borbidge (State Premier) and Kev Lingard (Aboriginal and Torres Strait Islander Affairs Minister) —Queensland Parliament House, February 1996.

Sean Leahy's cartoon that appeared in the *Courier Mail*, 26 April 2002.

Godsall Street house in the centre of a planning dispute with the Toowoomba City Council, 2003.

With Russ Brown, the son of E.S. Brown, at the Athletic Oval following the announcement of the United Nation's ruling—April 2003.

3
Uncharted Waters

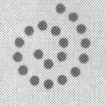

the N word

A Tropical Embrace

After putting out feelers to work in other parts of the country, in February 1990 I was offered a secondment to the DAA in Cairns. Soon after I arrived in the tropical town, the amalgamation that Charlie Perkins was instrumental in implementing came into effect with the ADC merging with the DAA and becoming the Aboriginal and Torres Strait Islander Commission (ATSIC). However, it would be several months before the amalgamation was completed and in the meantime, I took up my position with the DAA in their field operations division.

During one of my regular field visits to Innisfail to attend the Mamu Aboriginal Medical Centre meeting, I met a very attractive medical assistant who had an aura of conservatism about her. The absence of a wedding band on her finger indicated that this stunning young lady, Rhonda Appo, appeared not to be in a relationship. As I underwent a grand tour of the facilities with members of the management committee, I found myself in unfamiliar emotional territory. I asked a work colleague about Rhonda's marital status and my first impression was confirmed.

As an ambitious public servant I had kept extending the dates for when I should get married. At first, I said I would get married when I was twenty-four but that went up in intervals of two years as I kept

the N word

justifying my inability to find a partner. When my thirtieth birthday came and went I took a serious look at myself in the mirror and I didn't like what was looking back—an ageing, overweight, lonely, thirty-something man.

I'd kept telling myself that I was too busy to settle down, and besides, I was having too much fun. I had had a few longer than usual relationships with wonderful women but they were not with any view to longevity in mind. I wasn't particularly looking for a partner when I visited Innisfail on that warm day but as soon as I set eyes on Rhonda she took my breath away.

The only problem for me was that as much as my infatuation was on the rise, Rhonda didn't seem to be reciprocating. I tried and tried but I just couldn't make any headway with the guarded medical assistant. I'd go out to lunch with staff of the centre whenever I went to Innisfail, which became more frequent, and occasionally Rhonda would join us and be hospitable. But as soon as lunch was over she would walk ahead of the group and busy herself as soon as she was back at her work desk.

Just when I thought all was lost, she agreed to attend a community barbeque with me after the first day of a regional forum I was chairing for Aboriginal organisations in Innisfail. However, we didn't get much of an opportunity to talk as participants from centres hundreds of kilometres away were keen to follow up on conference business. No one at the poolside barbeque would have suspected any great romance blossoming, but I did feel a hint of affection coming from the previously guarded Mamu employee during our infrequent conversations.

As participants commenced their short walk to the Crown Hotel for more refreshments, I asked Rhonda if she would like to join the crowd. Not only was I relieved that she agreed to join me for drinks at the popular watering hole but also that she later accompanied me to a nightclub. Here, we left no one in doubt that we were spending the evening together. At last, a promising start, I thought to myself.

the N word

After a most enjoyable evening of dancing and chatting, in between inquisitive stares and comments from her cousins, who appeared to be every second person we bumped into, I walked Rhonda to the nearest taxi rank. Being the gentleman, I insisted on paying her taxi fare home but I hadn't counted on the trip being some ten kilometres out of town on the Palmerston Highway.

Having attempted to impress Rhonda by handing over a significant note to the taxi driver with the passing comment of 'keep the change', I suddenly realised when I searched my wallet for my own taxi fare that I had no notes left at all and was low on coins. Still, I rather enjoyed my pleasant stroll back to the motel in the cool, subtropical air with only one thing on my mind. Later I found out that the large note I handed over to the cabbie was within ten cents of not being enough. My comment of 'keep the change' would have had Rhonda in fits of laughter I'm sure.

I couldn't sleep that night. I felt like a teenager and arrived at the community meeting the next day with red eyes, not just from a lack of sleep but possibly one too many nerve-settling drinks as well. By now the word had spread throughout the town, famous for its pawpaws, bananas and sugar cane. Everyone in the Indigenous community knew that they would be seeing a lot more of this besotted public servant from Cairns.

※

When you meet the only girl in a family of ten—Rhonda is the second youngest—you most definitely need the nod of approval from the matriarch. So after the conference I was delighted when I was invited to meet Rhonda's mother. From Mary's first warm embrace I felt at ease. I knew then that if Rhonda was happy to explore a relationship she would have her mother's blessing. Mary, who lost her husband Stan a few years before I met Rhonda, is a friendly, dignified lady who has total respect and admiration from all her boys. They steadfastly adhere to her rules of the house whenever they return home.

Mary was the only child of an Aboriginal mother, Mary Cuthill, and a Polish father, Walter Moczenski, who was a taxi driver and cook for sugar cane gangs. Mary Cuthill was the daughter of Bombeeta, a Mamu traditional owner from Silkwood, north Queensland, and a Scotsman, Alexander Cuthill. Walter was born in Germany to Polish parents and jumped ship to Australia at the age of 38. He and Mary Cuthill met in Innisfail and married two years later. Rhonda's mother Mary was born in June 1929. Sadly, her mother died when she was twelve years old, and she eventually moved in with her mother's sister, Nancy.

Rhonda's dad Stan was of Sri Lankan descent and had an equally fascinating lineage. In November 1882, Lucy Anna Wanetong and Haromonis arrived at the port of Bundaberg on the ship *Devonshire* from Sri Lanka (or Ceylon as it was then known). Their thirteen-year-old daughter Sarah met a distinguished Ceylonese gentleman by the name of Kallu Appo on the ship and they married not long after.

Sarah and Kallu had nine children. One of their sons, William, married Evelyn Singho whose parents were also Sri Lankan. Evelyn and William had twelve children and Rhonda's father William, known as Stan, was their first son.

Stan met Mary while in the Innisfail area cutting sugar cane and together they followed work to a variety of jobs from the Mt Isa mines to the Maryborough canefields and back. During the off-season they would travel with their growing family to Victoria to work the fruit-picking season, making their way back up to western Queensland where they tried their hands at stick picking.

When Rhonda was born in 1966, such was his delight at finally getting a long awaited granddaughter that Walter caught the train to Maryborough. After congratulating his daughter he gave his granddaughter a kiss and boarded the next train home to Innisfail.

the N word

Stan and Mary were so overjoyed at the birth of their special girl that they tried again for another daughter. But another handsome young baby boy arrived, signalling the end of any further offspring for these proud and devoted parents.

When her father died Mary inherited his house in Innisfail and moved the family there permanently. Rhonda was unaware that she had three much older brothers when she was growing up in Innisfail. It wasn't until she reached double figures that she met them. They had left home at a young age and travelled around the country, spending most of their time working in Western Australia and the Northern Territory.

Although Rhonda's father Stan, enjoyed the respect and company of all his children, he never got to be with them all at once as a result of the men working away from home. The only time the whole family got together was when they attended his funeral. Mary took the opportunity to have a family photograph taken at a local studio. Conscious of the significance of the event, she made allowances for an opening in the top row so a photograph of Stan could be superimposed.

※

Within five months of our meeting at the regional conference, Rhonda resigned her position at the Mamu Medical Centre. Being an intuitive person, as soon as she had made up her mind about our relationship she packed her bags and made the one-hour car trip to Cairns to join me in my new unit in Grafton Street.

Rhonda began working at the Wu Chopperan Medical Centre, a former sponsor body for Mamu. The change of jobs wasn't that big a transition as she knew most of her new colleagues.

After all those years of kidding myself that I was enjoying life, I finally got a taste of what fulfilment was. Rhonda became my fiancée

the N word

within several months of the move to Cairns and from that moment to now she remains my best friend as well as my wife and mother to our children. We were different in many respects but similar in others. I was a brash political operative, or at least I thought I was, and she was the homely girl who returned to Innisfail to be with her mother after her father passed away.

However, I believed we had the same moral fibre to bind us and help us grow together spiritually. Today we are proud to pass on our strong family values to our children and, although we aren't churchgoers, we exhibit the same commitment to the Almighty as dyed-in-the-wool Christians do. Our god is our spirit being who personifies our traditional cultural values.

It wasn't until Rhonda moved to Cairns that it dawned on me that I was heavy in love but very light on possessions. Like many young men and women, I had left home, gained employment and promptly started spending my hard-earned dollars as if there was no tomorrow. To begin our life together in downtown Cairns, we bought a queen-sized bed, some kitchen utensils, a cupboard full of groceries and borrowed an old fridge from one of Rhonda's brothers. We struggled happily together until our joint income allowed us the luxury of tastefully fitting out our ground floor unit and adorning the walls with Indigenous artwork.

A couple of days after celebrating our engagement, on Rhonda's twenty-fourth birthday, we decided that it was time to focus our attention on the south-western corner of the state. August in Cunnamulla is when the town holds its annual Opal Festival and I thought it would be a great opportunity to introduce Rhonda to my family and many relatives.

Dad and Mum picked us up at Brisbane airport and we drove to Cunnamulla. As we approached the small town eight hours later Rhonda asked where all the mountains were. She had never been in country as flat as the western plains. It was vastly different from the

the N word

mountain range around Innisfail. From the back porch of her family home on the Palmerston Highway you could clearly see the peak of the majestic Mount Bartle Frere, at 1622 metres the highest mountain in Queensland.

Rhonda was impressed with the hospitality shown by my relatives in the small town and I know they were equally impressed with her. We attended the Friday night Opal Festival Queen Ball, the Saturday street parade and the Sunday World Lizard Racing Championship in Eulo, sixty kilometres to the west.

I also took the time to show Rhonda around the old Yumba campsite and pointed out where my family lived. The council had demolished all the dwellings and built a rubbish dump in the centre. Most landmarks from my childhood had been bulldozed into the ground and even century-old trees that had stood the test of time had been no match for the Paroo Shire Council's heavy machinery. I took Rhonda up to the top of the sandhill and explained how we walked to school, the movies, and the pool where we amused ourselves. We drove past our old house in Bedford Street, which has been wonderfully preserved by Mum's first cousin.

After this quick visit to the town of my birth we drove back to Brisbane and returned to Cairns content in the knowledge that both sides of the family had given their blessings to our relationship. We were convinced that we wanted to spend the rest of our lives together and commenced the meticulous planning of our wedding. We wanted it to be an event that our families and friends would remember for many years to come.

A week out from the wedding, family members started arriving from all parts of Australia. When at last the big day arrived I was voluntarily restricted to the Pacific International Hotel where I tried to calm my nerves and those of my best men by watching pay TV. Rhonda was kilometres away at her matron of honour's house, being pampered by her mother and aunties. She had booked our favourite

the N word

hairdresser for the day and I believe he would have had a good yarn or two to spin after a day with the ladies.

My wedding party consisted of five men (including my brothers and brothers-in-law) and my three nephews. Rhonda had five beautiful ladies and three gorgeous little princesses, including her nieces and goddaughter, attending her. The entire wedding party, all eighteen of us, was of Aboriginal descent. Looking back on the photographs today, I marvel at the range of skin shades from olive to dark, a reflection of the large number of mixed marriages that have taken place over many generations in the past two hundred years.

At St John's Anglican Church I was warmly greeted by the Rt Rev Bishop Arthur Malcolm, the only Aboriginal Anglican Bishop in Australia at the time. After a respectfully late arrival my beautiful bride walked down the aisle. I don't know what possessed me but I was so nervous that I couldn't raise a smile even though Rhonda looked stunning.

I didn't look left or right during the whole service until after we said our vows and kissed. I was still pretty rigid when I nervously signed the register and only started to lighten up when I marched down the aisle with Mrs Rhonda Hagan, well-wishers on both sides shaking our hands, patting us on the back and snapping photographs. I didn't know we had so many friends until I looked up and saw the benches full, upstairs as well as down.

Half an hour later our bridal party made a grand entrance at the reception at the Pacific International Hotel. The sun was just sinking on the horizon as we walked among our guests and I caught the last rays of sunshine streaming across the sparkling blue of the swimming pool, a fabulous backdrop for our pre-dinner drinks. I couldn't stop smiling, knowing that less than an hour earlier I had married the beautiful Rhonda Appo of Innisfail.

the N word

As life for Rhonda and I returned to normal after our honeymoon in Honolulu, I agreed to a change of jobs. On a secondment basis I went from ATSIC to the Department of Employment Education and Training (DEET). I enjoyed my time at DEET and in late 1991 was promoted to the position of Manager of Aboriginal Programmes.

I had responsibility for the approval of vast sums of money for community employment and training programmes and I assisted in the development of community business plans for communities such as Coen, Ravenshoe, Mareeba, Croydon, Atherton, Innisfail, Kuranda, Mona Mona Mission and many communities in between. To see the response on the faces of the community leaders was enough to tell me that they enjoyed such tangible results after years of being overlooked by bureaucrats while the money was allocated elsewhere.

One of the most rewarding aspects of my role as manager was working with senior field officer, Ruth Lipscombe. Twenty years my senior, Ruth had a wealth of knowledge from working with Indigenous people in the Northern Territory and Queensland. She was an absolute gem and I feel privileged to have worked with her.

One experience that stands out to this day was when Ruth and I travelled to the Lotus Glen Prison, about 100 kilometres from Cairns on the outskirts of Mareeba, a rich sugar cane and tobacco-growing region of North Queensland. We were to discuss training programmes with inmates.

Visiting a prison for the first time, although daunting, was a humbling experience. I got to talk to many Indigenous inmates about what education and training programmes they felt would be immediately relevant to them and which skills they would like to take back into the community on their release from prison. The inmates requested basic numeracy and literacy courses, but most importantly they wanted an art teacher and supplies to assist them

the N word

with their work on canvas, boomerangs and didgeridoos. I approved the programmes and was later informed by the manager of the prison that the inmates had greatly appreciated our visit. He told me we were among the first government officials to show any interest in their needs, let alone action their requests.

⁂

Towards the middle of 1992 I was offered the position of CEO at the Kummara Aboriginal Dance Theatre at the Gold Coast Arts Centre. I initially knocked back the offer to work in this new enterprise but was convinced to rethink my position when the directors made a surprise visit to see me in Cairns. They offered an employment package that I could not refuse and Rhonda and I were on the next plane to Brisbane.

Kummara was marketed as celebrating Australia's heritage, her people and her future. The daily shows presented soul-stirring didgeridoo and clapstick playing, haunting songs, comedy and rhythmic contemporary and traditional dance. I soon got into the swing of things and started to develop a new accounting, filing and reporting system. The administrative staff and dancers accepted my new style of open management as well as the strict alcohol-and-drug-free work environment I insisted upon. The dancers knew they either toed the line or became former employees.

Every day, on the hour, I would call Rhonda who was resting at home in our townhouse in Benowa Waters, to check how she and our soon-to-be-born baby were going. When her mother Mary arrived, I knew that the time was fast approaching for our world to be graced with a new arrival.

At 3 am on 30 October 1992, I gathered a small travel bag, carefully assisted Rhonda into our car and drove the short distance to the Gold Coast Public Hospital at Southport. After the tenth hour of

the N word

witnessing Rhonda in excruciating pain, I begged the doctor to give her pain relief. To my surprise the doctor produced this enormous syringe and administered an epidural injection. Although it served its purpose, the sight of the needle almost made me faint.

As I sat helplessly beside Rhonda I thought of the story my sister Pam told me. In the final hours of her first pregnancy in 1976 when she was carrying her twin boys, she was in severe pain and asked a nurse for some pain relief. She never forgot the vicious words of the nurse. 'You're a silly little black bitch. You got yourself pregnant too young, so serve you right. I hope the pain teaches you a lesson.'

The hours ticked by at Southport Hospital until 9.30 pm when the medical staff decided to deliver by caesarean section. I sat beside Rhonda and held her hand gently until I heard the excitement from the staff. Cradling our new arrival, a nurse said to us in a jubilant voice, 'Congratulations, you have a healthy baby boy.'

I hugged Rhonda and kissed her softly on the forehead as the nurse placed our little boy in the arms of his tired, but extremely proud mother. Tears welled as I stared at my elated wife and beautiful baby. A week later Rhonda and Stephen Victor William arrived home.

After almost six months at the Gold Coast Arts Centre things didn't look too good. The businessmen who owned the company weren't prepared to inject any more money into marketing and as everyone in business knows, if you don't market your product you will be no more than a best-kept secret. The business liabilities started to exceed our income and the Kummara Aboriginal Dance Theatre sadly ground to a halt. I believed we had a going concern—all we needed was the same level of commitment from the directors as the cast had been giving.

the N word

As a farewell gesture I organised for most of the dancers to travel with Rhonda, Stephen Jnr and myself to the Whitsunday Islands to do several performances. We received a great response, as I expected, and management of the upmarket resorts, impressed with our performance, offered short-term contracts for shows. But after the experience of the Gold Coast I wasn't about to put the dancers through the uncertainty of promises that could lead to further disappointment. Rhonda and I bid them farewell at Airlie Beach and continued on our way to Cairns.

Early in 1993 soon after my arrival back in Cairns, I resumed work with ATSIC. During my term on the Gold Coast I'd had several heated discussions with ATSIC management who opposed me taking up the Kummara job as I was only on loan to DEET at the time. It was their belief that I should have returned to them instead of accepting another position elsewhere. I picked up where I left off in ATSIC's field operations division, but by then my relationship with ATSIC management was strained.

※

It wasn't long before I was accepting an invitation from a respected friend, Mick Miller, to join his staff at the Aboriginal and Torres Strait Islander State Tripartite Forum (STF) as its administrator. The STF had been established as an Indigenous advisory group to the Queensland Minister for Health and Mick and his staff, who were not public servants, worked in the same building in the centre of town as the Regional Manager for Health.

I had always held Mick in high regard and had admired his work as an Aboriginal activist who came to prominence with Fred Hollows' trachoma team, which visited remote Aboriginal communities tending to serious eye infections. Later I'd come to know Mick better from his many trips to Canberra as ADC Deputy Chairman and as

the N word

Chairman of the Miller AEDP (Aboriginal Employment Development Programme) review team. He'd earned quite a reputation among both black and white bureaucrats and businessmen as the author of the 'Miller Report', which addressed major employment issues such as employment equity within the public and private sectors. In short, he was another prominent leader on my small list of role models.

By now my résumé was growing distinctly longer with my propensity for accepting new and attractive work offers. However for my young family, the move to the STF in Cairns was to be the most challenging of all my jobs to date.

Staffed by experienced, hand-picked Indigenous people, there was an air of excitement every time Mick walked through the door of the STF office. You never quite knew what the day held for you or who you would be having lunch with. Mick was a popular identity in Cairns, a magnet to all people from the unemployed to blue collar and white collar workers. But most of all he was a very kind-hearted man who would give his last dollar to a stranger in need of help. Even on a busy day he gave generously of his time, often to the first person who came knocking on the door without an appointment.

Of all our shared experiences, my fondest memories of Mick are of seeing him racing to check-in counters at airports minutes after a final boarding call. Mick had a problem with time management and was notoriously late most of the time.

With a beautiful wife, a healthy baby boy and a challenging job my life seemed complete. What more could a man ask for? Well, I didn't ask for it but I was about to enter a new chapter in my life, one that I wish I had never entered.

the N word

An Unhealthy Alliance

Working with Mick Miller, I quickly became aware of the political clout he had developed over the years. Mick told me that as a long-term member of the ALP he'd been offered the number one position on the State Senate ticket. However, he had declined and Margaret Reynolds (an academic at James Cook University and my former lecturer in early childhood education) accepted, serving several terms as the ALP Senator for Queensland.

It appeared that every State or Federal politician who came through Cairns rang Mick or visited him in his office—all wanting to discuss his perspective on Indigenous matters, locally and nationally. Mick was always very accommodating and shared his time with both sides of politics. He could converse on all matters and surprised many of these political leaders with his grasp of Latin and Roman history when general interest topics arose.

It was early December 1995, during a visit to Goondiwindi on the Queensland–New South Wales border, that Mick, Victor Jose (a Cairns-based senior confidant to Mick on health worker training) and I devised a strategy that would lead to serious political ramifications for the office of the STF.

After meetings with health workers at the Toomalah Aboriginal Community Health Centre and community leaders, Mick tried to coordinate bilateral talks between the Minister for Health for Queensland, Peter Beattie, and his counterpart in New South Wales, Dr Andrew Refshauge.

Mick had learnt from the local Aboriginal leaders that community people felt some staff at the Goondiwindi Hospital were displaying a racist attitude towards them. They claimed the resentment stemmed from hospital staff who begrudged ambulance call-outs to the Boggabilla and Toomalah Missions on the New South Wales side of the border. Apparently the staff felt they were spending an inordinate amount of Queensland Health money on what they viewed was primarily a New South Wales problem—and a black one at that.

Mick felt the message wasn't getting through to Minister Beattie. Previously Mick had enjoyed a good relationship with Beattie's predecessor, Ken Haywood, Member for Kallangur. If Mick needed additional resources for the STF he would call Haywood direct to state his case.

Fed up with having to jump through hoops to get to Minister Beattie, Mick decided he would take up the issue with Mike Horan, the Queensland State Opposition spokesperson for Health.

Mick, Victor Jose and I met with Mike Horan in his electorate office in Ruthven Street, Toowoomba on Tuesday 5 December. My younger brother, Lawrence who was living in Toowoomba at the time, came along as a silent observer. Horan received us in his smallish, ground floor office in an arcade opposite the Toowoomba City Council building. He asked us if we would like a beer and quickly organised a couple of stubbies.

After agreeing on a course of action to address the border issue, Horan the consummate politician, asked if there were any other issues that we would like him to follow up on. Mick, equally at home playing politics, brought up the urgency of expanding the operations of the STF and the need for an injection of significant funds into our operations in order to address the appalling health statistics of Indigenous Queenslanders.

Horan concluded the meeting in a jovial mood and suggested we meet again soon. He left us with a thought he had—to form a partnership between the Coalition and the STF. We knew what he was talking about as he had already touched on the issue of the upcoming Mundingburra by-election, the outcome of which would determine whether the Labor Party would remain in government in the state of Queensland.

The by-election for the Mundingburra seat had been called by order of the Court of Disputed Returns which had identified discrepancies in the State election held on 15 July 1995.

That night, over a few drinks at the Toowoomba City Golf Club, Mick raised the prospect, previously unheard of as far as we were concerned, of getting into bed with the conservative Coalition parties in Queensland. We initially expressed reservations, especially given the disastrous record the National Party had on Indigenous issues under the ultra-conservative Bjelke-Petersen administration.

Nonetheless, we thought we would give it a try and see how far we could go. If it looked like failing we could always pull out of the agreement. Who in their right mind would believe that Indigenous people with left-wing political leanings would ever collaborate with the Coalition?

Within a week the telephone at the STF was running hot, initially with calls from Horan and then from Kev Lingard, State Opposition spokesperson on Aboriginal and Torres Strait Islanders Affairs and Deputy Leader of the National Party. It was clear that they wanted to secure the jewel in the crown, the seat of Mundingburra, and become the government of the day.

the N word

The Opposition knew, and we did too, that there was a large Torres Strait Islander population in the seat of Mundingburra, many of whom in all probability hadn't cast a vote in the last State election. The general consensus was that if our group could convince them to vote for the Coalition's man Frank Tanti, then the numbers in Parliament would be tied up. There was a strong view within the Coalition ranks that Independents, Liz Cunningham and Peter Wellington, both former National Party supporters, would come into line and if so, then the government in Queensland would change.

We knew we were playing for big stakes and our office soon received regular visits from conservative politicians Naomi Wilson, National Party member for the seat of Mulgrave, and Lyn Warwick, Liberal Party member for the seat of Barron River. The amount of attention and number of promises we were receiving from the right side of politics rose exponentially the closer we got to the election, leaving us in no doubt that we were squarely in the driver's seat.

⁂

Mick's large, ground-floor office at the STF looked out onto Lake Street. With the blinds constantly wide open it wasn't difficult to observe his visitors from street level, or from the front entrance steps which led to the elevator of the Queensland Regional Department of Health office. I suspect the Regional Manager for Queensland Health was becoming a little wary of the comings and goings of prominent Coalition members and their staffers.

As the date of the Mundingburra by-election approached it was time for the big guns to demonstrate their commitment to the STF. They didn't disappoint, coordinating a meeting in Townsville on 17 January 1996. Mick and I drove the four hours south from Cairns, along the Bruce Highway to meet Horan's flight at Townsville airport. It was strange watching a customarily unflappable Mick nervously search the transit lounge and airport walkways for any sign of Labor buddies who might happen to be passing by. Not knowing the outcome of the meeting to be held later that day, we were conscious of being seen with the Coalition politicians outside of Cairns and how it might be perceived.

It was with relief and a touch of trepidation that Mick and I greeted Horan on that sun-drenched afternoon in Townsville. We collected his luggage and drove him to the Banjo Paterson Motel. A couple of hours later Mick and I picked Horan up from his motel and set off to dinner at the renowned Ming Dynasty Chinese Restaurant where we would meet with the Deputy Leader of the National Party, Kev Lingard.

It didn't take long for Mick and me to hit it off with Lingard, a jovial, extroverted man. We had previously met Lingard with fellow National Party member Howard Hobbs, at a lunch organised by Naomi Wilson and Lyn Warwick at the Cairns RSL in November the previous year. Mick and Lingard gelled like long-lost friends. An hour into the meal, Horan raised the subject of the by-election and searched for something to write on. He found an unused table napkin and asked me to jot down for him the points the STF sought confirmation on as part of any partnership.

Meanwhile, Lingard continued to chat with Mick who it turned out was not the only Labor identity in the room that night. We spotted a couple of leading ALP officials, obviously in town to do some lobbying ahead of the by-election.

❖

It was only on the way to Townsville that Mick and I had developed the finer points of our strategy for this meeting. The deal that we thought would be best for the STF was to enter into a partnership with Queensland Health and the Aboriginal Coordinating Council to develop ongoing health policies which would allow the expansion of the STF by six offices, thereby ensuring that Aboriginal health programmes were successfully undertaken statewide. The primary targets for the STF would be drug and alcohol education and preventative programmes for diabetes, nutrition and eye infections. These programmes would be met by making more places available for health worker training at higher education institutions, and by undertaking a review of the basic infrastructures on communities with a particular emphasis on sewage treatment centres.

Mick and I felt confident that Horan would deliver these points as part of the Opposition's health policy for Indigenous people and we left the restaurant to adjourn to the Townsville Breakwater Casino for a drink and to chance our luck on the tables.

The next day Joan Sheldon, State Deputy Opposition Leader and Leader of the State Liberal Party, held a joint press conference with Mick outside the Townsville Base Hospital. Horan and I stood off to their left. As Sheldon reiterated the promises agreed upon the night before, I did feel rather awkward standing with the conservative politicians and noticed some of the media offering more than a cursory glance at us Murries.

Mick commented to the media that he was pleased to hear the Coalition's new policy direction on Indigenous health and said he was confident they would deliver on their promises. The advantage of this media coverage was that it seemed the STF had come out in response to the Opposition's policy—although I'm sure some reporters smelt a rat before Joan Sheldon's announcement. Nonetheless, we all left Townsville content in the knowledge that there was now a commitment on public record and that we could work cooperatively

the N word

on achieving our goal of winning the seat of Mundingburra for the Coalition parties.

Back in Cairns, the STF was abuzz with telephone calls on strategies and updates for the State by-election as well as the upcoming Federal election for the seat of Leichhardt.

⁂

I respected Mick. He was a people's person with an enormous capacity to win over the hearts and minds of ordinary folk and often did his best work in social situations. Our friendship with the State Coalition politicians seemed genuine, and on occason we were invited to dinner at their homes. Lyn Warwick and Naomi Wilson also joined STF staffers and friends for a meal at the Taj of India Restaurant to celebrate Mick's birthday.

Once the March date for the Federal election had been announced, aspiring politician Warren Entsch, who was contesting the Federal seat of Leichhardt, became another agreeable politician who frequented our office for a yarn. He was a knock-around sort of fellow who was more at ease chasing cattle on horseback and fossicking for minerals in the harsh terrain of the Cape York Peninsula than doing political advertisements on radio or hosting a fundraising party. We were often returning calls to his office and he was regularly canvassing us on Indigenous issues.

The Liberal Party brought in a full-time campaign manager from Darwin to look after his interests, which I believe assisted greatly in Entsch's success. One day, his campaign manager rang me at the STF to ask what I thought of Entsch's radio advertisement. I said I felt he should not have done the commercial with such a bad cold—only to feel like a right goose when I discovered it was just his gravelly voice hardened by a tough life in the bush.

the N word

During the lead-up to the Federal election Horan flew to Cairns and I joined him at a breakfast address at the Pacific International Hotel by the Deputy Prime Minister, Tim Fisher.

A couple of days later, just when I thought I wouldn't be seen dead at such an event again, I found an invitation on my desk to the best show in town—lunch with the Prime Minister John Howard. Mick and I turned up at the Cairns International Hotel to hear Howard deliver the keynote address. This lunch was to launch Warren Entsch's campaign and there were over 400 people in attendance. After the official part of the function, Entsch organised a photograph with the Prime Minister, himself, Mick and me, for the Queensland daily, the *Courier Mail*. Fortunately, it wasn't published as part of the next day's coverage of the event.

It wasn't long before we began to receive requests from the Liberal's PR machine to provide the names of high-profile Indigenous people who would be prepared to go public against criticism the Prime Minister was receiving from certain sections of the Indigenous leadership—namely the Dodson brothers, Mick and Patrick.

My response was to ask whether the government had a register of Indigenous people who were card-carrying members of the Liberal Party. I said I thought it would be more appropriate to contact people on that list and I was then asked to assist in putting one together! When I spoke to Mick about this he simply said he would be surprised if many high profile Indigenous people would be courageous enough to admit to voting for the Liberal Party.

※

On 24 January 1996 I accompanied Victor Jose and Torres Strait Islander leader Jim Akee to Townsville to continue our campaigning for the Coalition parties in the lead-up to the Mundingburra by-election. We headed straight to the Nathan Village shopping centre

the N word

to hear Bob Katter, Federal National Party Member for the seat of Kennedy, and Frank Tanti make their public addresses.

This was the first time we were introduced to Tanti, the political aspirant. We also met Joan Sheldon again and her adviser Cameron Thompson, now Federal Member for the seat of Blair. We were introduced to the Liberal Party support staff and it was made clear to them that the resources of the campaign office could be accessed by us whenever we visited Townsville. That same day members of our team were also happy to receive some funds to assist with our campaign expenses.

After their spirited speeches, Bob Katter invited Akee, Jose and myself to join him at the Hotel Townsville to discuss our role in the forthcoming by-election.

❖

The following day, 25 January, Jose, Akee and I had breakfast with Opposition Leader Rob Borbidge, and Liberal staffer Cameron Thompson, to discuss our campaign strategies to date with the Indigenous population, in particular the large Torres Strait Islander population living in the electorate.

Borbidge was a magnet for curious eyes as we ate breakfast in the ground floor eatery of the Lowths Hotel. He talked about a range of issues—including our partnership agreement previously worked out with Horan and Lingard and confirmed by his Deputy, Joan Sheldon, at her press conference. He made mention of the critical role we were playing in the campaign, saying he believed any increase in Indigenous voter numbers on the day would change the outcome of the election and effectively the government of the State.

We discussed briefly the transportation available for Indigenous constituents to cast their vote at the Mundingburra Primary School and whether we were required to hand out how-to-vote cards in front

the N word

of the polling booth. Conscious not to offend us, Borbidge said it might be awkward for non-Indigenous people to receive how-to-vote cards from Indigenous volunteers. He suggested an alternative arrangement was for us to hand out to 'your people' on the bus or at their homes prior to visiting the polling booth. We understood what he was saying and seeing that we had put a considerable amount of our time and energy into this campaign were prepared to overlook his remark—just this once.

Throughout the breakfast Cameron Thompson took down notes. He was dressed like an executive from the big end of town and looked every bit the politician he would graduate to within a relatively short space of time, post-Mundingburra. We found Borbidge to be a charming fellow who was quite receptive to our views. After thanking us for our efforts, he politely excused himself and departed for another meeting.

※

Later that day Jose, Akee and myself drove to the Townsville airport to pick up Horan. After the customary greetings around the baggage carousel we drove him to his accommodation at the Banjo Paterson Motel. Horan checked in and after he'd freshened up we headed off to our only scheduled appointment for the night, an address to the large Torres Strait Islander community meeting in Flinders Street in the centre of town.

Francis Tapim, the Maguni Malu Kes Administrator, warmly greeted us at the entrance and took delight in showing the shadow Health Minister around his office. Tapim introduced Horan to his staff as he walked through the building and explained the purpose of the organisation was to assist his people with housing and a range of social welfare needs.

the N word

While I was organising a cup of tea for Horan, large numbers of people were slowly making their way into the meeting room ahead of time. It wasn't long before the room was packed with Islanders chatting cheerfully in language. They were greeting each other and waving to others seated away from them and the smallish meeting room soon took on a carnival atmosphere. The large roll-up was a clear indication to me that they were eager to find out what Horan had to offer them.

Horan commenced his speech singing the praises of the Coalition and their commitment to improving the conditions of Indigenous Queenslanders. He again made mention of his commitment to the STF and promised to open an office in Townsville which would work in partnership with Maguni Malu Kes to address health matters. He also said they would have direct access to the Minister responsible for Aboriginal and Torres Strait Islander Affairs on matters that concerned their community.

The next day Horan, Jose, Akee and I visited the Townsville Aboriginal and Islander Medical Service and spoke to Chris George, the Administrator, and her staff. Like another local Indigenous leader we had spoken to the previous day, Chris appeared bemused that we were singing the tune of the Coalition parties' propaganda. We had all known each other for years and had marched together in protest against the Bjelke-Petersen regime in days gone by—now they were hearing conservative rhetoric from us.

◈

On 3 February 1996 I joined Miller, Jose, Akee and our supporters in celebrating Frank Tanti's by-election victory. He won with a three percent swing in his favour. As we celebrated I sensed we were entering a new chapter in Queensland history. We were confident that the hundreds of extra votes gained by the Coalition, predominately coming from the Torres Strait Islander population, with a small number from the Aboriginal population, were a direct result of our efforts. I believe this may well have been the first time in Queensland that Indigenous people had assisted a conservative party to win a crucial seat.

Several weeks later the Coalition parties came to power with the expected support of Independents, Peter Wellington and Liz Cunningham. The calls from Members of Parliament to the STF office after the declaration of the polls indicated to our team that they also thought our campaign had succeeded.

I received congratulatory messages on my answering machine at home from Horan and from the sound of his voice I sensed that he was a very happy chappie.

the N word

Political Deceit

After a couple of weeks of back slapping and congratulations from politicians and party faithfuls, Mick Miller and I flew to Brisbane to start the ball rolling on the commitments made to the STF prior to the elections. Tony Koch, at the time Chief Reporter for the *Courier Mail*, looked a little perplexed when he arrived at Parliament House to interview Mick and me for a story which was to focus on the agreement entered into by the STF with the Coalition Government to improve Indigenous health in Queensland.

Tony had been a recipient of the prestigious Walkley Award for his articles on Indigenous issues in Queensland and is highly respected by Indigenous communities throughout the State. A big man, who likes a cigarette and a beer, Tony tackles his stories with passion and attention to detail. He tells it like it is and is not frightened of treading on toes if it means exposing the truth. His recent articles on Indigenous corruption have contributed significantly to charges being laid against a number of Indigenous leaders.

ATSIC was put under the microscope for its inability to deal with financial mismanagement and in my view, Tony's exposure of this flaw in the ATSIC administration influenced the Federal government in its final decision to make legislative changes. In the middle of 2004, ATSIC was relieved of its funding role and replaced by

Aboriginal and Torres Strait Islander Services (ATSIS). The bulk of the former body's funds—estimated to be $1.4 billion—was handed over to the new organisation. Applications for access to the funds were thereafter to be assessed by bureaucrats instead of the elected arm of ATSIC.

I valued Tony's work and got to know him over the years as a result of several stories I'd provided to him from Cairns. However, on this occasion, on the first floor balcony of Parliament House, I could sense that he felt awkward about my choice of venue and partners. Posing for a photograph with Mike Horan, Rob Borbidge, and Kev Lingard, Mick and I, however, thought we were off to a good start. We had succeeded with our goal of gaining the ear of the politicians in charge of running Queensland.

That evening I invited Dad for a meal courtesy of the government. A long-standing Labor Party supporter, Dad was pleasantly surprised at the VIP treatment we were receiving at Parliament House from the Coalition powerbrokers. Although he didn't say anything to me at the time, I sensed that he was also somewhat uncomfortable with the company we were keeping. But, always diplomatic, he agreed to support our cause, interested to see how our game plan played out.

During the third course of our meal, Premier Borbidge and Deputy Premier Joan Sheldon joined us. Sheldon told us that earlier that day she had announced the sacking of the Liberal Party candidate for the Federal seat of Oxley, Pauline Hanson.

When I asked why Hanson had been disendorsed, Sheldon said it was over remarks Hanson had written about the Federal Minister for Aboriginal Affairs Robert Tickner, in a letter published in the *Queensland Times* in January. Hanson had been damning of comments made by Tickner about Aboriginal deaths in custody. The letter had sparked widespread debate and panic within the Liberal Party ranks after it was exposed in the national media.

Borbidge said he supported his Deputy and that this was a good way for the Coalition Government to start shedding its redneck image. They appeared proud of their stand and although I hadn't been aware of the Pauline Hanson debate, I was delighted that they had taken such a proactive stance to remove her from their ranks. No one in that room could have predicted what was to come and the controversy that would follow with the unexpected election victory of Hanson as a Federal Independent member for the seat of Oxley.

After the Premier and his Deputy left our table, we devoured our dessert and adjourned to Kev Lingard's office for a yarn and a serious drink. Lingard said he was looking forward to the day when he could move into bigger premises. The handover wasn't yet completed and he was still 'in a pokey little Opposition office'. We played some country and western music and then moved on to the more palatial Treasury Casino to chance our arm on the gaming tables.

During the next couple of weeks Lingard became a regular caller to the STF office, asking for ways in which he could better improve the administration of his Aboriginal and Islander Affairs portfolio. Our office started doing position papers for both Queensland Health and the Department of Aboriginal and Islanders Affairs. Lingard invited Mick Miller, Victor Jose and myself to Brisbane to discuss the paper we had developed for his Department. Mick was in demand and went off to meet with other government officials while Jose and I met with Lingard.

Our proposal was to establish an Indigenous Advisory Group with an office based in the Executive Building, a high rise in Brisbane's CBD which housed, among other things, the Premier's Office. It was adjacent to Parliament House and we felt the location met our vision of placing the CEO in the heart of the power and decision-making precinct. Lingard was impressed with our proposal but said he would

the N word

like to put a bit more meat on the bone and asked us to supply him with the names of Indigenous leaders from the Torres Strait and rural and urban Queensland who we would like to see comprise the advisory group.

On return to Cairns, Jose and myself put together the names of ten leaders who we thought were representative of the State's Indigenous population and after having them endorsed by Mick, passed the names on to Lingard.

At the same time, Horan was enjoying his elevated status as the new Minister for Health. He was in regular contact with us and said that he had done his figures on the six new STF offices throughout the state as per his pre-Mundingburra commitment. When he asked if we could reduce the number by two, we reviewed our original list and suggested Toowoomba, Rockhampton, Townsville and Mt Isa as communities that could make the most of additional resources and staff to address the endemic health problems of Indigenous people.

Everything was going along famously and I started to wonder if it was all too good to be true. However, there was a hint of a cool south-easterly breeze wafting slowly through Cairns which at the time I mistook for seasonal changes and not those of a political nature.

※

On the evening of Thursday 2 May 1996 at a Parliament House dinner organised by Frank Carroll, the Liberal Party member for Mansfield, I commented to those present that I was grateful for the support of the Coalition during the by-election campaign.

At some point in the evening, the Speaker of the House, Neil Turner, approached our table and invited us to his chamber to celebrate his wife's birthday. In the privacy of the Speaker's chamber, I repeated my thanks to the Members for the Coalition's support. Turner's hat was in a prominent place on the hat rack. Being in a jovial mood after the pleasurable meal with new friends, I joked with him that Katter had a bigger hat than his. 'The bigger the hat, the smaller the property,' Turner quipped.

I also expressed my delight at seeing an Aboriginal painting by Geoffrey Manthey hanging prominently in Turner's chamber. Geoff and I had been junior high classmates back in Cunnamulla and it turned out that Turner was a friend of Geoff's father Frank, from the time when he was actively involved in the National Party in far south-west Queensland in the 1970s and 1980s. The rest of the evening passed quickly and after several drinks I bid them all goodnight and caught a taxi back to my parents' house, blissfully unaware of a storm brewing.

The following day I sensed a change in mood. Although it had never been my intention to upset the Coalition by openly acknowledging their support, it appeared to be more than coincidence that events now changed quite dramatically for me.

Within a short time of the Parliament House dinner I was informed by Mick Miller, on advice from the Director-General of Queensland Health Dr Robert Stable, that I was to be suspended from work pending the outcome of a police investigation into misappropriation allegations.

Following the Mundingburra by-election a snap internal audit of the STF had revealed certain irregularities which would not only allow Horan to renege on his pre-election promises but would also signal the demise of the STF.

I was absolutely devastated that I was the subject of these allegations but I was told it was only a technicality and that I would receive full pay until the matter was resolved in my favour. It was alleged that I had breached the State Public Service regulation which provided that a public servant should stay at an approved hotel, motel or boarding house when in receipt of a travel allowance from Queensland Health.

At the time it never occurred to me that I had in fact stayed in approved accommodation. Mum and Dad ran a boarding house for the Brisbane Broncos' Rugby League Club and I stayed with them and paid the sixty dollars per night fee like all their other boarders. It soon became apparent to me that all the meetings with Horan in Brisbane and an associated trip I took to Goondiwindi would also come back to haunt me. These were the only trips identified in the 'wilful false promise' charges that were later to be raised by Queensland Health. Horan had been aware that I was staying with my family as he had contacted me at their residence on several occasions.

Given all this, I sought further clarification from the Premier's office, the President of the Liberal Party Bob Tucker, the President of the National Party David Russell QC, and the Speaker of the House Neil Turner, as to why the investigation was still proceeding. I was eager to rid myself of the charges and return to work. I was advised to accept advice offered by Frank Carroll, Member for Mansfield, the only lawyer in the Government ranks. Carroll was evidently being nominated by his party mates to handle my problem.

Tucker assured me that I was in good hands and advised me to cooperate with him fully. When we met, Carroll told me that he'd recently represented a woman who had misappropriated $30,000 from the Department of Social Security. On his advice she pleaded guilty and repaid the money. She was let off without a conviction being recorded.

Within days a Senior Policy Advisor from the Premier's office informed me that she had spoken to several senior officials at Queensland Health and everything looked good about the matter being resolved in my favour. She also suggested that I was still a strong candidate for the Executive Officer position of the soon-to-be created Indigenous Advisory Group, but I was subsequently removed from the short-list. Prior to my demise, I had been introduced to Doug Slack, Minister responsible for the Premier's office, and his Director-General Peter Ellis, to talk about the composition of this new body—the objective of which was to monitor all Commonwealth funds allocated to State departments and ensure that money was spent on specific Aboriginal programmes and not squandered on administration.

I had also been asked to speak to Neville Bonner, former Queensland Liberal Party Senator, who was to chair the interview selection panel. Some time later Bonner went straight from being the Chairman of the interview panel into the Executive Officer's position.

※

As the weeks went by it became obvious that I was not commanding the attention that I was previously afforded and I became increasingly frustrated by the lack of progress. As a last resort I told officials that if I was going to be treated this way then I might go public over pre-Mundingburra promises the new government had yet to fulfil in addressing the Aboriginal health problems.

The expression of my concerns only appeared to exacerbate the situation. My predicament went from bad to worse. On 4 June I was interviewed by CIB detectives at the City Police Headquarters, Brisbane. After informal discussions prior to the interview, the senior detective told me he was satisfied that I was telling the truth and that I didn't have a case to answer. He left the room and phoned Tony Hayes, Director, Internal Audit, Queensland Health, to inform him of his view.

The detective returned to the interview room a short time later and informed me that he had been instructed to proceed with the interview. After two hours of interviewing during which I admitted to staying at my parents' house in Brisbane instead of a hotel, the detective, in the presence of his partner, repeated that he believed that I didn't have a case to answer. He went on to say that of all the interviews he had conducted, mine was one of the most honest and straightforward, and in his opinion the case did not warrant any further action.

In hindsight, I made a mistake at that interview. I assumed the rules of the Commonwealth, which I worked under as an ATSIC official, were the same as the State, whereby public servants could stay wherever they chose provided it was for the number of days stipulated in the approved travel program. If I had informed the interviewing detectives that I had paid sixty dollars per night when I stayed at the boarding house Mum and Dad were running, I believe the interview would have been terminated there and then.

On Thursday 25 July 1996, a Senior Advisor to the Police Minister rang me at home to say he wanted to help. He asked me for the name of the most senior detective handling my case, saying he wanted to sort the mess out. At last someone believed in me and was going to help or so I thought.

Unfortunately the next day the Senior Advisor resigned over a Memorandum of Understanding agreement between the Police Union and Premier Rob Borbidge and Police Minister Russell Cooper. I sought help from his successor but he claimed he was not familiar with the case.

As the trial date approached, I organised a telephone hook-up with my solicitor from the ALS in Cairns and Frank Carroll. Carroll's advice to my solicitor was for me to plead guilty. He said that with my unblemished record I should get off without a conviction. My legal team at the ALS ultimately concurred with Carroll's advice and confirmed that I should enter a guilty plea. They seemed to take the view that a simple case like mine should be an in-and-out case with no conviction recorded.

◈

At the trial on 19 September, the Police Prosecutor had only one charge to read from instead of the six which my solicitor Matt McLaughlin, from the ALS had before him. The magistrate adjourned the case until the next day so the prosecution could gather all the relevant documents. The following day the same magistrate was informed that I had repaid the money in dispute and was handed a receipt for $1,940.00, evidencing payment of that amount to Queensland Health.

However, the Police Prosecutor had a different figure to ours as a result of Queensland Health's failure to deduct the twenty dollars per day that I was entitled to claim if I chose to stay privately. The magistrate once again adjourned the case until the afternoon session in order for the prosecution to get its figures right.

The Police Prosecutor, frustrated by the imprecision of Queensland Health, told my solicitor he did not want to take the matter further and would recommend that the charges be dropped. During lunch, my solicitor and the Police Prosecutor put a call through to Queensland Health. They were informed that the case must continue and that the revised figures would be faxed through within the hour for the hearing to proceed.

In the afternoon session, Magistrate Errol Wessling recorded a criminal conviction and gave me a four months' suspended jail sentence. This shocked not only my solicitor but also the *Cairns Post* court reporter who told me she was staggered to see such a harsh penalty handed out to someone with no previous conviction and for such a small amount of money which had since been repaid. I departed the courthouse feeling dumbfounded and appalled.

the N word

A week later I received a disturbing telephone call from the prosecuting CIB Detective who had handled my case from day one. He informed me that Queensland Health had found more claims of misuse of travel allowance that they were going to charge me with. As the new claims of misappropriation related to the same time period as the first ones, he thought that no further action would be taken against me. He told me he felt I had already been dealt with quite harshly in the first trial and believed no further penalty would arise from a court appearance, which was necessary to tidy up the loose ends.

At this stage I was devastated. However, as my solicitor also advised me that it was unlikely that I would be further penalised, I agreed to plead guilty once again.

On the day of this trial, 11 October, Rhonda and I drove young Stephen to his preschool and arrived early at the Cairns Courthouse, with our two-month old baby daughter Jayde in arms. We'd allowed plenty of time to talk to my solicitor before the hearing. My three business colleagues from the Rainbow Serpent Cruises—all non-Indigenous—came to wish me well. I told them not to worry about sitting in on the hearing as I would be in and out quite quickly and would see them back at the marina within the hour.

Rainbow Serpent Cruises was a tourism venture of which I was a director. After my experience on the Gold Coast I'd decided to form my own dance company by recruiting a couple of my Gold Coast dancers and some locals to test the market in Cairns. I spent most of my time after work at rehearsals and choreographing dance routines to perform at the large international tourist hotels in the area. It was at one of these performances that we were noticed by a couple of businessmen who decided to invest their money and expertise into a

the *N* word

harbour cruise showcasing the Gulbari Wata dancers, under the name of Rainbow Serpent Cruises. (The Kullilli words 'gulbari wata' mean 'emu at play'.)

As it turned out, I was not to meet up with them again that day. As we walked into the courtroom everyone seemed upbeat. Sitting on the bench was Magistrate Trevor Pollock, who I'd been led to believe was on vacation. I'd been warned that Magistrate Pollock, like Mr Wessling, was not the most sympathetic of magistrates.

I stood as confidently as I could given that I was a criminal defendant in a courtroom. Pollock studied the new charges and without any hesitation ordered that I be detained in the watch-house until he had time to consider his decision over lunch. I was in a state of shock as two burly police officers escorted me by the arm out of the courtroom.

As I walked out I glanced across at Rhonda who, cradling Jayde, stood in a trance-like state, not quite comprehending what the magistrate had just ordered. I tried to give her a reassuring smile but I was very upset that she had to witness me being led away by police. As I walked up the slight incline to the cells in the rear of the courtroom I felt tears roll down my face. I kept telling myself that I wouldn't allow a magistrate to break my spirit and proceeded to follow instructions from the attending police.

In the holding cell I noticed a very thin white man pacing his cell. He looked like he was in a daze. I tried not to stare at him, as I had enough problems of my own to worry about. However, this scrawny man kept pacing and pacing and then all of a sudden it dawned on me that he was the man I had heard about on the news. He was being held over the heinous crime of pouring petrol over the young boy, Tjandamurra O'Shane, in a Cairns primary schoolyard and setting him alight. He continued to pace his cell and didn't appear in the slightest agitated or remorseful for a crime that shocked the nation and made Tjandamurra a household name.

the N word

After a short time in the cell, Matt McLaughlin visited me with what I thought was good news. He tried to reassure me that Pollock had placed me in a cell to put a scare into me and that he would free me when court resumed after lunch. He sounded convincing—but then again he also thought I wouldn't have been convicted if I'd pleaded guilty in the first trial before Magistrate Wessling.

When I was led back into the courtroom after what seemed like an interminable two hours, I was asked to stand in the dock while Magistrate Pollock read out his decision. I gave an encouraging smile to my wife in an attempt to reassure her that everything would work out okay. Then Magistrate Pollock read his decision. I was 'to serve a term of six months in prison'.

My heart missed a beat and I looked quickly towards Rhonda. She was in an extremely distressed state, crying and nursing Jayde. Our daughter had been delivered by normal birth at the Cairns Base Hospital on 28 August, two days after her mother's birthday, and I remembered little Stephen nursing her when she was just a day old—two beautiful children staring into each other's dark brown eyes.

I was fortunate that a young Indigenous policeman who had recently graduated from the police academy was on duty. Rhonda and I were friends of his parents and on completion of the standard paperwork for new prisoners he rang his mother and asked her to come down and care for Rhonda, who by now was inconsolable.

His mother came immediately and after making sure Rhonda got home safely, she promptly contacted Rhonda's mum Mary and her brother in Innisfail. Both of them dropped what they were doing, packed their bags and made their way to Cairns.

Meanwhile in the watch-house the white police officers working behind the counter commented that there was only one magistrate in Cairns, if not all of Australia, who would have the audacity to hand down such a sentence. 'Padlock Pollock,' they said in unison.

the N word

I kept hearing that wretched nickname for hours after the prison doors were shut behind me. In another place and in another time I probably would have laughed. But as things stood, I was in no mood for humour.

Incarceration

Concerned for my welfare, the police agreed to place me in a cell by myself. However, as the afternoon slowly turned to evening there was a change of shift and the new officer, aware of my case, said he would move me to a cell with someone I would be able to identify with. He had to place a prisoner with HIV/AIDS in my cell to isolate him from the rest of the inmates.

My solicitor had been trying all afternoon to get me out on bail pending an appeal, but later that day he informed me that the Director of Public Prosecutions, based in Brisbane, had opposed bail. I was devastated. I had never been before the courts in my life and had no convictions. I had committed no crimes that would make me a threat to society. I didn't have money hidden in a tax haven on a remote island and I wasn't about to do a runner and go abroad.

If I were to offer advice to people, black or white, male or female, about the worst day to appear before court, I would nominate Friday. Bail and other legal relief can be frustrated by officials having an early mark on a Friday afternoon. As I found out the hard way, once the weekend arrives there is not a lot that can be done to try and bring some attention to your plight except wait until the following Monday. Friday night is the busiest of the week, with the cells full to overflowing with all sorts of offenders.

the N word

I shared a cell with a young Indigenous prisoner who had been in for a few days and soon discovered that prisoners were allocated cells at the Cairns watch-house based on race. After many hours of reflecting on the events of the past six months I felt myself drifting in and out of sleep. I would only have been asleep for an hour when I was awoken by a major commotion involving a prisoner being placed in the padded cell. I sat upright, not sure how to prepare myself, and looked in the general direction of the noise. I couldn't see the prisoner as he had already been manhandled into the cell by the duty officers and was now venting his spleen at anyone within earshot, which was the entire prison population.

Many prisoners started screaming obscenities, yelling at him to shut up and go to sleep, but the new arrival appeared too mad with the world and threatened to tear off their heads when he was released from his cell in the morning. I was anxious to see what this man looked like and had an image of a heavily muscular, wild man from the west. I thought to myself he must be handy with his fists as he was shouting abuse freely at prisoners he hadn't even seen. But when morning finally arrived the police led out this short, chubby fellow.

At 8 am when all the cell doors were opened for prisoners to stretch their legs in the narrow corridor and take a shower, most prisoners made their way to this noisy person's cell to get a closer look at the cause of their interrupted sleep. To my surprise some of the prisoners, in spite of the closed circuit TV monitors, walked into his cell and assaulted him. Others threw food at him and one prisoner hurled a bucket in his direction. I waited for intervention from the morning duty officers but there was none forthcoming.

After witnessing all this I lined up to wait my turn for a shower. After a not-so-private wash in an open booth I put my clothes back on—minus my belt and socks which had been taken from me—and followed the others out into the courtyard, a concrete pavement measuring six square metres. This was the only place we could fully stretch and see a bit of sunlight for the thirty minutes allocated daily.

the N word

On an exercise break the following day I noticed two young men from Cape York Peninsula fill their mouths full of water and without attempting to swallow walk slowly towards the rear of the courtyard. I strayed behind everyone else, curious as to what they were up to. To my surprise they stopped at the door of the female prisoners' cell and emptied the water along the edge of the door entrance. The men then asked the women inside to take their pants off and stand over the puddle. Feeling uncomfortable at their request for a peep show I didn't stay around.

I was really a novice in there. I wanted to sound tough but had trouble convincing the seasoned white criminals in particular that I was indeed a bad guy who had earned the right to be locked up. I wanted to tell the prisoners who asked why I was in jail that my fraud case involved hundreds of thousands of dollars. Instead I told them the truth about Mundingburra, the subsequent charges that resulted in my conviction, and the refusal of bail on the grounds that I was a risk to society. One prisoner asked me if the amount wasn't so great why hadn't I paid it back to avoid prison. I told him that I had repaid the money but this only made my story even more baffling.

There were a couple of heavily-tattooed prisoners who didn't buy my story and hinted that I was insulting their intelligence. I couldn't win so I didn't bother going down that path again and spent most of my time reading and trading books. When I received my first opportunity to use the public phone, one of the white prisoners shouted out, 'Don't forget to say hello to Premier Rob for us.' A day later the same group of prisoners were asking me to write letters for them and to assist them with their appeals as they had received word from the outside that I was indeed telling the truth.

On another occasion, I asked my cellmate if he minded if I invited another Indigenous prisoner, who I'd spoken to during our courtyard breaks and found to be a pleasant fellow, to bring his mattress to our cell. (Officers in charge had no problem with prisoners changing cells provided there was nothing suspicious or untoward going on.) I was promptly told that this guy was awaiting court on charges of killing his baby. I was shocked and didn't make any further requests for other prisoners to share our cell.

I received a visit from the Murri Watch cell visitors who asked if I needed anything from home, such as books or toiletries. Murri Watch is a critical contact for Indigenous prisoners who use them as a conduit to get messages to their families if they are unable to visit the jail for whatever reason. When I explained my reason for being in prison, the Murri Watch woman told me to relax and take it easy and advised me not to rock the boat by appealing. She suggested I do the time and get it over and done with, adding that I would probably be out after doing two months of my six-month sentence!

When Rhonda came to visit me on the second day, she told me Stephen was asking about me. She said she told him that I was away on business and would return home soon. It was incredibly sad talking to her through the wire mesh. I had played a major role in changing the government in Queensland and now here I was shedding tears with my wife in a non-contact visit, not knowing when I would be returning home.

Rhonda tried to fill me in on everything that was happening at home and around town but her briefing was punctuated with bouts of emotion. She did manage to tell me that I was receiving literally hundreds of messages from well-wishers, family and friends around the nation who had heard of my ordeal and telephoned our home to offer support.

the N word

At night I tossed and turned under the flickering of the dim florescent light thinking of how the gamble of aligning with the conservative Coalition parties had backfired. I was disappointed in myself that I hadn't seen it coming, especially after dealing with politicians who appeared to be largely unaware of the plight of Indigenous Queenslanders. I recalled one politican's frank admission during the by-election campaign that he didn't know that Torres Strait Islanders had curly hair!

I managed to get my quota of calls to Rhonda with some help from a couple of supportive officers in charge who sympathised with my incarceration. But after four days I started to become very disillusioned with my situation. Although I remained confident of being released on bail, I didn't want to spend another Friday night in the Cairns watch-house.

The seasoned prisoners had told me of the easy life at Lotus Glen Prison and assured me that I would be placed in the lowest classification and possibly be sent to the prison farm. They described life at Lotus Glen as like being on a vacation at a strange but comfortable motel. You could have a feed whenever you wanted to, work out in the gym and even take classes in the adult learning programmes run by Technical and Further Education (TAFE). I knew a bit about these programmes as I had funded a few of them when I was Manager of Aboriginal Programmes with DEET. In fact, I had launched a similar one with senior prison officials about twelve months prior. What a strange situation to not only be the creator of the programme but also a participant, I thought.

It was simply the luck of the draw as to who would be offered one of the limited bus seats to Lotus Glen on the Friday run. By now, I had convinced myself that if I was to wait any longer for my legal team to get me out on bail I would be better served waiting at Lotus Glen Prison than sitting around in a watch-house with artificial lighting. I didn't know if it was cloudy or sunny outside. If it wasn't for the meal call I would have been none the wiser about the time of the day or night.

※

I was lucky, if you can call it that, to be chosen to be relocated to Lotus Glen Prison on that Friday's run. As I was being processed and handcuffed I met another Indigenous police officer at the front counter. She had been a mature-aged entry into the police academy having completed an entry qualification at the South Johnstone TAFE College in Innisfail. I had also provided funding, as Manager of DEET, to support the TAFE justice programme at Innisfail for Indigenous people who required extra tuition in order to gain entry into the Brisbane-based academy.

I remembered being the guest speaker at this officer's graduation class. Now I was avoiding eye contact with her as I sat shackled, awaiting transportation to the Lotus Glen Prison. I felt most uncomfortable, edgily waiting for orders to board the bus and for a fleeting moment wished that I hadn't made myself available to be on the Lotus Glen run.

As soon as the last prisoner was signed out of the watch-house we were directed onto the bus. As we drove through the city of Cairns I tried not to look out the window in case someone recognised me. Other prisoners, however, were eager to spot and acknowledge family and acquaintances as the armed bus slowly made its way along the Bruce Highway. They seemed to wear the criminal title like a badge of honour. By now I was starting to feel the discomfort of the heavy handcuffs and we hadn't even reached the outskirts of the city.

It was quite intimidating arriving at the prison and passing through the huge gates surrounded with razor sharp wire. I wondered how anyone could possibly escape as we were ordered off the bus and walked single file into a processing room where we waited until our names were called. I was towards the end of the line and reluctantly stepped forward on finally hearing my name announced by the warden.

The prison officials ordered me to shed all my clothes for the humiliating strip-and-cough routine. Then I was handed a cake of coarse soap and told to scrub under my armpits and fingernails. The sandpaper-like soap was about as far removed from the Palmolive I used at home as one could get. I gave the impression of scrubbing vigorously but in reaility I avoided any direct contact with the soap, fearing I would shed my skin in the process.

When it was my turn to fill out the paperwork, the prison official, in his sixties, couldn't stop shaking his head in disbelief. He asked me if I had any tattoos to which I replied I didn't. He asked me what the highest grade I attained at school was. I told him I had completed my matriculation and had graduated from university with an arts degree. He asked me what I was sent to Lotus Glen for, to which I replied misappropriation.

Without lifting his head he asked how much money I'd misappropriated, all the time trying to get a fix on the seriousness of the crime. I told him the amount and said that I had repaid it. After exhausting his list of questions he then surprised me by blurting out words I still vividly remember to this day. 'Look mate, I've never had anyone here on charges like this before and I've been here for a hell of a long time. This is obviously politically motivated.'

He ended by saying he didn't expect to see me at Lotus Glen for very long. I asked him if he had heard anything about my bail application but he hadn't. I tried to remain upbeat and confident in my solicitor's ability to get bail granted.

the N word

❃

After I was fitted out with my basic prison clothes and boots I was taken to the medical facilities where I waited to be blood tested. Soon a young nurse called out my name and proceeded to brief me on the purpose of the test. At first the simple process was going smoothly. Then, without warning, the nurse thrust the needle into my arm a little deeper than normal. I jerked my arm and blood squirted all over her snow white uniform. When I asked her what she thought she was doing she replied that she wasn't getting enough blood for a sample and needed to extract more. I told her she only had to tell me what she required and I would've been more than happy to oblige. Not a good start Steve, I thought. I needed to remind myself that I was in a prison—not in a boardroom where you gained bonus points for being self-assured.

After that ordeal I was instructed to proceed with my possessions to my designated block. I walked along the path and observed the other prisoners, the majority of whom were Indigenous, performing a range of duties from mowing lawns to taking laundry and equipment between buildings. They knew exactly who I was—a nameless, new inmate.

When I arrived at my block I made another mistake. Instead of stopping on the yellow line I stepped over it and into the office of the warden who admonished me with an outburst, the likes of which I hadn't heard since I was in primary school.

After that unsavoury introduction, I walked a further twenty metres to a new division of the prison, eager to locate my name on the wall and find out what classification prison officialdom had allocated for me. I half-expected to be given the highest risk classification and be thrown in with the murderers and serial rapists after the dubious bail application refusal earlier in the week.

As I walked down the corridor I passed a familiar face—an Aboriginal liaison officer I knew from Cairns. He told me that another colleague of his was waiting to give me a lift down the Kuranda Range. I was excited, thinking this was the confirmation that my bail application had been successful after all. I didn't know whether to laugh or cry but thanked the officer and continued on my way, anxious that the warden, a short distance back, would begin barking out more orders. At last I arrived at the designated prison wing and searched frantically for my name on the list taped to the window to find out the all-important classification. I was relieved to see 'low classification' beside my name.

I found it difficult to hear the new set of instructions from the next warden, who was sitting behind a thick glass window, and asked if he could repeat himself. I also asked if he knew the status of my bail application and was told that he hadn't been given any instructions but would page me if any news came through. He then pressed a button, telling me I would be sharing a room in the second last cell on the left side of the long corridor of cells.

The thought of being locked up with another stranger was disconcerting but the situation was out of my control. At least it wouldn't be a serial killer as they were housed in the high risk wing in a separate block. As I made the long, fifty-metre walk down the row of cells I observed prisoners watching television and eating toasted sandwiches and other snacks. Some of them I'd seen around the streets of Cairns. What they'd said in the Cairns watch-house seemed true. There was the freedom to move around the cells and eat outside the normal meal times. So far so good, I thought. If my stay here became a little more permanent, I knew I could make the most of a bad situation.

I walked through my cell door and saw a bunk bed—a tall thin, blond-haired man was sitting on the bottom bed. As I entered the room he stood to greet me and we introduced ourselves. He informed me that he had the bottom bunk and I was more than welcome to

the N word

borrow any of his belongings if I needed to. I gathered he was referring to the radio and books sitting neatly on his shelf.

As we talked I noticed a separate room with a shower and toilet. I was relieved. It would at least make prison life a little more bearable given the demeaning six nights I had just endured at the Cairns watch-house with no privacy. As I warmed to the idea of showering in private and not having to strategically plan to go to the toilet, I convinced myself that I had made the right choice catching the bus.

It didn't take long for my cellmate to ask what crime I had committed to warrant being sent to prison. Here we go again, I thought, but rather than get frustrated I soldiered on. I told him about the Mundingburra by-election and subsequent breach of agreement by the new government. I told him about the dogged determination of Queensland Health to press on with the charges even after being advised by the initial interviewing detectives and then the prosecutor to drop the charges. When I completed my story, one I had narrated often in the past six days, he looked intently at me, with a peculiar expression on his face, not quite knowing if I was lying or telling the truth.

Not long after, one of the traditional inmates from a Cape York community, who had travelled with me in the prison bus, came to my cell and invited me to meet his relatives in another cell. Most of the Cape inmates were in their late teens or early twenties and appeared to be comfortable among relatives and friends in prison.

By now, about half an hour had passed and I had a good knowledge of the various groupings of prisoners out on the exercise oval, which I could see from my cell window. The traditional men were congregated together and most of the others, black and white, were playing touch football. I noticed a few loners walking around the oval and some inmates jogging.

At a quarter to five I started to get worried that I might indeed be spending the weekend—maybe even longer—at Lotus Glen as I had not heard a word from my solicitor. I hadn't even bothered to unpack my prison issues, wrapped in a blanket, in anticipation of being called to the warden's office at any minute to hear news of my imminent release.

As the minutes ticked by, conscious that five o'clock was fast approaching and the front administration office would soon shut, I started telling myself to stop dreaming and face reality. Resigning myself to no news coming through, I undid the knot and commenced unpacking my toiletries. Then, at ten to five, I heard the sweetest message I have ever heard when the warden's voice came over the internal public-address system with the message 'Prisoner Stephen Hagan to report with his belongings to the front office.'

My heart almost stopped beating as I hastily retied my blanket knot and gathered up my swag. I was overcome with emotion and felt a tear roll down my face as I shook hands with my temporary cellmate. The poor fellow thought he had gained a sensible roomy and now he would have to wait for the next prison bus run from Cairns to find out if it delivered good or bad news for him.

My legs felt like jelly as I made my way towards the warden's watch tower and I sensed envious eyes staring in my direction. They would have heard these public-address announcements many times before and known that it was the last day for that prisoner. However, in my case they had only seen me walk into their wing a little under an hour earlier.

The warden told me I was required at the main office and that it had something to do with my bail notice coming through. After he released the door I walked politely through and along the left side of the yellow painted path, careful not to offend any over-zealous prison staff along the way.

As I left the prison wing and made my way along the walkway to the main office, I felt like skipping and shouting out loud 'I told you so'. But I dared not appear arrogant, as I still had to be formally advised of the result of the bail application. Another ten minutes and

the N word

I would have had to spend the weekend in prison, irrespective of positive news being forthcoming.

I was introduced to one of the senior managers who said he remembered me from my last visit when I was the manager of DEET. I vaguely remembered his face but waited patiently and submissively to be told of my release. I wasn't in the mood to reacquaint myself with past adult education courses and their successes.

Eventually I was told that I was free to go and that I should have been notified of the decision on arrival. He said I had not needed to have been processed and sent to the low security block and that earlier one of the Indigenous counsellors had offered to give me a lift to Cairns but had to leave without me. The good news, he said, was that he had made contact with Rhonda and she was now on her way to the prison because the last public bus to Cairns had already departed. The manager was only permitted to release me onto the outer perimeter of the prison and if Rhonda had not been on her way, I would have had to make alternative arrangements or wait by the road and hitch a lift. All this information, so quickly, made me feel light-headed and I didn't know whether to be angry or happy.

Once I'd completed my discharge papers, the senior manager released several doors for me to walk through. The final barrier to my freedom was the high steel gate with razor wire on top. As I walked towards the gate I had a funny feeling I would be called back to the office and told something had come up that prevented my release. Every step I took without hearing a booming voice over a loudspeaker brought an extra spring in my next step. I knew I only had to complete a half dozen more paces to secure my anxiously awaited freedom. The huge gate was yet to be opened by the central controller and I still had four long steps to go.

the N word

I continued to walk, without looking over my shoulder, past the visitors' car park and towards the road. Then I heard someone call out my name. For a second my heart missed a beat and I was tempted to make a dash into the sugar cane fields. I could hear the prison guard approaching fast from behind and started to prepare myself for further bad news.

However when I turned to surrender, I was greeted by a smiling face of the senior manager who had just completed the paperwork for my release. He was offering me a lift to Mareeba, half an hour's drive away from the prison. A knight in shining armour, I thought, as we drove silently away from the prison, still curious as to why he was providing me with transportation when he had distinctly informed me only five minutes earlier that, as a prison official, he was not permitted to privately assist prisoners with a ride into town.

He explained that he had remembered the excellent work I had done a year earlier funding the successful adult education course at Lotus Glen, and volunteered that he had been following my astonishing case in the media and felt I had been badly treated by the justice system. As far as he was concerned I should not have been convicted for such a minor offence. He also told me that he had contacted Rhonda on her car phone to tell her that she could pick me up at the KFC outlet in Mareeba. I was truly moved by his gesture. Then, as we approached KFC, he asked if I was hungry. When I replied that I was he opened his wallet and gave me his last five dollar note. I thanked him profusely and said I would repay him some day.

I walked into KFC with my six-day growth and asked for a 'combo' meal. The young attendant said it would be five dollars and ninety-five cents. When I asked her what could I order for five dollars she must have gathered I was very hungry and offered me the meal

the N word

for that amount. I told her that I would pay the difference when Rhonda arrived.

As I sat by the window contemplating my release I suddenly caught, from the corner of my eyes, the familiar sight of my brown Ford Fairmont pulling into a vacant parking zone on the main street immediately outside. Rhonda was on the passenger side and her brother Bradley in the driver's seat. A steady flow of tears was running down Rhonda's beautiful face as we warmly embraced. Then before she could say a word, I asked her if I could have a few dollars to repay the attendant. It was difficult for me to say the words that I really wanted to after six days in a cell, but at least my question was the circuit breaker I needed right then. I could speak with Rhonda later.

On the hour-long journey back to Cairns the three of us engaged in small talk, mostly about the Rainbow Serpent Cruises. It broke the ice a bit and took a couple of extra nervous minutes off our time together as we drove down the Kuranda Range.

⁂

That night, after I had hugged and played with Stephen and Jayde and thanked Rhonda's mum and brother for their wonderful support, my wife and I had a long talk. We cried on each other's shoulders as we tried unsuccessfully to work our way through the political and legal machinations that had led to my conviction and incarceration. Clearly there seemed to be a perception on the part of the government that following my acknowledgement at the Parliament House dinner of the Coalition's support during the Mundingburra by-election, I might be a loose cannon. What I do believe is that Queensland Health was in a position to have the allegations discontinued when first raised and later to have the charges dropped when recommendations to that effect were made by police.

After a couple of days of getting my thoughts and house in order, I returned to work as an Executive Director of the Rainbow Serpent Cruises. I had no intention of reacquainting myself with either Queensland Health or the STF so I resumed work with my other business. I was pleased to be back seeing friendly faces on the black, red, yellow and green boat. They were happy to see me too and passed on messages of support.

A requirement of my bail was that I had to report to the local central police station, in downtown Cairns, three times a week. Although I felt embarrassed having to go in and sign a special register at the front counter I did so without fuss. Of greater concern to me was raising money to pay for the expensive legal representation for my planned appeal to the Supreme Court of Queensland.

I rang the Queensland Aboriginal and Torres Strait Islander Legal Service Secretariat (QATSILSS) for assistance on the appeal but was told that the advice from their legal representatives was that there was a low chance of success and the money should be spent elsewhere. QATSILSS was funded by taxpayers and had been established to provide legal assistance to Indigenous people throughout the State. I knew then that I would have to do everything by myself if I was to succeed in having my case overturned.

I made an offer to my business partner to sell part of my shares in the Rainbow Serpent Cruises and was fortunate in being offered a satisfactory price. The amount was enough to pay for my solicitor Matt McLaughlin, and Brisbane barrister Tony Glynn SC, to represent me in the appeal.

Weeks after selling my shares and just prior to our first cruise for the day I received a call on my mobile phone from Matt McLaughlin who joyfully announced that Tony Glynn had been successful in the appeal hearing. The judgement of the three Court of Appeal judges delivered on 15 November was unanimous. However he said the court ruled that the conviction was to remain unaltered.

I didn't quite know what this meant exactly. Was I to be sent back to prison? Matt repeated the Supreme Court decision and it became clear when I later read from the court document.

> ...In our opinion, the magistrate who sentenced the applicant on the second occasion erred when he ordered him to serve a period of actual imprisonment; especially having regard to the course adopted by the magistrate who sentenced the applicant on the earlier occasion, the proper course on the second occasion was to extend the term of imprisonment imposed – as was done – but to wholly suspend it.
>
> We would grant the applications for leave to appeal, allow the appeals and order that the sentence imposed on the applicant on 11 October 1996 be varied only by an order that the period of imprisonment be wholly suspended. Otherwise, the sentences should stand.[10]

At that point however I was just relieved to be a free man. But out of curiosity, I asked my business partner from Singapore if he thought I should appeal the decision not to remove the conviction. To my amazement he informed me that in parts of Asia people went missing never to be found again when they innocently got involved in politics at the same level that I had. He suggested I enjoy my freedom, get stuck into business as a free man and make bucket loads of money.

Back on the wharf at the Marlin Marina, Pier Marketplace, I was overjoyed at receiving the news from my solicitor and I immediately phoned home. Rhonda shed tears with me at the good news and told me to hold my head high, adding that she never once doubted my ability to work my way through the legal quagmire. But we agreed that we didn't have the money to appeal the decision of the Supreme Court. I'd been waiting weeks to hear of the decision and was feeling quite emotional so I walked a short distance away from the boat to continue making my calls. I called my parents and a few close friends and knew that once I had spoken to the people on my shortlist the word would quickly spread. I was ecstatic.

the N word

That night I took Rhonda out to celebrate. The next morning I went to the station and handed the police a copy of the *Cairns Post* with the headline 'Jail sentence lifted for convicted fraud'. They said they didn't need to see any official documents on the Supreme Court's decision and announced that I was no longer required to report to the police station.

4
A New Direction

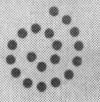

the N word

Moving South

In the months after the Supreme Court decision our business started to decline, the result of an ineffective marketing strategy and a number of other variables associated with boardroom indecision. I felt I was deserting a sinking ship but believed it would be for the best that I seek another career change. It wasn't long after I sold my remaining interest in the company that bills started to flood our address at Smithfield; our liabilities were exceeding our income. Rhonda and I agreed to pack up and head to Innisfail to spend time with her mother on her block of land on the outskirts of town and to once again reassess our family's future. Hopefully, it would be free of any politically motivated plots.

In Innisfail young Stephen changed from a private preschool environment to a public school education and soon got to make new friends. Rhonda stayed home with Jayde and her mother while I tried unsuccessfully to gain employment through Centrelink.

It was a little difficult for me at first, lining up to fill in forms at the unemployment office, but after a couple of weeks the pride starts to loosen up and I accepted the fact that I was just another person in the queue, just another Commonwealth statistic. Many Centrelink employees were familiar with my face from regular visits to their office in my previous capacity as Manager of the DEET office

the N word

in Cairns. Occasionally I'd be offered preferential treatment ahead of others in the queue but I sought no special favours and chose to wait my turn to be processed.

After I'd been out of work for several months, Rhonda and I took a good, hard look at our predicament and decided the best option was for us both to apply for entry to the University of Southern Queensland (USQ) in Toowoomba. By now Mum's health was starting to deteriorate—in fact that had been the main reason for me staying at hers and Dad's boarding house in Brisbane rather than at a hotel in the city. If Rhonda and I were accepted into the university, it would mean we could be closer to my parents.

Simultaneously, Rhonda and I received positive news from USQ. Rhonda, who had completed several years of a teaching diploma years earlier, was about to embark on a Journalism degree and I was to start my Masters degree in Business Administration.

So it was in July 1997 that we bid farewell to Mary and other family members and drove the 1400 kilometres south to Toowoomba. Rhonda and I were determined not to let our horrendous experience destroy us. We wanted to occupy our time in a new community with fresh interests and new friends and career paths and as far as we were concerned our children would be provided with every possible opportunity to develop their own personalities in a loving and warm family environment.

My family and friends were delighted to see us healthy and in good spirits even though our bank balance had been severely depleted and the mental scars from our ordeal were still fresh. My youngest brother Lawrence, offered us a room in his house with his partner and children but it didn't take long for us to find a nice four-bedroom house a kilometre from the university.

the N word

Dad had recently retired from the public service and returned home to Toowoomba to spend more time with Mum whose health continued to cause him and the rest of the family great concern. They visited us regularly and quickly became attached to their beautiful grandchildren who they had only seen fleetingly over the years. Mum also became fond of her daughter-in-law and tried to get Rhonda to go to bingo with her. It didn't appeal to Rhonda at first but she soon got the hang of the game and enjoyed the companionship of the other female members of the Hagan clan when she did go.

Choosing a preschool for our children was not difficult as the Mirrembena Day Care Centre, next door to the university, was recommended. We enrolled Stephen and Jayde and it wasn't long before the centre added the Kullilli word 'yathi', meaning 'laughter', to the welcome board at the entrance.

Towards the end of the year Rhonda and I drove around town looking for a suitable primary school to enrol Stephen for the following year. We agreed on two prerequisites for our son's new school—it had to be close to both the university and home.

Driving south along Hume Street one day we came across the Martin Luther Primary School. We looked at each other. The first thing that sprang to mind of course, was the famous civil rights leader from the United States, Dr Martin Luther King Jnr. It didn't click at first that the school's name actually referred to the German Luther. But it sounded good and was close to home so we enrolled Stephen and started making plans for Jayde.

Although the fees were a worry, the school fitted our needs. There was one class per grade and everyone knew each other. From the first day the other parents were cordial and appeared genuinely interested

the N word

in the affairs of the school. We were especially delighted to see Stephen settling in after just a couple of days.

However after a week, Stephen came home and told me that he didn't want to use Aboriginal words in conversation anymore—words like 'muntha' (bread), 'yurdi' (meat), 'boida' (red kangaroo), 'gulbari' (emu), 'bungu' (money) and 'munga' (ear) to mention a few. He also said he wasn't happy with all the Indigenous artwork adorning our walls at home. The next day I made an appointment with the principal and explained that for the first six years of his life I had encouraged in Stephen immense pride in his heritage. Now, within six days, someone at his school had ridiculed his racial origins to the point where he no longer wanted to identify with them.

The principal assured me that he would get to the bottom of the complaint. True to his word he got back to Rhonda and me within a day to say he had found the culprits—two children in a higher grade. Their parents met with the principal and since that day, Stephen has not experienced any more racial name-calling or other forms of bullying at the school. He was the first Aboriginal student to attend and today there are several others, including Jayde, who enjoy the warmth and friendship of all their fellow students.

One of Stephen's proudest moments occurred a few years later in Grade 4 when he raised the Aboriginal flag with his grandfather during the school's National Aboriginal and Islander Day of Observance Committee (NAIDOC) week celebrations.

Today the Aboriginal and Torres Strait Islander flags fly beside the Australian and Queensland ones at the entrance to the office. Every child at the school knows the flag colours and what they represent: black for the colour of our skin, red for the blood we shed for the land and yellow for the sun, the giver of life and the colour of mother earth. Year 7 students are charged with raising the flags each morning and Rhonda has only needed to remind them on a couple of occasions that the black must always fly at the top of Australia's Aboriginal flag.

Studies at the university started slowly for me but after a while I became familiar with research and understanding the complex concepts taught at postgraduate level. Rhonda too enjoyed the new challenge of tertiary studies after many years away from the textbooks, and formed a strong bond with other mature-age Indigenous women students.

On the political front I started to get approaches from family and friends who asked me to make representations on their behalf to various Aboriginal organisations that they believed were not adequately addressing their needs. Many complained that the majority of ATSIC-funded organisations, located in Bowen Street, Toowoomba, looked after family members and friends but as outsiders they felt they were not made welcome.

In October 1998 during a meeting with the Federal Member for Groom, Ian Macfarlane, to discuss the possibility of establishing a cultural centre, the subject of the Indigenous funding was raised. The next day's *Toowoomba Chronicle* (27 October), which was to carry the story on the cultural centre, instead ran a story on Indigenous accountability accompanied by a photograph of the local member and myself:

> Mr Macfarlane met with local Aboriginal community leaders yesterday to find out how much funding was coming to services being used by Aborigines, and if it was being used to the best advantage.
> He said: "I think it's about establishing that the funds are being used in an accountable way, or establishing the better targeting of those funds or that we need more.
> "The community is asking for visibility and transparency and accountability and even the Aboriginal community aren't able to say

specifically how much money is here, how many people are resourced to the task and what the success or otherwise of those projects are."

Aboriginal leader Mr Stephen Hagan said he was confident Mr Macfarlane would make inroads in issues that were of concern to the Aboriginal community.

He said he had been contacted with concerns that the Aboriginal community did not know how funding was being utilised.

"I've had a lot of complaints. We need to follow through to ensure that the complaints are addressed. Now if it means getting a bit of extra information and enlightening those people who have made the complaint, so be it.

"But if there's a legitimate complaint where people are being paid money for their respective jobs and are not performing their jobs, what we're saying is either do your job or stand down and let someone go in and perform the task themselves."

The phones were running hot all that morning and I immediately came under attack from the Aboriginal powerbrokers of Bowen Street which housed the legal service, the housing company, the land council and the childcare agency in two separate buildings. They alleged I was an outsider who had only been in Toowoomba for five minutes and how dare I voice an opinion on something I knew nothing about.

Although it wasn't my intention to offend them, what I said obviously touched a raw nerve. My relationship with the Bowen Street tenants deteriorated considerably and today I'm afraid to report my relationship with them is just as frosty.

A community meeting was called and the results were reported the following day in the *Toowoomba Chronicle* (28 October) under the headline 'Aborigines split on talks with MP':

A scrap has developed within the Toowoomba's Aboriginal community after a small group met with Member for Groom Mr Ian Macfarlane on Monday.

… Yesterday, Mr Walter McCarthy from the Aboriginal Legal Service called a meeting of more than 40 other community members, saying they were "insulted" at not being invited to Monday's discussion.

Mr McCarthy said: "(Mr Hagan) has no right to make any representations on behalf of the Aboriginal community and has insulted the elders in arranging a meeting."

However Mr Hagan said on Monday he and the four other people involved were not acting in any official capacity but were part of a "group of concerned persons".

Mr McCarthy said: "The meeting was unfair. We didn't know where it was or what time and who was going."

But Mr Macfarlane said Monday's discussion "was at the request of those people who attended".

"I wasn't issuing invitations. My door is always open to any group or individual who wants to come and talk with me about anything," he said.

Mr Macfarlane said he was surprised he was not notified about Mr McCarthys' meeting yesterday.

Meanwhile, last night Mr Hagan said he did not meet Mr Macfarlane on the basis that he was speaking with any authority on behalf of the Aboriginal community.

"The meeting with Mr Macfarlane was to try to obtain some sort of record of the amount of money coming into Toowoomba for all agencies," he said.

"If it was determined that there was some sort of shortfall they would seek to address that."

Mr Hagan said yesterday's outcry was healthy in that there would now be an understanding of what money was being spent and determination of whether existing allocations were being spent properly.

After this meeting I became the focus of further attacks and the usual stories of me being a convicted fraudster started doing the rounds. Fortunately I did not try to hide my past. With Rhonda's support I had completed an interview with Stephen Lamble, journalist with the popular *Sunday Mail* a year earlier when we had first arrived in Toowoomba. The story, 'Unfair, says ex-diplomat', published on 5 October 1997, ran in part as follows:

> A former Australian diplomat says it is unfair that federal politicians accused of rorting travel expenses still have jobs while he lost his and was jailed over similar allegations.
> Stephen Hagan, 37, became the first Aborigine to work overseas as a diplomat when he was posted to the Australian consulate in Sri Lanka in 1983.
> A highly qualified professional public servant, Mr Hagan ... had pleaded guilty in Cairns Magistrates Court to accepting accommodation expenses when in fact he stayed with his parents.
> The false pretences charges related to claims Mr Hagan lodged between August 1995 and February 1996 while working as a field officer for Queensland Health's Aboriginal Tripartite Forum in Cairns.
> ... Although he pleaded guilty, Mr Hagan told the court he had not deliberately made false claims as he believed he was entitled to expenses irrespective of where he stayed.
> A person with an otherwise unblemished record, Mr Hagan ... was released from jail six days into the six-month sentence after three judges sitting in the Queensland Court of Appeal unanimously found he should not have been imprisoned.
> But the judges did not quash his conviction. Because it still stands, Mr Hagan cannot be employed as a public servant or hold a position as a company director.

the N word

The publication of the story was a load off our shoulders. Rhonda and I were not going to go underground or be consumed with guilt for the rest of our lives. The same month I had prepared a letter to Frank Clair, Chairman of the Criminal Justice Commission (CJC), asking him to investigate my complaint of political conspiracy by the Coalition parties. I was concerned that in several instances there had been breaches of the Electoral Act. I also sent a copy of the letter, with attachments, to Peter Beattie, at this time Leader of the Opposition. I received an acknowledgment letter several months later from Beattie's Chief of Staff, Rob Whiddon.

It wasn't until the following year (5 June 1998) that M.A. Barnes, Chief Officer, Complaints Section, Official Misconduct Division, CJC, wrote to me advising that the CJC had considered and investigated some of my claims (the remaining did not warrant further investigation) and that they would not be taking any of the matters further.

I was most disappointed with this response and told Rhonda that one day I would clear my name and expose the real story of the Mundingburra by-election and the related events.

In Toowoomba I became involved with the Toowoomba Multicultural Committee promoting cultural diversity and also with Councillor Dianne Thorley who was working on street kids' programmes. Councillor Thorley was passionate about the plight of street kids. I wanted to learn more and agreed to do a television report on allegations of street kids sleeping on the rail siding at night.

A WIN TV reporter and his cameraman picked me up from home after midnight to drive around town in search of the street kids. I became distressed when I tried to talk to four young Aboriginal children who were hanging out on the railway line in the CBD. I asked the kids their ages—eight to eleven years—and then the names of their parents. It was a shock to realise that I was distantly related to them.

I went home and told Rhonda about this experience, saying that I thought I'd have difficulty completing the report. I couldn't sleep worrying about those young kids and wondering if they made it through the night unharmed. I hadn't realised until then how close to home the issue really was. The next day I got in touch with senior members of the children's extended families and asked if they could have a talk to the kids' parents. I believe that meeting took place but I did not want to meddle in their affairs and so didn't pursue the matter further. Nor did I complete the TV report.

That autumn Rhonda and I got very excited about the approach of winter, not for the sub-zero temperatures that came with those three months of the year, but for the rugby league. Over the previous four years we had enjoyed watching our twin nephews, Andrew and Darren Robinson, graduate from being schoolboy footballers to playing with the Brisbane Broncos. The twins had represented at state and national level during their junior football years and had returned home to Toowoomba in the past year to play in the local competition before considering their future.

Sunday at the footy was a huge event for my family. Those who had money would make regular trips to the canteen to buy burgers, chips, pies, sausage rolls and soft drinks. Mum on the other hand, would insist on Dad cooking a roast of lamb or beef the night before the big game so that she could make a pile of sandwiches for the family to eat at the game.

I wasn't sure if this habit of packing a lunch basket stemmed from our days of attending the Wallel Cup Rugby League games in Cunnamulla when all the family would turn up to the John Kerr Oval

the N word

to cheer on my two cousins, Henry and Johnny Hagan, or whether it was because Mum was light on finance. It made no difference. The family would still feast on Mum's sandwiches even after they had their fill of takeaway.

⁂

It was in June 1999, when I took Rhonda and the children to watch the twins play at the Athletic Oval in Toowoomba, that I made the decison to go to the authorities seeking to have the word 'nigger' removed from the sign on the southern stand.

My children were growing up and rapidly becoming more aware of the world around them. As a parent with a social conscience I was determined that they would not have to be confronted with such blatant racism at their local sportsground.

I knew that the stand had been named in the early 1960s in honour of Edward Stanley Brown, a highly regarded international footballer and businessman from Toowoomba. Not only is there a large sign on the grandstand but at the front of the Oval there is a plaque with the 'Nigger' reference and inside the ground there is a mural with a list of the sportsman's achievements. There is also a sign within the ground pointing to the stand.

Edward Stanley Brown's birth certificate did not include the word and, irrespective of how he received the nickname, the word itself was racially offensive and definitely not a term of endearment. The nickname 'Nigger' was bestowed—and later included on the sign—in a time before Indigenous Australians were even allowed to vote or be counted in the nation's censuses.

the N word

Toowoomba's Response

Several days after the game I attended a Multicultural Day Committee meeting where I had a discussion with the President David Curtis, a solicitor with a proactive stance on multiculturalism and Indigenous affairs. He hadn't seen the sign but it didn't take long for him to drive past the Athletic Oval. He asked me why I wanted to pursue this issue given its potential for division. I told him the word 'nigger' is an insidious slur and is without doubt the most disparaging epithet used for black people.

I admired David's passion and commitment to social justice and when I asked him why he was so supportive of my campaign, he told me of his background. David's first real exposure to Indigenous culture had been during his four years working in Vanuatu. Then known as the New Hebrides, it was jointly administered by the French and the British. In 1975 David was elected to government in the first poll held in the country. He was closely aligned politically, and as a lawyer, with the Nagriamel Movement—essentially a customary law movement opposed to Western religions bastardising the integrity of Indigenous culture and spirituality.

David 'connected' to Australian Aboriginal spirituality when involved in the management of Mt House Station in the Kimberley

the N word

Region in Western Australia where he was appalled at the attitudes to and treatment of Aboriginals. Later, as a solicitor with the Aboriginal Land Council in Toowoomba, he was given the task of developing the concept of an Aboriginal Cultural and Education Centre at the old quarry site. Here he experienced the racism directed at the local Aboriginal community and Indigenous people generally.

During this period David was physically 'shouldered' in the main street of Toowoomba and advised that the League of Rights had him in their sights. He received phone calls telling him he was 'too smart for his own good' and warning him that he should watch his back. He was also described as a 'gin jockey'.

David's response was to moot the idea of Toowoomba Day—a celebration of all the cultures that make up the Toowoomba community—as part of the city's signature event, the annual Carnival of Flowers. However, when the Toowoomba Day Committee passed a resolution supporting my efforts to remove the word 'nigger' from the grandstand, David was formally advised that if the Committee persisted in supporting me, the Carnival of Flowers Board would withdraw its endorsement and publicly disassociate itself from the cultural event.

David cautioned me against taking on the Toowoomba Athletic Oval Sports Ground Trust (managers of the Athletic Oval complex), saying that it would be like taking on the world—a David and Goliath scenario. He suggested I talk to Councillor Dianne Thorley, the first female appointed as a member of the Sports Ground Trust. I took David's advice and spoke with her about my concern. When I asked for her assistance in removing the signage permanently, she said that she too was concerned and suggested that I write a letter to the Trust.

I addressed my letter of 23 June 1999 to John McDonald, Chairman of the Sports Ground Trust, and sent a copy to Councillor Thorley, care of the Toowoomba City Council.

the N word

The letter read:

I write to request that you and your board take immediate action to have the E.S. "Nigger" Brown Stand public sign removed from the grand stand at the Athletic Oval complex. I personally am offended by the name whenever I attend football matches at the ground.

As you may be aware I do have the option of lodging a complaint under the Racial Discrimination Act 1975 Section 18C, with the Human Rights and Equal Opportunity Commission.

The Commission also has responsibility to inquire into complaints of racial hatred. Racial hatred is defined as being a public act, which is likely to offend, insult, humiliate or intimidate a person or group of people and which is based on race, colour, and descent, national or ethnic origin.

I would like to think that in these enlightened times your committee would view the display of such an offensive sign, identified above, as being outdated and in urgent need of change.

I wish to make it very clear to your committee that I have the greatest respect for the sporting achievements of Edward Stanley Brown and also wish not to offend his family. However I am very serious in seeing a positive outcome to this rather protracted public debate ...

A couple of weeks later I received a reply from John McDonald in which he advised that based on representations and responses made by a range of Indigenous people, the Board had unanimously resolved to take no further action.

In my mind it was patently obvious that with her eye on the next elections, Alderman Di Thorley had jumped the fence. When the dispute was raised in the media, initially by me, the Toowoomba Sports Ground Trust appeared to adopt the policy that the best form of defence was attack and made a concerted effort to discredit my position by enlisting the support of prominent local Aboriginals. It felt to me like the divide and conquer strategies of the colonial days.

the N word

I was not so surprised to learn that my adversaries from Bowen Street, who'd had difficulty with my public call for accountability and transparency in the Indigenous organisations they represented, joined the civic leaders saying that 'nigger' should be retained in the sign at the stand. What initially appeared to be a straightforward fight along racial grounds now took on a new dimension. The union of people—black and white—who normally wouldn't say hello to one another on the street made my task much more challenging than I ever would have thought.

From within the Indigenous community the main opposition appeared to come from three key players—Dick Rose, the former captain of the Toowoomba Clydesdales rugby league team, Arthur Beetson, former captain of Australia's rugby league team, and Walter McCarthy, community leader.

With renewed vigour, the Toowoomba Sports Ground Trust declined my request to take the sign down and spoke with pride of the support they had gained after consultation with Indigenous people. Journalists had a field day. Wayne Smith's story in the *Courier Mail* of 10 July 1999 was one of the more moderate:

> The Toowoomba Sports Ground Trust has held out against the forces of political correctness ...
>
> Steve Hagan, a prominent member of Toowoomba's Aboriginal community, had requested the trust remove the word "Nigger" from the grandstand because of its racist overtones.
>
> However, trust chairman John McDonald yesterday said his committee had decided no change would be made ...
>
> "We regret if Mr Hagan is offended by it, but we also have had a lot of support from other members of the Aboriginal community who are not offended by it." Mr McDonald said ...
>
> "I think this decision sets back the process of reconciliation by several decades," Mr Hagan said.

the N word

On 13 July 1999 I lodged a complaint to the Human Rights and Equal Opportunity Commission (HREOC). I stressed that I was personally offended by the sign and stated that I would like to see the name removed and a public apology given. I added that I would be happy if the name was altered from the E.S. 'Nigger' Brown Stand to the Edward Stanley Brown Stand or E.S. Brown Stand.

The Sports Ground Trust directors, in particular John McDonald, President, and Di Thorley, Secretary, immediately went into overdrive by making public comments—with the support of Rose, Beetson and McCarthy—in an attempt to discredit me before the story escalated any further.

The *Toowoomba Chronicle* was instrumental in applying enormous pressure. Steve Keating's editorial of 13 July 1999 summed up the views of the conservative elements of the town:

> Grandstanding and point-scoring!
> Political correctness has gone too far.
> The issue of the name of a Toowoomba Athletic Oval stand is now out of hand.
> Such a name would not be placed on any grandstand today, but the name was placed there in the 1950s.
> Why is it an issue now? It is all grandstanding and point-scoring of another kind.

I was already saddened that Indigenous people were prepared to take sides on what I believed was obviously a clear-cut case of racism. But it still came as a surprise to read Beetson's attempt at dismissing the word as inoffensive. The *Toowoomba Chronicle* quoted him on the same day:

> "I just can't believe it." Mr Beetson said yesterday.
> "I have heard about it and I'm absolutely amazed.
> "I don't know what's going on it the world. I don't have a problem with it and when I read about it I found it quite laughable."

... "But this whole thing is just stupid, that was the bloke's name."

He said some members of the Aboriginal community "had lost the plot".

"I can only think they have a lot of spare time on their hands."

"I think you could ask anyone with Aboriginal blood in them and they wouldn't have a problem with it.

"I've got mates with nicknames like coon and things like that and they don't worry. Soon I won't be able to call them anything."

As I read those words my mind flashed back to grand finals he played in the 1970s. I recalled sitting at home in Bedford Street, Cunnamulla dressed in my red, white and blue Eastern Suburbs jersey, watching him play a leading role in the Roosters' victories. Cunnamulla had the same colours as Easts and I wore my number two jersey with pride when I went shopping and travelled away on school trips, such was my fondness for the team and my hero Arthur Beetson.

Many times during this period I asked myself why the race issue, as epitomised by my fight about the 'n word', took hold so quickly in Toowoomba. I was shocked at the swiftness and viciousness of the media attacks on me and surprised at the broad acceptance by the Toowoomba public of the position adopted by the Sports Ground Trust. I guessed the community, both black and white, didn't feel very comfortable about me raising such a divisive issue as race. To many I was like a bad nightmare that wouldn't go away—some even told me so.

Once I had made the decision to do everything I could to have the word 'nigger' removed from the sign at the Toowoomba sportsground, at no time did I imagine the strength of the personal backlash against me or the effect it would have on my family. It took me completely by surprise and for some time I found myself retreating indoors and spending more time at home. The controversy also took its toll on my friends, some of whom kept their distance from me while the battle raged in the media.

the N word

On 29 July 1999, just when I was thought things couldn't get any worse, there was another Indigenous community meeting—this time supporting the decision of the Trust. It was no surprise to me that it was held at Bowen Street. John McDonald and Di Thorley would have been aware of the divisions in Toowoomba's Indigenous community, especially between the Bowen Street workers and myself, and possibly taken advantage of the rift.

The meeting at Bowen Street was attended by thirty-five people. A 'community meeting' was how the media referred to it, but I believe it could be better described as a gathering of staff, relatives and friends aligned with Bowen Street. Dick Rose, who like Beetson had a long association through football with John McDonald, chaired the 'community meeting'.

The meeting passed their own resolution stating that the sign should remain on the stand to honour "E.S. Nigger Brown" but that in the interests of reconciliation, derogatory or offensive terms should not be displayed in the future. I thought the resolution was a contradiction of the worst kind. As a strong supporter of the principles of democracy and freedom of speech, I was also aghast when I read in the minutes the comments of one member who believed that Indigenous people in the Toowoomba community should take their concerns to a community meeting before publicising it in the media.

After several weeks of anxiously waiting I finally received a response from the HREOC to my letter of complaint. I was informed that they were sending a conciliator to Toowoomba to convene a meeting of the parties. Conveniently, the meeting was scheduled to take place at City Hall. Since my campaign commenced, Di Thorley had graduated from local councillor to the position of Mayor.

At the conciliation meeting on 7 September, John McDonald and Di Thorley represented the Toowoomba Sports Ground Trust and

David Curtis came along with me as an observer. Before I could take my seat Mayor Thorley accused me of tipping off the media, an obvious reference to some journalists stationed at the entrance to the Council chambers. I suggested that she call the managers of the media outlets and ask if I had spoken to them about the meeting.

We proceeded with our talks but the tension rose by the second. For a meeting that was to be conducted with goodwill from both sides it soon degenerated into a farce. Di Thorley recommended to the conciliator that she and McDonald adjourn to her office to conduct their meeting with him, separate from David Curtis and myself. I found it hard to believe they could excuse themselves from face-to-face discussions so early in the piece, but according to David it can often take some time for parties to air their grievances and find common ground.

In this case it took a good while. The HREOC officer was walking from one room to another, obviously finding the going tough. He looked exasperated as it became clear to him that this meeting wasn't going anywhere. I was used to shaking hands at the end of disputes of all sorts, from football to politics, but McDonald and Thorley didn't return to our room to close the meeting.

As I descended the stairway of the Mayor's chamber, I saw the media waiting patiently for a comment. I didn't disappoint and told them that I was deeply offended that Mayor Dianne Thorley and John McDonald had recoiled from the HREOC conciliation process.

I will always remember that sad day for what it didn't achieve. So much could have been resolved in the spirit of reconciliation. Thorley and McDonald could have made their mark in the history books as progressive civic leaders who had the foresight and strength of character to make the hard call and lead the town's population into an era of respect and tolerance.

Not quite sure what the conciliator from HREOC would say about our meeting, I waited several anxious months before I received a response. I was finally advised by letter that there had been changes to the law administered by HREOC which came into effect on 13 April 2000 and that although my complaint had been referred to the HREOC prior to that date, because there had not yet been a public hearing, the new law stated that the complaint must be terminated. The letter also advised that I could make application to the Federal Court to pursue the matter.

As I turned the page the termination notice jumped out at me and I knew the time had come to make a decision on whether to proceed with the matter before the Federal Court or ignore it and regain some degree of normality in my life.

※

I put all this to Rhonda. Knowing how I felt about the issue, she gave the matter a lot of thought. We had both been feeling stressed with the amount of media attention the debate had been receiving and knew full well that proceeding would continue to have a huge impact on our family. However, with extraordinary courage and an appreciation of the cause I was fighting for, Rhonda gave her consent for me to take the case to the next level.

I wasn't quite sure what the next level was—but I suspected it would cost a little more than the forty-five cent stamp it had cost me to have my complaint formally assessed by the HREOC.

the N word

Legal Foray

I didn't know the first thing about making an application to the Federal Court and I was conscious of the twenty-eight day deadline, at the same time fixing my eyes firmly on the USQ study calendar. My university studies were beginning to suffer but I was forced to make a judgement call and I knew that if I were to advance this case I would have to find a solicitor to undertake the legal preparation—and soon.

The biggest problem was that I didn't even have enough money to make phone calls to the numerous law firms in Brisbane to discuss the complexities involved in undertaking a case of this nature. The second biggest problem was trying to convince a reputable law firm to take my case on. I didn't even bother to contact the ALS for legal support or advice as I knew from past experience what their response would be.

With time running out I sought the assistance of a barrister friend Kathryn Feeley, a former entrepreneur, pilot, author and a practising barrister who was involved in native title work for my father's Kullilli tribe. Kathryn pounded the streets of Brisbane on my behalf, searching for a law firm with an interest in social justice and, more importantly, which would agree to do the work on a pro bono basis. From my own general inquiries around Toowoomba with friends in the know, I knew that very few law firms would be prepared to go down the long, untried, legal quagmire this type of case would present. To my surprise Kathryn called me back after a few days and suggested I beg, borrow or steal some money for a bus fare and travel to Brisbane to meet Peter Black.

From the first day I met Peter I was impressed with his easy-going, laid-back attitude. Pete never once spoke down to me or refused to take a call from me whenever I rang, which was often over the next four years.

A Brisbane-based lawyer, Peter is a senior partner of the city law firm Drakopoulos Black Solicitors that has been operating since 1995. Prior to this he had been with the larger firm Phillips Fox. He had extensive experience in anti-discrimination law and litigation and in recent years had pursued cases with a social justice bent.

His longstanding desire to use the law to make a difference to the rights and fortunes of the average citizen flourished when he was at university, although it initially arose from his humble beginnings in the northern NSW town of Casino. Growing up as the son of Greek immigrant café proprietors, he gained a great love of political and social justice issues from the long discussions that would take place at the back of his father's shop.

He also had considerable contact with Aboriginal families who would come into the shop from the settlement at Tabulam. His mum sold plenty of 'cooked chooks' to them, particularly on pension days and that money helped to pay Peter's way through university.

Pete had experienced discrimination at school where he, like others, was labelled a 'wog', 'dago' and 'wop'. These jibes were hurtful and to Peter beyond comprehension. But if he confronted the perpetrators he was always met with the standard response 'just joking, mate'.

When the E.S. 'Nigger' Brown Stand issue arose Peter embraced it because he knew immediately what I was talking about. He saw that the cause was just and that the racial vilification sections of the Racial Discrimination Act needed to be given a more liberal interpretation.

Peter ended up devoting countless hours to my case, working around the clock to prepare applications first to the Federal Court, then to the High Court of Australia and eventually to the United Nations. He suggested I should make an application for financial assistance to the Attorney General's Department.

To support the application I supplied him with original documents to confirm my impoverished status at the time and so meet the Department's criteria. With both of us being full-time students, Rhonda and I were struggling to make ends meet and often had to borrow a couple of dollars or so to see us through until the next fortnightly Abstudy allowance arrived.

We were confident I met the criteria for assistance with the Attorney General's Department and expected a positive response. But when a subsequent letter from Chris Meaney, Assistant Secretary in the Legal Assistance Branch of Attorney General's Department, arrived it stated that our claim failed to meet the 'prospects of success' criteria. Peter and I had extensive discussions as to how to best respond. On 5 July 2000 Peter sent a letter to Meaney addressing a number of critical issues. In it he presented a novel argument which was slightly different to the arguments that would later be put to the courts:

> ... the term "act" is not defined in the Racial Discrimination Act 1975. We argue that the term "act" can mean a failure to act as well as an overt act, as is the case in the common law of negligence, which recognises acts of non-feasance.

As an analogy we submit that the failure by a hotel for example to allow someone of Aboriginal extraction into a public bar because of established rule that such persons are not allowed access would constitute an act in several ways. (1) The failure to act to alter the rule to allow a person access would cause offence as much as (2) the act of physically refusing entry to the bar.

Accordingly the act of failing to change the rule would be reasonably likely to offend indigenous persons and in all likelihood would dissuade them from in future attempting to enter the bar. In much the same way the decision of the Toowoomba Sports Trust to name the stand the "E S 'Nigger' Brown Stand" was an overt act which no doubt over time has caused offence and insult to indigenous persons. An act perpetuating the continued public display of the name "Nigger" would be analogous to a refusal to change a rule relating to the access of indigenous people to a bar as referred to in the example …

Clearly this is a matter, which is within the public interest criteria as its determination will decide "new" issues of law and it will benefit the reconciliation process.

In the circumstances we ask that you reconsider the initial decision refusing the grant of aid in this particular case and we await your earliest response as the matter has now been set down for hearing in the Federal court at Brisbane on 6 and 7 November 2000.

We received a reverberating 'no' to our detailed and what I thought was a more insightful appraisal of our initial application from the same officer who had disqualified our application in the first instance. This negative response gave us a fairly good gauge of how the bureaucracy was going to view my complaint in both the short and the long term.

It's worth noting that the only response we got from our other letters was from Senator John Herron, Minister for Aboriginal Affairs. Dated 14 August 2000, this letter suggested we contact the manager of QATSILSS to arrange a meeting to determine whether they could help. However, I didn't even consider that option given my previous dealings with QATSILSS in Cairns. Besides, it reeked of a bit more buck passing.

In any case, with or without government assistance, Peter made a commitment to take on the case and represent me at the Federal Court hearing. However we were still in need of a barrister to make the presentation to the court as it was highly unlikely that the opposing camp would be represented by a solicitor alone.

Peter arranged for us to meet with a prominent Brisbane barrister in his chambers so we could present our case and win him over on the merits of our arguments. I met Peter on the ground floor of the high-rise building in George Street and was quietly optimistic of signing up the legal counsel to the case, as we ascended in the elevator to the top floor.

Even so, I was on edge for the meeting. I knew the significance of gaining a barrister was of paramount importance to the success of our court application and Peter had told me that this was by no means an open and shut case.

It wasn't long before the barrister emerged from behind a sturdy wooden door to usher us into his impressive office. I took my seat opposite him as he grasped his glasses to study the brief. The barrister lifted his head from reading and came straight to the point. He declared that in his opinion we could not win the case and therefore wasn't interested in taking it on.

As soon as I caught my breath I asked him, 'Why do you only take cases that have an above average chance of winning? And when do people like you feel comfortable about taking on social justice cases?'

After muttering something inconsequential he turned and engaged in a bit of small talk with Peter before bidding us farewell.

I felt my trip to Brisbane on the McCafferty's bus had been a complete waste of both time and my limited resources. With those few words from the barrister I'd been brought back to reality. This case wasn't going to be a walk in the park.

the N word

As hard as I tried to block the barrister's words out of my mind, I kept hearing them on the slow bus trip back to Toowoomba. I acknowledged that at least he'd been honest but wondered if his views reflected the general feeling among his peers.

❊

By now time was running out so Peter sought a favour from barrister, Dimetrios Eliades. With Peter's assistance he prepared what I thought was a first-rate attempt at addressing the relevant sections of the Racial Discrimination Act.

I began to get a little excited, although at times there were twinges of anxiety as the date for the Federal Court hearing approached. I knew I would have to give evidence and worried about how I would cope. I also shuddered at the thought of being in the same courtroom as some of my adversaries from Toowoomba, both black and white, although I knew that John McDonald wouldn't be present in the courtroom as he was in England attending a rugby league test match between Australia and the 'mother country' in his capacity as Chairman of the International Rugby League Board.

On the morning of 6 November 2000 I met with Peter in our barristers' chambers at the Inns of Court to go over the finer points of law on which the case would be argued. As we walked along North Quay, in the direction of the Commonwealth Law Courts, we were relaxed and tried to engage in small talk about the weather and other news items. We were unexpectedly interrupted when we turned up Tank Street from North Quay to the Commonwealth Law Courts. Awaiting us was a media scrum the likes of which I had never seen. Certainly my legal team had never had to work their way through such a mob before. 'How do you feel Mr Hagan?' 'Do you think you can win Mr Hagan?' 'What do you hope to achieve today?'

the N word

Although Peter advised me not to make any comments I felt compelled to speak. Channels 10, 9 and 7, SBS, the ABC and many radio stations had followed the story and all wanted a grab for their afternoon or evening news. I told them I was deeply offended by the word 'nigger' and was sure Justice Drummond would support our application and order the removal of the racist sign. He was highly regarded by many Indigenous political figures, especially for his landmark decision in support of several native title cases in northern Queensland, so I was quietly optimistic.

Unfortunately I was to see the more uncompromising side of Justice Drummond, as he did not give any ground in his handling of my case before a packed courtroom. I was the only witness for my team while the defence had Mayor Di Thorley and Dick Rose as their principal witnesses.

Time went fast in that courtroom. It wasn't long before my name was called out and I found myself taking the oath. My barrister asked me to tell the court in my own words why I chose to take the matter to court in the first instance. I stated that I was disturbed by the physical presence of the sign and by the commentary over the loudspeaker system. I told him I was concerned for my children and the message it was sending to our youth.

The next thing I remember was taking my seat and instead of facing the packed gallery I was staring curiously at the judge. I couldn't gauge from his body language which way he was interpreting the law but it became a lot clearer as the case progressed.

Thorley and Rose almost repeated word for word that the Indigenous community meeting gave a clear mandate to the Toowoomba Sports Ground Trust to retain the sign as is, as it did not offend them. They did not tell the judge that thirty-five people from the organisations in Bowen Street, called to a meeting the morning it was announced, did not constitute a legally advertised and convened meeting.

the N word

Their legal team, headed by barrister Dan O'Gorman, pushed home the fact that Rose and other community leaders in attendance at the meeting were not offended by the sign and therefore felt it should stay. He also identified Arthur Beetson as another creditable Indigenous sportsperson who did not take offence at the word.

Justice Drummond asked my barrister if there were any other Indigenous people other than me who were offended. Dimetrios Eliades said there were many who had expressed offence at the sign and had offered their support. However the judge was taking evidence before him literally and commented that in our submission there were no witnesses identified other than me.

My barrister argued that one could assume that there would be many others who would be offended. He asked if we could adjourn the case in order for his team to provide a list of Aboriginal people who were also insulted by the sign. But the judge's denial of the request made me realise that it was all over and that I'd better get my thoughts together for my walk through the media scrum outside.

Although my barrister had claimed that under the Racial Discrimination Act it wasn't necessary to demonstrate that more than one person was offended to fit the criteria, the judge obviously thought otherwise. He went on to shock the court by giving an example of a way in which the word 'nigger' could be used and not be considered offensive. He made mention of the phrase 'niggerhead reef', which refers to an outcrop of dark coral jutting out of the ocean, making the point that fishermen use the term without taking or causing any offence. As big as I am, you could have knocked me over with a feather.

Before I knew it the court case that was set down for two days had finished before lunch on the first day. When Justice Drummond departed the courtroom, I asked my legal team what was the next step. They promptly informed me that the judge had reserved his decision and would notify us when he had made up his mind. They

the N word

said it could take a day or a week or even a month and added that I would need to remain positive.

As I left the Commonwealth Law Court building and walked towards the cluster of journalists I reminded myself to hold my head high and be upbeat about what I was about to say. But I couldn't help myself. The first comment I made was to attack the judge for making such a feeble analogy to the 'niggerhead reef'. I said I wasn't optimistic of a positive outcome and thought Justice Drummond hadn't provided my barrister with a fair hearing. If we were to lose the case, I added, I would immediately appeal the decision to a higher court.

On the bus home to Toowoomba that afternoon I literally did a phone interview every twenty minutes with radio stations around the nation. Some might argue that I was seeking media attention and to some extent they would be correct. But I was simply motivated by my desire to inform the broader community of how ridiculous this whole saga was.

I tried to remain positive just as my legal team told me but my Murrie intuition told me to start preparing an appeal. As sure as day turns to night, round one looked like it was going to be awarded to the opposite corner.

⁂

Prior to the handing down of Justice Drummond's decision, I had to attend a national Community Development Employment Programme (CDEP) conference in Canberra in my capacity as the interim Coordinator of the Toowoomba Aboriginal Corporation for CDEP, a job I had won in recent weeks. While everyone was getting acquainted with each other at the venue, the Australian National University (ANU), I was being pursued by Channel 7's *Today Tonight* who wanted an interview for their programme that night.

the N word

The conference gave me an opportunity to catch up with many old friends I hadn't seen since my days working in Canberra. Most had returned home to work for their communities, coincidentally in the same line of work as me. We talked about the old days and our families, and of course my stand over 'Nigger' Brown came up.

On the first night all conference participants were invited to the celebrations of the tenth anniversary of the ANU Centre for Aboriginal Economic Policy Research. It was during refreshments that I introduced myself to an elegant woman studying a large map of Australia with coloured labels representing the towns of delegates in attendance. Her name was Mary Louise Willheim and she was attending the function with her husband. When I asked her what he did for a living she said the sweetest words I could possibly want to hear at that moment—'Ernst is a constitutional barrister and does part-time lecturing at ANU.'

I asked her if she would introduce me to him. She nodded and we made our way towards a small gathering of men who were huddled deep in conversation. As we approached I immediately knew that the distinguished looking man with the exquisite bow tie was her husband, Ernst Willheim.

After waiting for a joke to be told, I introduced myself to Ernst and asked if he was aware of my case. When he said he was, I felt the need to cut to the chase and asked if he would be interested in representing me for the appeal if I lost the Federal Court case with Justice Drummond. Although retired Ernst, took on one or two cases a year and said he would be happy for Peter Black to forward him a copy of our application to the Federal Court. Thus began a relationship that would grow over the next couple of years.

Unfortunately, while my legal fortunes were on the rise, my position as CEO of the Toowoomba Aboriginal Corporation for CDEP came to an end when the board sacked me soon after I took up my appointment (following the Canberra conference I had taken on the position of CEO). The Toowoomba CDEP employed over 100 workers under the federally funded work-for-the-dole scheme.

I enjoyed the new challenges and believed I was being well received by both directors and workers. Everyone seemed contented and life could not have been happier for the family for the first couple of months.

The sacking, three months into a three-year contract, came a few days after I suspended the daughter of the chairperson for abusive language in the foyer of our administration building and in the wake of the suspension of a senior director's husband for breaching a fire ban that required three fire brigades to extinguish an out-of-control fire on our five-hectare property.

I also suspended my nephew, who was a director and a CDEP worker, for his part in the verbal tussle with the chairperson's daughter, an administration officer. In addition, I made the difficult decision of standing down my top ganger for unauthorised use of the organisation's vehicle.

I believed my decision to suspend prominent staff members was correct so early into the life of the CDEP. I felt I needed to send a clear message to other workers and the Indigenous community that under my management this organisation would be run without nepotism and preferential treatment.

I was comforted when the majority of the workers went on strike in support of me. However, the threat of non-payment of wages by desperate directors soon had workers rethinking their stance and reluctantly they returned to their duties. In the end, a couple of senior staff members who supported me were stood down and the board of directors had control of the CDEP again.

❖

Within weeks of the dismissal I organised for Drakopolous Black Solicitors to issue the organisation with a writ for unfair dismissal claiming breach of my contract. Counter-claims of mismanagement and failure to implement the organisation's policy and procedure guidelines were widely circulated throughout the community by the directors.

Almost immediately, I gained employment as the Coordinator of the Minimbah Day Respite Centre (for frail Indigenous aged and disabled young people) but six months later my position was terminated by the board of directors. In this instance, three carloads of men, connected with my political rivals, ensured I left the premises within ten minutes of receiving my written marching orders. I was told in no uncertain terms that I had lost the confidence of the board and should leave the premises immediately. I walked into the conference room, looked a couple of the directors in the eye and immediately knew from their bowed heads that they were complicit in this eviction. I was tempted to ring the police to lodge a complaint about the standover tactics being used but as the mood was becoming more volatile by the minute I decided to cooperate and leave without getting into a physical altercation.

I packed my possessions, walked outside to the side of the road, five metres from the front entrance, and phoned Rhonda. Fifteen long minutes later she pulled up and I climbed into the car. 'Here we go again,' was all she could say as we drove off. She cast a look of contempt at the carloads of men parked close by but I told her not to worry about them. Within weeks the State Government had closed the Centre down and I had no recourse for seeking compensation.

the N word

Needless to say, my legal journey continued to be made difficult by our financial situation. Rhonda by now was in full-time employment while I received minimal family support payments from Centrelink and occasional consultancy work.

On 10 November 2000 I received a call from Peter saying that Justice Drummond was about to hand down his decision and that I should prepare for the worst. We hadn't fared too well in the court Pete reminded me, saying that it would follow that we had a less than a fifty percent chance of success.

Justice Drummond released his decision within twenty minutes of Peter's telephone call. It was fifteen pages long and contained forty-three paragraphs, but my fate was clearly spelt out on the last two pages:

> ... On the evidence in this case, I do not accept that the trustees' decision to keep the sign in place unaltered was an act that involved treating members of the Aboriginal race differently, let alone less favourably, from other members of the community. I have referred to the evidence that the word complained of is only used in the sign as part of the customary identifier of a well-known and respected, now deceased member of the general Toowoomba community and that, in the context of that use, it has long ceased to have any racial or racist connotation (if it ever did have that). I have referred to the evidence confirming this to effect that the general view of the Toowoomba Aboriginal community is that the use of the word complained of in this particular context causes no offence to such persons considered as a racial group.
>
> ... Even if, contrary to what I believe to be the case, the act of the trustees can be said to have been based on race, that can be so only in the sense that racial considerations provided the, or at least one motive for the doing of the act. But since those racial considerations were taken into account to satisfy the trustees that maintenance of the sign would not give offence to Aboriginal persons generally, as

distinct from offence to Mr Hagan personally, it cannot be said that the act, even if based on race, involved any distinction etc having either the purpose or effect of nullifying or impairing the recognition, enjoyment or exercise, on an equal footing, of any human right or fundamental freedom of the kind referred to in s9. Only Mr Hagan's personal feelings were affected by the act. Because there was no distinction etc produced by the act capable of affecting detrimentally in any way any human rights and fundamental freedoms, there was no racial discrimination involved in the act.

… The application is dismissed.[11]

The following day the *Toowoomba Chronicle* ran a full front-page story with the headlines '"Nigger" stays–Hagan vows to take it to higher courts'. The headline was accompanied with a headshot of Mayor Di Thorley on her mobile phone and a caption which read: 'We Won: Toowoomba Mayor and Toowoomba Sports Ground Trust member Cr. Dianne Thorley phones England to discuss the victory in the "Nigger" Brown case with trust chairman John McDonald.'

The caption under the photograph of me, also talking on a mobile phone read: 'Knockback: Aboriginal activist and ATSIC councillor Stephen Hagan, standing outside the Athletic Oval, hears by mobile phone of the judge's decision against him.'

I was appalled at such headlines, even if they were in a rural paper. The *Toowoomba Chronicle* is sold throughout southern Queensland and on that day you could not walk into a newsagent without being confronted with the word that had triggered the fight in the first place. If before that front page article people still hadn't seen or cared about the sign, the issue was now well and truly in their faces.

Justice Drummond had cited the vocal minority of no more than thirty-five local Aboriginal people as the main reason for striking my application out. This was in spite of the fact that there had been no advertisements for that meeting and that the record of the minutes

the N word

does not list those in attendance or mention any objections or abstentions to the resolution to retain the sign at the Stand.

After the first court case I'd observed two strategic changes to the way people looked at this debate. The first change was that the winners and their supporters actually looked more like the losers as I became relentless in my pursuit of justice and made it clear to them that they were defending the indefensible. The second was that both Aboriginal and non-Aboriginal people started to put their hands up in greater numbers in support of my stance and demanded to be heard, thus ensuring further controversy in the community.

All along though, most social commentators would much rather I rolled over and played dead than insist on appealing at the next level in the judicial process.

Four days later, on Tuesday 14 November 2000, the *Toowoomba Chronicle* ran a story that began:

> Stephen Hagan's lawyers are bracing for a claim of up to $10,000 in legal costs after losing the "Nigger" Brown case to the Toowoomba Sports Ground Trust.
> But activist and ATSIC councillor Mr Hagan is pushing on with the court battle.

the N word

|<|<|<

As I had throughout my campaign I kept asking myself questions about the motives of my adversaries and to this day am perplexed as to why some people feel so threatened by others wanting to pursue social justice issues?

The increase in publicity of the case sparked an exponential rise in the intensity and regularity of hate mail and personal attacks. When it became clear that I was going to take the matter further the attacks went up tenfold. Blacks and whites alike were doing their best to discredit me within the Toowoomba community.

However following Justice Drummond's ruling I also started to receive more vocal support from various quarters. It gave me that little bit of inspiration I needed to keep me focused on the appeal as many friends and people I didn't know, rallied around saying they would have been active earlier if they had known I was going to lose the court case. They assumed it was going to be an open and shut case in my favour. I couldn't sleep some nights wondering why people weren't lending their support on a critical social justice issue and now these new supporters were shining some light on their past inaction.

Nevertheless, my family, although stalwartly supportive, were growing wary of the increased personal attacks I was receiving and worried for my safety. I kept asking myself if it was all worth it and

the N word

wondered whether I should call it quits. Had Rhonda told me enough was enough, I would have immediately walked away. She had gone through plenty in recent years with my incarceration and sackings and although she felt I should let others worry about solving the ills of the world, it was her support that allowed me to pursue issues of unjust racial practices. In this case it was a racist sign but those who know me would attest to the lengths I would go to have any racially discriminatory practices addressed.

I knew the decision of Justice Drummond ensured the task ahead was going to be a mammoth struggle for my legal team. We would need to present clear evidence of serious flaws in the original judgement to the Full Bench of the Federal Court. I thought long and hard about what road my father Jim and his father Albert would have taken and I knew that there was only one way to go. Over and again as I pondered the future. I thought of a saying my father was fond of repeating when I was younger, 'A quitter is not a winner and a winner is not a quitter.'

※

An article by the *Courier Mail* journalist, Margaret Wenham on 7 November 2000 sparked a reader into writing one of the vilest pieces of hate mail I ever received. The envelope bore a postcode confirming its origin as Gatton, fifty kilometres east of Toowoomba and its author as a well-known international sportsperson.

The letter was written on the back of a TAB form guide and enclosed Margaret Wenham's article with disturbing language scribbled over it. When I sent a copy to Margaret she told me she cried, not so much for me, but for the person who has so much hatred that he put pen to paper in such a way to air his bitterness. The 'author' made explicit comments about his desire that I be sent to jail and pack-raped in the hope that the experience turned me white.

The police extradited the man in question from south of the Queensland border to Toowoomba for a series of forensic tests. He was subsequently proven not to be the author of the letter. Instead he had been used in a sinister ploy to intimidate me.

For some time I had been concerned for my family's safety and had reported numerous disturbing threats. I had an arrangement with Queensland police that whenever I received suspicious-looking mail, I would grasp the envelope with a tissue or handkerchief and without opening it, place it in a plastic bag before contacting them so the letter could be sent away for forensic examination.

As my phone number wasn't listed, all hate mail was delivered to me via the USQ or to any one of the many Aboriginal organisations in Toowoomba listed in the white pages. Even so, it got to the stage that I became sensitive about where I stood when television journalists interviewed me at home. I made sure the front of my house and the number on my mailbox weren't in view.

Much of the mail had letterheads depicting images of white-hooded Ku Klux Klan figures and bearing the words 'White Pride, White Power'. One letter concluded with 'AND REMEMBER—DON'T SNIGGER NIGGER THE KLAN IS GETTING BIGGER' with an image of a Klansman holding a noose at the bottom of the page. Another read:

> STEVE HAGAN — YOU LOW LIFE 'NIGGER' MONGREL
> HOW DARE YOU ATTEMPT TO EXTORT MONEY FROM THE
> WHITE AUSTRALIAN TAXPAYERS OF THIS COMMUNITY.

the N word

WE WILL NEVER SUBMIT TO YOUR DEMANDS REGARDING
THE NIGGER BROWN STAND.
BE SILENT OR WE WILL PAY YOU A VISIT.
REGARDS—FROM THE BOYS IN THE HOOD
CC: TO THE MAYOR OF TOOWOOMBA —A COPY OF THIS
LETTER HAS BEEN SENT TO THAT TROUBLESOME 'COON'
STEVE HAGAN—KEEP IT IN MIND THAT WE ARE
ON YOUR SIDE.
BEST WISHES THE KKK

It was difficult to know whether these letters were from genuine operatives or the work of some weirdo sitting at home alone experimenting with a cut-and-paste operation on a computer. However, there were known KKK clusters in the region and I had to take the threats seriously.

Needless to say, the letters put me on edge and I tried desperately to keep them away from my family. That was not always possible as I was often away on business relating to Kullilli native title work, in most cases representing Dad who was unable to be there.

On one trip I rang home one evening and Rhonda informed me that I had some mail from the university. I asked her to open it, thinking it might be a result from one of my assignments and waited in eager anticipation for her to read it to me. After a long pause her distressed voice came over the telephone as she tried to describe the contents of the letter. Immediately I knew that it was more hate mail. I felt an intense migraine coming on and for a moment words escaped me as I stood alone in that public telephone booth in Eromanga in the far south-west of the State, oblivious to other people waiting to make their calls.

After Rhonda gained her composure I asked her to take the children with her to my sister's house as I didn't want her to be alone in such a distraught state. I felt useless being over 1200 kilometres away in that small opal-mining town. I wanted to get in the car and

the N word

drive back but I knew the night would come and go before I made it home to my family.

I left the booth and waited a long thirty minutes so the other people who were queued behind me could use the phone. By the time I got through to Rhonda at Pam's house she had settled the children down to watch television and was having a cup of tea. She had also contacted her brother in Brisbane who had commenced his 140 kilometre journey up to Toowoomba to stay for a few days until I returned home.

It was clear Rhonda wanted to have a frank conversation about the letter but I could sense she felt uncomfortable discussing it in front of her in-laws and the children. I said I was sorry she had to find out about the hate mail that way, told her I loved her and asked her to give the children a kiss from me.

I couldn't sleep that night and tried to watch television in my motel room but my thoughts kept drifting back to Rhonda and the kids. Gently I pulled their photograph out of my wallet and stared at it throughout the night, constantly cursing the cowardly men draped in white bed sheets. The most upsetting thing for me was that I had broken a promise with Rhonda. Early in our marriage we had agreed we would not keep secrets from each other. We promised that we would work through the difficult times by being upfront and honest with each other.

When I returned home a few days later I received, and deserved, a very cold reception from Rhonda. I told her about the letters I hadn't opened and about my discussions with Queensland police. From that day forward I kept no secrets from her although for some time we both found it difficult to sleep at night, worried that cars might pull up and place burning crosses on our lawn. This did not seem such a far-fetched notion given the bizarre and violent nature of the threats contained in the KKK hate mail. However, it was reassuring to know that local police were doing regular nightly patrols in our street and the neighbourhood as a result of the threats.

the N word

I had developed a good rapport with Det Sgt Steven Stewart who I reported to on matters relating to the KKK letters. I also had a good relationship with Police Inspector Gary Wells and Assistant Police Commissioner Alan Honor and would contact them if I needed to talk about issues of importance to the Indigenous community.

Since my clash the previous year with some members of the local Indigenous community, many others continued coming to me for assistance as they claimed they weren't getting much help from the funded Indigenous organisations. For instance, at the time of my complaint about the Athletic Oval back in June 1999, skinheads in the area were terrorising black people, including children. My brother Lawrence and our nephews had been confronted by these hoons at the Norville Hotel in Russell Street where they were playing pool and having a couple of drinks.

As these attacks became more regular and violent I decided to go public with the story. Unfortunately my political opponents at the ALS went public with statistics from the service and denied that these attacks took place. I believe they were misrepresenting the truth for their own political gain.

On 7 June 1999 the *Toowoomba Chronicle* had reported:

> Members of the local Aboriginal community are rejecting claims of a "muscle-bound group of men" targeting and bashing Aboriginal people.
> Toowoomba Aboriginal Legal Service (TALS) administrator Mr Sonny Martin said the comments by Mr Stephen Hagan last week in The Chronicle were misleading and could cause unrest in the community. Mr Martin said the TALS was perfectly positioned to deal with such problems but Mr Hagan had not consulted with them to help find a solution.

the N word

But while the representatives were justifying their position, in town the youth continued to raise their concerns with me. Some of these issues I brought to the attention of the media, others I took direct to the police.

Weeks after the reports in the local paper, one of the senior staff of the ALS approached me to report an incident. The same group of skinheads had accosted his daughter and her friends. He apologised for his colleagues' denials and asked if I could help. I told him to contact the police and provide them with a description of the offenders, whom I imagined fitted the profile supplied by me in my complaint to the *Toowoomba Chronicle*.

Another incident that became very public was the threat, found in a student's diary, to kill Aboriginal students at the ninth hour of the ninth day of the ninth month in 1999. Once again the Bowen Street clique said that I was only chasing publicity—until their sons, daughters, nephews and nieces confirmed that a real threat had indeed been made against black students.

On the day of the planned attack most Indigenous parents kept their children home as did several non-Indigenous parents. There was a big media presence at the school but fortunately the day came and went without incident. As the police raided the house of a boy and his friends and found questionable items of interest, the media built the story up as a copycat of the Columbine High School massacre that occurred in the United States earlier that year.

It wasn't until weeks later that the truth behind the harassment of Aboriginal students by this disturbed boy became clear. It was alleged that his father had arrived at the school weeks earlier and passed a baseball bat through the window of his car, telling his son to take care of the 'troublesome niggers'. The 'troublesome niggers' were my nephew and his friends.

I have no regrets about going public. If the threats had been carried out, I would not have been able to live with myself for suppressing the information that came to hand.

※

In the middle of 1999 I had stood for the ATSIC elections on the platform that the minority voice within the Aboriginal community had too much power over the Commonwealth funds allocated for our people.

I ran on a ticket with several people who unfortunately came under pressure from a number of influential people within ATSIC in our region. They were given the usual misinformation from the spin doctors who insisted they would have a better chance of success if they announced their departure from my team.

When the Australian Electoral Commission (AEC) announced the successful candidates in August, I was relieved that I had made the final twelve that would make up the ATSIC Regional Council for the Goolburri Region. I was also looking forward to the opportunity to go head to head against 'Sugar' Ray Robinson who would stand again as the incumbent for the position of Commissioner.

I sent out letters to most of the twenty-four candidates from the Goolburri Regional Council and the Rockhampton Regional Council who would be charged with electing the Commissioner to represent them at the national level for the next three years.

On the morning of the joint sitting of the regional councils in Hervey Bay in November that year, I met with a number of councillors who were interested in backing someone to stand against the incumbent. To my disappointment, Peter Savage from the Rockhampton Region also had his eye on the top job. As time was running out for nominations to be tabled, I informed the councillors who were in the room that we had no chance of beating Robinson if both Savage and I stood. Since it was obvious Peter wasn't going to surrender his nomination, I decided to stand down and consider my position in three years time.

There was an enormous amount of tension in the room as the nominations were put forward. The place was packed with ATSIC bureaucrats from Canberra and Brisbane who would have heard the rumours of an imminent challenge coming from me. I suspect they liked the idea of a new kid on the block up against the forceful, ex-boxing champion incumbent. When only two names were read out by the scrutineer I noticed the disappointment etched on the bureaucrats' faces. They'd been present three years earlier when Peter Savage ran against Robinson and received only a few votes.

When Robinson trounced Peter Savage again, I didn't get to test if those present at the early morning strategic planning session were simply spies for Robinson or if they were there to support my challenge. Either way, it didn't take long for the fireworks to begin as Robinson launched an unprovoked attack on me in front of all twenty-four councillors. He said I was making a fool of all Aboriginal people in the region by my public stances over the 'Nigger' Brown and Coon Cheese issues. (Several months after I lodged my complaint to the HREOC about the 'Nigger' Brown Stand I decided to do likewise with a grievance about Coon cheese. It had concerned me for some time that this brand of cheese was sold throughout Australia and Coon accepted as a legitimate trade name. I lodged a complaint against Dairy Farmers, the makers of the cheese, on the grounds that it was a racially offensive trade name.)

To the astonishment of the packed room I stood and directed my question at the chairman, asking for a point of clarification on the rule governing the use of inappropriate language. I told Robinson and Bertie Button, Chairman of the Goolburri Regional Council, that they did not intimidate or threaten me and that as I was going to be around for three years, they had better get used to my presence. I added that I thought Robinson should be ashamed of himself for swearing in front of our elders, some of whom were women.

You could have heard a pin drop. Concerned by the deterioration in the proceedings, the neutral chairman adjourned the meeting for lunch. I wasn't exactly being rushed with offers for lunch so I followed the crowd and headed for the public bar where the boys club were having a drink.

I decided I wasn't going to be intimidated and stood in line to place a bet at the TAB and watch the races on the monitor. After I made my point, I went back to the conference room where I talked to some of the bureaucrats. To my surprise they commented that they had never seen anyone take such a public stance against Robinson as I had. They wished me well and said they would keep a close eye on my progress.

On reflection, I am not sure if I actually did make any progress. As with all democracies, ATSIC was governed by the numbers game. I might have had the vision and know-how to tackle major enterprises within the Goolburri Region but I did not have the numbers. To put it bluntly I had a discreet fan club behind closed doors and over the telephone, but when it came to a show of hands in the meeting, the numbers were found wanting.

The biggest disappointment during my three-year term was the intensity of the attacks on me from Indigenous people. Some took the form of resolutions moved against me and in support of the retention of the E.S. 'Nigger' Brown sign at the Athletic Oval.

On one occasion in 2000 the Regional Council moved a resolution when I took a day off from the meeting to drive my mother to an appointment in Brisbane to have major eye surgery. When I was

the N word

contacted in Brisbane by the *Toowoomba Chronicle* about this I agreed to make a comment.

After being briefed on the wording of the resolution, I told the newspaper that I found it insensitive and accused the regional councillors of being cowards. They didn't have the guts, I added, to front me when I was in the meeting but instead waited for me to be absent in Brisbane before launching their attack.

A couple of months later in Warwick, at the June meeting, Chairman Button called an in-camera session and ordered all secretariat staff and non-councillors out of the room. When the door was closed the Chairman commenced his attack on me over the *Toowoomba Chronicle* article. He slapped his fist into the palm of his hand, looked me in the eye and said that he'd had enough of me and that the gloves were off. I responded by saying, 'I'm not exactly shaking in my shoes. Where do we go from here? It's your call.'

There was an embarrassing pause before the Chairman changed tack. He altered his tone a little and said it had been a dirty act involving my mother in the media story. He went on to say that they all had mothers, aunties and grannies and if I'd told them of my purpose for the trip to Brisbane they might have shown more lenience with their media release.

Another resolution at a meeting in 2002 resolved to send letters to the editor of several newspapers saying the Goolburri Regional Council did not support me in my legal actions regarding the 'Nigger' Brown Stand or the Coon Cheese issue. I had to excuse myself from the meeting as they discussed and voted on this resolution.

I had been elected to ATSIC to represent my constituents and argue on their behalf for an equitable share of the Goolburri Regional Council budget of $26 million. It wasn't my expectation that I would be belittled by other representatives simply because we held contrary views. As with my previous battles, when I started my Coon cheese campaign I never envisaged that so much time would be taken up fighting my own people in the media.

I thought back to an article I'd read in the *Toowoomba Chronicle* on 27 November 1999. Under an editorial entitled 'Forget the squabbling, says elder's son' the story read:

> Mr Michael McCarthy was speaking after Mr Stephen Hagan lodged a complaint with the Human Rights and Equal Opportunities Commission, alleging Coon cheese was offensive and should be renamed.
> In Thursday's Chronicle, Mr Hagan said many Toowoomba Aborigines did not support his fight to have Coon cheese renamed.
> He said: "I respect the Aboriginal people, but maybe the assimilation procedures of the Government have been effective. Maybe their intolerance of obscene names has been watered down."
> Mr McCarthy, son of Aboriginal elder Mr Walter McCarthy, said his family believed Mr Hagan's comments were a personal attack on their father.
> Mr McCarthy Snr told media this week he did not find the name Coon cheese offensive, and he has previously made it clear he does not share Mr Hagan's views on the "Nigger" Brown stand at Toowoomba's Athletic Oval.
> His son said yesterday: "The cost of having opinions which conflict with those of Mr Hagan is that our father has been painted by Mr Hagan as some sort of traitor to his Aboriginality."

I had lodged a complaint to the HREOC against Dairy Farmers, based in Lidcombe in New South Wales, on 23 November 1999. I requested the discontinuation of the brand name Coon, which I felt was racially offensive. It seemed a natural progression to engage the public in further debate over another use of inappropriate language—and 'coon' sat high on my list of racist words. However, I never in my wildest dreams imagined that this controversy too would spark such huge interest nationwide as well as internationally.

'Toowoomba man complains cheese brand racist' shouted the headlines for Leigh Jabs' story in the *Toowoomba Chronicle* on 25 November 1999. Australian Associated Press ran the story nationwide a day after I lodged the complaint when my once political ally, former State Premier Rob Borbidge, came out with both guns blazing:

> Opposition Leader Mr Rob Borbidge has labelled Toowoomba's Mr Stephen Hagan a professional agitator following the Aboriginal man's objection to cheese giant Coon.
> ... Mr Scott Watkins, Dairy Farmer's cheese division marketing manager, said the company was disappointed with Mr Hagan's comments but did not intend to change the brand name which was named after Dr Edward William Coon in the 1930s.
> Mr Borbidge yesterday said the complaint against Coon cheese was "an overdose of political correctness".
> "The time is fast approaching where, as a society, we've got to draw a line and we've got to say 'this is stupid, this is over the top, and there needs to be some sort of check and balances in the system'."

Six weeks later I received an anonymous letter that was postmarked from Shepparton, Victoria. Its contents confirmed what I'd always thought about the origins of Coon cheese:

> After reading Cheese Brand stays, I had a chuckle to myself as my mother's nickname was nigger or nig all her life. Didn't worry me when young but I think about it now.
> Can I offer a confidential method of proving the Coon situation as if I remember correctly from 1939 to 1946. I grew up alongside a cheese plant, which used to stencil a black coon monkey's man's head on the 10lb and 15lb loaves of rinded cheese before we dipped the cheese in hot clear paraffin wax. The black coons head later changed

to red stencil and later to I think just red coon letters. As a lad of 12 years old I used to help the workers and later became a cheesemaker. Now plan your attack. Through State Gov't Dairy Departments and Commonwealth Export Departments, seek out the trade marks for cheese as all butter and cheese wraps are still on record as old labels are coming back all the time.

The old man gave me other important historical data, but his final comments provided an especially enlightening perspective.

> I won't give my name or address but hope you can read my writing. Perhaps Dick Smith our Ozziemite man may be interested as P/M co. just registered his brand and upset him.
> Coon cheese is normal cheddar cheese and this matured fulltime 6-12 months.
> Dr Coon to me is all bullshit and was invented in USA to counteract, the coon monkey man image.
> But I can still visualise the Coons head in black as the cheese was stencilled before waxing.
> Hope I have thrown some light on the subject as I see and know it.
> Good luck Stephen.
> My advice is to keep this info confidential to yourself and start quietly perhaps at Qld and seek out any info from people in Quinalow and Kenilworth.
> Just another late thought.
> Kraft operated a small factory on Kind Island from 1939 to 1952 and the old building is still there and no doubt made coon 10lb loaves.

I was deeply moved by the letter and acted on his advice. The findings are quite disturbing and when the real story is known about the origins of the naming of this cheese and the inventor who lent his name to the patent, I expect many critics will be left speechless, including the former Premier of Queensland, Rob Borbidge.

the N word

Back on the broader Indigenous issues front I continued to be isolated from major policy decisions of the Goolburri Regional Council and instead focused most of my attention on my court cases. I made appeals to the NSW Land Council and other prominent national Aboriginal organisations for financial assistance with my legal forays but I always came up with a negative response.

When it came to my 'n word' battle, I was still on my lonesome, supported neither by the Attorney General's Department nor ATSIC. Civil liberties lawyers weren't interested in supporting me legally, and most major Indigenous bodies weren't prepared to endorse my stand or provide me with financial assistance. Fortunately I did have my family, legal representation and a growing number of individuals and groups who did give a damn about my stand.

Later that year, on 7 December 2000, Greens Senator Bob Brown raised the matter in the Federal Parliament. His motion in the Senate called for the removal by the Toowoomba Sports Ground Trust of the word 'nigger' from the E.S. 'Nigger' Brown Stand. Bob Brown's motion was supported by one Green and nine Democrat Senators, but was defeated, with all other parties voting against it. However it meant my campaign remained in the public eye and, despite the lack of support from elected representatives, there was increased public support from both Indigenous and non-Indigenous quarters.

I was moved to tears when I read a letter to the editor of the *Koori Mail* of 21 May 2003 that had been written by Linda McBride of Brisbane. Linda courageously resigned her membership of the ALP over Peter Beattie's handling of the 'Nigger' Brown case, so disappointed was she that he didn't show leadership on the issue. I was extremely grateful for such displays of support and hoped they might influence attitudes in the broader community.

the N word

Not long afterwards, my sister Pam stopped at the traffic lights in the centre of Toowoomba. She was alone in her car when a vehicle pulled up beside her. She was overcome by a strange sensation of fear, but couldn't help herself and glanced to her right. Two skinheads in their hotted-up old car were sneering at her. Then the one closest to her, without uttering a word, rolled up his sleeve to reveal a swastika tattoo on his arm. On another occasion, a group of Nazi aspirants drove past a small group of Aboriginal youths screaming obscenities, including the word 'nigger', before roaring off.

Once we were aware of such incidents, Rhonda and I agreed that it would be best, at least during the height of the controversy, for us to do our shopping when the supermarkets weren't so busy. I'd already had experiences when I was shoulder-charged in crowded shopping centres. On each occasion however, I had chosen not to make a scene or get into any physical altercations with the offenders. It wasn't hard to imagine the headlines—'Hagan charged with assault on innocent bystander at major shopping centre'.

Sometimes support came from completely unexpected quarters. On one occasion I stopped at the Stock Exchange Hotel on Anzac Avenue with my brother Lawrence and parked the car directly in front of the public bar. I wasn't aware until I walked into the pub that there was a large gathering of labourers, presumably from a nearby building site, having a few celebratory drinks. My brother arrived back at the car before me and was seated in the passenger side as I descended the pub stairs. As I was nearing the car Lawrence warned me to watch out as one of the construction workers was fast approaching me from the public bar.

Not quite knowing what to expect, I assumed a clenched fist. What occurred next took me totally by surprise. The construction worker put out his hands, offered me his congratulations on my stand against the racist sign and wished me well in my future campaign. I thanked him and drove off. What made this event stand out from

the N word

others was that the young man made his gesture in full view of his work mates, clearly not giving a damn about what they thought.

As the debates — 'nigger' and 'coon' — raged on, I started to grow in confidence. Where once it felt like it was all getting a little too difficult with so much hostility directed at me, the shows of support I was now receiving helped me feel more focused—and more determined. Whenever the media asked me how I was going, I would simply reply, 'I'm not the one trying to defend the indefensible.'

the N word

An Ernst Approach

With the date of my appeal to the Full Bench of the Federal Court approaching, this new confidence began to grow. Much of it stemmed from the fact that Ernst Willheim had agreed to take my case on. When I thanked my previous barrister, Dimetrios Eliades for his efforts, he'd agreed with Peter and me that we would need an experienced constitutional barrister if we were going to successfully appeal. Now we had one.

Specialising in constitutional law, international law and human rights, Ernst worked for the Commonwealth Attorney-General's Department from 1967 to 1998. He also worked closely with ATSIC and Aboriginal Affairs Minister Robert Tickner towards the end of the 1990s, appearing as counsel in numerous Aboriginal matters.

He had led numerous Australian delegations to international conferences and has appeared as counsel for a range of Australian Government clients in the High Court, Federal Court, Industrial Court, Family Court and State Courts of Appeal in constitutional and public law cases.

Following his retirement in 1998 Ernst was Visiting Fellow and Visiting Scholar in the Faculty of Law at ANU for three years. He is currently a Visitor in the Law Program at the Research School of Social Sciences at ANU and has published widely.

the N word

He has made submissions to parliamentary committees critical of government legislation on human rights and assisted with submissions to the United Nations challenging Australia's compliance with international human rights obligations, particularly in relation to the 1998 amendments to the Native Title Act.

In 2002 he was invited to Oxford to present a paper on Australia's response to the *Tampa* incident (the previous year the Norwegian ship, the MV *Tampa*, had rescued over four hundred asylum seekers from a sinking boat in waters between Indonesia and Australia).

Born in Sweden, Ernst came to Australia in 1948. His father had been a prisoner in Nazi concentration camps and had risked his life by interposing himself between SS guards and an elderly man who was being beaten because he was too weak to meet his work quota. Perhaps some of that concern for the underdog engendered Ernst's own personal commitment to human rights and social justice, as throughout his working life he has taken a keen interest in human rights issues.

※

Ernst was a welcome addition to our legal team. After weeks of consultations he and Peter finally sent me a copy of the application for appeal they had signed off. After reading it I knew for sure that Peter's task would be much easier the second time round thanks to Ernst's knowledge and experience in the area of constitutional law. I was convinced that we would have no trouble winning the appeal before the Full Bench of the Federal Court, and independent legal advice from solicitors in Toowoomba indicated that in terms of its language and argument, the document that Ernst had drafted could not be faulted.

There was still plenty of time before the appeal so I thought it would be useful for me to work more with my supporters.

Increasing numbers of them were becoming more vocal. Almost immediately after the decision in the 2000 hearing many people came out of the woodwork to make a public stand. Quite a few admitted to me that they hadn't acted earlier because they were convinced the Federal Court would order the offending word be removed. They'd been shocked and dismayed when Justice Drummond handed down his decision.

One of these newly emerged supporters was Dr Libby Connors, a lecturer in History at USQ. She felt guilty that she hadn't acted earlier and told me that she'd waited and waited for someone of stature to stand up, for leading whites to take a stand, at least against the persecution of me if not against the sign itself. But the only critical voice was that of the local community group, the Toowoomba Multicultural Association.

Libby Connors had become politicised in high school when a nun introduced her to social justice issues. She soon found herself in trouble with the headmistress for selling the poems of Indigenous author Maureen Watson to raise funds for land rights campaigns. These were the 'Joh' days when everyday politics were both humorous and heartbreaking and protest was to the fore.

In the 1980s she became involved in peace and anti-nuclear campaigns, which led directly to green politics. With her husband Drew Hutton she toured the state in 1991 to establish the Queensland Green Party, now part of the Australian Greens.

Libby felt it had now become impossible not to take a public stand on the issue. The local paper not only ran editorials attacking me personally but printed stories attacking my credibility and racist letters to the editor were published as if they were legitimate commentary. The notion that the city would change a sign because a black person objected was presented as absurd. Sometimes by implication, sometimes overtly, I was put forward as being too sensitive or as an uppity Aborigine who needed to be put in his place.

the N word

Libby's view was that I had become, metaphorically, a punching bag for anyone who wanted a chance to laugh at and ridicule an Indigenous activist. She bought into the issue in her professional capacity as an Australian historian. Here she was teaching students about the way in which colonialism had divided and ruled when in our own city local officials and the media were constructing images of 'good' blacks versus the nasty out-of-towner stirring up trouble.

Some wrote letters insisting that they found that there was nothing offensive in the name, that the name was part of their history, their heritage. There were opinion polls run as if it were a democratic right of the majority to decide what minority groups could or could not find offensive.

Although most proponents of retaining the 'Nigger' Brown name insist that they aren't racist, Libby Connors began to receive anonymous racist literature in the mail once she was publicly identified with the campaign. She also received abusive phone calls at work and for her it was an insight into what Rhonda and I had been going through. Having Senator Bob Brown raise the issue in the Senate lessened the sense of isolation and helped to restore our faith in the Australian people, she said.

During November 2000 Libby Connors and her supporters decided to organise a Walk for Practical Reconciliation. The publicity poster, circulated widely, had a question and answer format.

> Why should 'Nigger' be removed from the name of the E.S. Brown stand?
> 'Nigger' is a racist derogatory term. Today nowhere else in the world would allow it to be used in public signs because of its offensive meaning.

the N word

But isn't it just an amusing nickname for a football player?

E.S. Brown was a white footballer. Sportsmen often use derogatory names and terms among themselves. Brown's name was in use in the 1920s when Australians supported white supremacist views. The stand was nicknamed E.S. 'Nigger' Brown in 1962 when indigenous Australians were still not recognized as Australian citizens and were denied basic human rights that white Australians took for granted.

But isn't the stand just recognizing a great footballer?

The use of Brown's proper name for the stand would be a fitting tribute to him. Footballers still give one another derogatory names but they are not used publicly. By retaining the 'Nigger' nickname the sports ground trust is memorialising Australia's racist heritage and policies which Australians no longer agree with.

But don't sports people who use the ground say that they don't find it offensive?

A number of football and sporting codes have outlawed racist and offensive language on the field. If a player called another player a 'Nigger' they could suffer disciplinary action including fines up to $10,000. If it is offensive on the field it is even more offensive among supporters and spectators off field.

Didn't the courts say it wasn't racist?

Justice Drummond ruled that 'Nigger' was a racist term but that the complainant had not proved that a nickname was in breach of the Racial Discrimination Act. That does not mean that it is not offensive. A nickname that was offensive to women, the disabled or ethnic groups would not be tolerated on a public sign. The name is in bad taste and reflects badly on the city of Toowoomba.

What has the Toowoomba sports ground got to do with Reconciliation?

Earlier this year more than half-a-million Australians took to the public streets across the nation to support reconciliation. The reconciliation process must begin with a commitment to racially inclusive public spaces. That means removing or modifying historic signs which cause offence.

the N word

Impressed with Libby's enthusiasm and commitment, I asked how I could be of assistance, only to be told that everything would be taken care of. All she asked was that I attend. And attend I would. This was one march I was not going to miss, and with Rhonda's blessing nor would the rest of the family.

As the rally before the march got under way on 3 December 2000, I noticed many of my Indigenous adversaries from Bowen Street driving up and down the block, monitoring numbers, while others sat in their cars a safe distance away to listen to the speeches. Even Russ Brown, son of the legendary footballer E.S. Brown, made an unannounced visit to the rally to see for himself what all the fuss was about.

I stood to the left of the main assembly with my son Stephen holding our placards. I was genuinely moved when I saw the expressions of sadness and strength in the faces of both the black and white protesters and heard what the speakers had to say. I was especially impressed with my immediate family. None of them, with the exception of Dad, had been involved in a protest rally or procession before. Rhonda, Stephen Jnr and Jayde were strong and proud on that day and that in itself made it all worthwhile. Rhonda and I had agreed not to shield the kids from my campaign. The issue was frequently on the television and in the local papers and we felt the children had a right to know what was happening.

The next day's newspapers told the story in words and pictures. 'Nigger protest not just one man standing,' said the *Toowoomba Chronicle*. The story commented in part:

> A traditional Aboriginal smoking ceremony was held near the gates of the oval at a plaque bearing Edward Stanley (Nigger) Brown's name. ATSIC councillor Mr Stephen Hagan, who lost Federal Court action to have the Athletic Oval trust remove the word from a grandstand, did not speak at the ceremony and told The Chronicle the day was not in support of him personally.

The march was held in conjunction with interstate reconciliation marches.

"It's certainly more than (Toowoomba mayor and Toowoomba Sports Ground Trust member) Di Thorley has been saying – that there is only one man objecting," Mr Hagan said.

University of Southern Queensland history lecturer Dr Libby Connors, her partner Queensland Greens spokesperson Mr Drew Hutton, Aboriginal woman Jennifer Bonner and Toowoomba Multicultural Association member Mr David Curtis condemned the signs.

Mr Hutton said there was no ambiguity in the word nigger.

"White Australians use such terms to reinforce the idea that certain persons are inferior," Mr Hutton said.

"If they use the term in an affectionate way it was with E.S. Brown, it is because those people looked nothing like the people it is being used against. That's why we have names like Snowy, Lofty and Shorty – because it's the opposite of what those people look like."

Dr Connors said she did not disapprove if people who knew E.S. Brown used his nickname among themselves.

"But once that goes on a public sign it's a way of saying 'Not everyone is welcome in this sports ground. We know we're dominant and have the right to say who is welcome'," Dr Connors said.

Mr Curtis said there was only one use of the word nigger – to insult and offend.

"(Toowoomba Sports Ground Trust chairman) John McDonald as head of the Australian Rugby League should hang his head in shame when he pretends that the football code is serious in eliminating racial vilification in the sport," Mr Curtis said.

Ms Bonner said nigger was a "filthy, evil word." She said the name did not have to be used for a public figure.

"If his family want to use it that's their prerogative, but we are a proud race that have been degraded for too long," Ms Bonner said.

the N word

>Mr Hagan is appealing to the full bench of the Federal Court after Justice Doug Drummond's decision that the signs are not illegal in their context. Mr McDonald declined to comment on the march.

'Marchers take stand against court ruling,' ran the *Courier Mail* headline. Its coverage ran as follows:

> One of the speakers, a niece of the late Senator Neville Bonner, said two of her boys played for the Queensland schoolboys football team and she had been upset by the sign, "It affects us spiritually. It cuts into your heart," she said.
> Aboriginal activist Stephen Hagan, who began the fight against the sign, on Friday, lodged an appeal against the court decision.
> He said the smoking ceremony was to pre-empt the decision of the full bench of the Federal Court, which would decide the appeal.

the *N* word

Pinky's Cement Mixer

In the weeks that followed the march, a petition, asking people if they were offended by the word 'nigger' in the E.S. 'Nigger' Brown Stand, was signed by over 300 people from many walks of life as well as many Aboriginal people from Toowoomba and throughout the country.

Peter and Ernst submitted the petition along with the appeal documents knowing that the three Federal Court judges would read it. Technically the document could not be accepted as it wasn't tendered in the original trial. Nevertheless, we thought an application to include additional evidence was worth a try. Still fresh in my mind was the way Justice Drummond had spoken down to my barrister as if he was a mischievous child who forgot his homework.

On the day of the appeal the legal team met in Ernst's borrowed chambers at the Inns of Court. After an hour of refreshing the legal elements of my appeal we gathered our briefcases and walked to the court. By now everyone except Ernst anticipated the media scrum that would greet us as we walked towards Tank Street to enter the Commonwealth Law Court. As usual I expressed confidence in a positive outcome and praised my legal team for the good work they had put into the appeal.

the N word

Nearby were a large number of supporters, including Drew Hutton, President of the Queensland Greens who was holding up a huge banner. Inside the courtroom were more familiar faces—academics, social justice advocates and grassroots people, all wanting to lend their support and to witness the legal debate about to take place. I sat anxiously waiting for court proceedings to commence as my legal team made their final preparations with notes and law books laid out across their bench.

The Clerk of Court signalled the arrival of judges Ryan, Dowsett and Hely and the appeal of Stephen Hagan v Trustees of the Toowoomba Sports Ground Trust was underway. The Queensland judge on the bench, Justice Dowsett, made his intentions known from the outset, saying to the assembled journalists, 'I won't have this courtroom turned into a circus.'

The legal debate hadn't even commenced and already his attitude had set the tone. David Curtis and Dr Libby Connors were sitting a few rows behind me, shaking their heads in dismay. I glanced across at Ernst's wife Mary Louise and from her expression I could tell that she too felt we were off to a bad start. It was obvious that we were going to be in for a long day.

The judges from the southern states afforded Ernst ample time to present his case and thoroughly cross-examined him on the finer points of law. However, they got bogged down on whether the act was done because of the race, colour or national or ethnic origin. I felt we had not addressed this technicality to the judges' satisfaction. Certainly they had seemed to expand on that line of questioning as a way of saying 'you've got no chance of winning this one'. They hadn't given my senior counsel much flexibility and I could tell by Ernst's voice at the time that he wasn't making ground on winning the judges over.

After what appeared to be an eternity, the three judges rose and departed the courtroom. I walked out with my legal team feeling absolutely flabbergasted.

the N word

I did not look forward to walking out to the assembled media, most of whom had also sat through the legal debacle. But I figured they deserved to get my response first-hand. I told them that I wasn't very happy with proceedings before the Full Bench of the Federal Court and said that I would take the matter to the High Court if I did not succeed.

On 23 February 2001 the Federal Court ordered that the appeal be dismissed and the appellant pay the respondent's costs of the appeal, to be taxed in default of agreement. The argument concluded:

> This submission should not be accepted. The issue is not whether the appellation "Nigger" was originally applied because of considerations of colour, but whether the acts of the Trustees were done because of such considerations.[12]

I'd been distressed enough after the first court appearance but now, after reading the decision of the Full Bench of the Federal Court, I was rendered speechless. Peter, Ernst and I agreed we should make application to the High Court of Australia for special leave to appeal. As Ernst explained, it was not an automatic right for anyone to have his or her case heard before the Full Bench of the High Court.

That night I clicked on the Internet to read up on the background of the High Court judges to see if any of them had a background on social justice or human rights. I didn't know what good the information would do but I needed to know that there was a small chance of success. After all, Peter and Ernst were working for free.

The weeks flew by and my legal struggle continued to gain plenty of coverage in the national newspapers and gossip magazines. Most stories highlighted my first two failures and predicted much the same outcome for the next test. Meanwhile, I was clearly still a source

the N word

of annoyance to those people who wished I would just disappear, literally. Hate mail flowed—and the police could not shed any light on its sources.

❖

When the big day, 19 March 2002, arrived for the appeal, almost a year after the decision from the Full Bench of the Federal Court my legal team and I were once again mobbed by the media. Journalists from media outlets across the country lined up outside the Commonwealth Law Courts, not wanting to miss out on seeing the highest court in the land throw my case out for the final time.

There was an air of expectancy at the case going before the High Court. As we opened the doors we were shocked to see the court was also full of reporters.

After standing against the wall for fifteen minutes, waiting for another case to finish, I decided to go outside for some fresh air and return when our case was called. Five minutes later I saw the team handling the case before mine walk out of the courtroom. There was a lot of victorious backslapping going on.

I waited for someone to call me inside but after another couple of minutes I decided to make my own way to the courtroom to take my seat. To my shock the case had commenced. Ernst was on his feet presenting our argument. Embarrassed, I took my seat immediately behind my Senior Counsel. I'd barely been able to look around the room to acknowledge friends when Justice Mary Gaudron commenced her infamous comments about, of all things, pink cement trucks:

> GAUDRON J: But your argument comes to this, does it not? Any person of any colour – let us assume pink persons who are offended because of any material, including, for example, a pink truck,

the N word

> cement-mixer, they think you should not use the pink – and it is called "Pinky's Cement-Mixer" – would automatically make out a complaint.
>
> Mr WILLHEIM: It would still need to satisfy section 18C(1)(a) and that is an act that is reasonably likely to offend a group of people.
>
> GAUDRON J: Let us assume for the moment that I am pink, which is not a bad assumption, and I am offended and it is reasonably likely that I will be offended by a sign which says "Pinky's Porkies". Now, is that made out?
>
> Mr WILLHEIM: The first question, your Honour, is whether "reasonably likely" imports an objective standard. It is a community standard. That would be a fairly difficult hurdle in the case of pink ...[13]

I looked around the courtroom. Journalists were furiously taking down her words. So sure was Mary Gaudron of the outcome that she told the defence Queens Counsel, Patrick Keane, to resume his seat; she didn't feel it was necessary to hear from his side. Then Justice Gaudron appeared to be consulting her colleague, something I thought would be done outside the courtroom away from the glare of the gallery. Soon after, she announced their decision:

> GAUDRON J: Yes, thank you, Mr Willheim. We need not trouble you Mr Keane.
>
> We see no error in the approach of the Full Federal Court to the interpretation and application of sections 9, 18B and 18C(1)(b) of the Racial Discrimination Act (Cth). That being so, the question whether further evidence should have been admitted by the Federal Court, which is raised in the applicant's written submissions, is academic. So far as concerns the costs of the Federal Court proceedings, that was a matter within the discretion of the Full Federal Court and is not a matter which of itself would justify the grant of special leave to appeal.

Accordingly, special leave should be refused. We see no sufficient reason to depart from the usual practice with respect to costs in this Court. The order will be special leave is refused with costs.[14]

The court proceedings started at 1.57 pm and they were all over by 2.20 pm. I barely had time to take my seat when Justice Gaudron and Justice Hayne stood up to leave the court. It had taken the High Court of Australia's best legal brains just twenty-three minutes to make their ruling.

I walked out to the waiting media and told them how disappointed I was and that I would take the case to the United Nations. I was confident I would find at least one judge there who would understand how offensive the word 'nigger' is.

The views of most media were summed up in Steve Keating's editorial in the *Toowoomba Chronicle* of 21 March 2002:

> It's fair enough to take a stand, but time to end 'Nigger' drama.
>
> Enough is enough regarding the E.S. "Nigger" Brown stand issue.
>
> Like him, loathe him, agree or disagree with his stance, Stephen Hagan must be respected for the battle he has fought to have the sign removed from Toowoomba's rugby league headquarters, the Athletic Oval.
>
> In a democracy, individuals each have the right to speak their mind and fundamentally it's healthy for society, in the long run, to openly debate controversial issues.
>
> However, a majority of Australians respect the ethos of "accept the umpire's decision" after being given a fair hearing.
>
> Mr Hagan was afforded an opportunity before the highest court in the land – his bid was rejected and he should now let the matter rest.
>
> The drama has become a personal vendetta – Mr Hagan's comments after High Court Justice Mary Gaudron's decision were emotive, not rational.
>
> To pursue the matter further with the United Nations will be a fruitless campaign.

the N word

An obvious question can be posed in response to a comment by Mr Hagan after Tuesday's court ruling: "We will get that word taken down from that grandstand so that the next generation of aboriginal sportsmen don't have to run on to Athletic Oval and play under that sign 'Nigger'."

If Aboriginal league players were so distressed about the sign, why have they never boycotted games played on that field?

As an ATSIC councillor, Mr Hagan should now concentrate on that role and harness his considerable energies in tackling and resolving key issues that can make everyday life better for indigenous people.

The appeal was covered further in the same paper by Steve Gray under the headline 'Hagan facing big costs bill':

While Mr Hagan's solicitor and barrister appeared on a "no-win, no-fee" basis, court costs of the Toowoomba Sports Ground Trust were awarded against him.

"I don't like the idea of paying these people any money," he said.

... He said he would now pursue the case overseas.

"If I've got to find the last judge in the world, I will have that sign removed."

Mr Hagan said he had been besieged by radio interviewers in the 24 hours since Tuesday's High Court decision.

Radio hosts included Howard Sattler, Stan Zamanek, and former Victorian Premier Jeff Kennett, on whom Mr Hagan hung up mid-interview.

My last hope now rested with the United Nations. I hoped and prayed that the stress I put my family and supporters through would not be in vain. All I could do in the meantime was keep myself busy and spend time with my caring but anxious family.

the *N* word

United Nations

On 31 July 2002 my legal team sent a submission to the United Nations Committee on the Elimination of Racial Discrimination (CERD) in Geneva. It was an awkward time, not quite knowing the process except that this was the last recourse I had available. I had difficulty organising even enough money for a return bus fare to Brisbane and asked Ernst if we were required to travel to Geneva to address the panel of judges who would hear our case. I was relieved when he said I need not worry myself about it. All submissions were in writing and there was no provision for personal representations.

On 23 April 2003, a year after Justice Gaudron's infamous 'Pinky's Porkies' comments, I finally received the decision I'd waited four long years for:

> The Committee ... notes with satisfaction the resolution adopted at the Toowoomba public meeting of 29 July 1999 to the effect that, in the interest of reconciliation, racially derogatory or offensive terms will not be used or displayed in the future. At the same time, the Committee considers that the memory of a distinguished sportsperson may be honoured in ways other than by maintaining and displaying a public sign considered to be racially offensive. The Committee recommends that the State party take the necessary

the N word

measures to secure the removal of the offending term from the sign in question, and to inform the Committee of such action it takes in this respect.[15]

When I received the call from Peter Black on that sunny autumn day, I was driving to the Logan Campus of Griffith University in Brisbane from Toowoomba. I had only recently been engaged there as a Research Fellow, studying 'Acquired brain injury of Indigenous men caused as a result of motor vehicle accidents and/or substance abuse in rural Queensland'.

I had borrowed my mother-in-law's mobile phone and after five failed attempts at answering Pete's call by pressing the button on the left I decided to press the right. When I finally heard Peter's voice he asked if I was sitting down.

Pete often delivers bad news on my 'n word' legal forays so I thought for a couple of seconds and tried to imagine what else could possibly go wrong. I told him to fire away because nothing could possibly upset me after the last couple of years of failed legal attempts at justice.

'We won,' he said rapturously.

As I pulled to the side of the Logan Freeway on the outskirts of Brisbane I asked him to repeat the words.

'We won at the United Nations. We've had our win at last.'

Tears came streaming down my face as I tried to be as calm as possible. But I wasn't doing a good job of it. All those hurtful memories came flooding back. When I did manage to compose myself I sincerely thanked him. If I'd been with Peter at that precise moment I would have kissed him through pure elation. I was so glad he'd persevered with me. I couldn't thank him enough for his tireless work and dedication. Many others would have given up on the cause much earlier.

Seeing as I was only ten minutes from Griffith University I asked Peter if he could fax me the UN decision. As I approached the final toll gate I was so excited I almost told the tollkeeper to keep the change, but still low on finance, I put out my hand.

I literally skipped through the hallway to my office at the university and after collecting the fax, phoned the media to let them know of the historic decision. By now I had a list of journalists who I had developed some rapport with over the years. I knew these reporters wouldn't require any five-minute briefing to give them background on the topic. In fact they were the source that other journalists went to for information on the 'Hagan v the Toowoomba Sports Ground Trust' case.

I told them to contact Drakopoulos Black Solicitors for the copy of the eleven-page decision and to call me on my mobile telephone if they required an interview. I was already preparing myself for an influx of media converging on the campus.

Within the hour I had completed interviews with the ABC as well as television Channels 10 and 9. The administrator of the university came down to ask what all the fuss was about, and after being satisfied that I wasn't saying anything controversial about Griffith University, smiled and walked away—although in hindsight I realised I should have followed protocol and obtained permission.

After the *Courier Mail* photographer had completed his photo shoot for his paper, to the curious stares of the students on campus, I packed a copy of the UN decision into my briefcase and rushed back to Toowoomba to honour a commitment made to *The Australian* to have my photograph taken at the oval. By now I was starting to feel fatigued from all the interviews and the long drive back to Toowoomba and it was only adrenalin that got me through the shoot.

the N word

While the photographer was at work, I received a call from a *Toowoomba Chronicle* journalist asking if she could meet me at the oval after I had completed other engagements. I agreed, a little surprised she didn't want to come while I was there with the photographer from *The Australian*, especially since the light was quickly fading.

Just as dark clouds began to roll in late that afternoon the reporter and photographer from the *Toowoomba Chronicle* greeted me. Within seconds I noticed a familiar face at the front entrance to the oval. With hands outstretched I greeted Russ Brown, son of Edward Stanley. He congratulated me on my win and agreed to be photographed with me in front of the sign.

※

Next morning I was delighted to discover the story was on the front page of most newspapers around the country. But the story that mattered most was the one in the *Toowoomba Chronicle*. Under the headline 'New Sign Of Respect—Black and white meet on "Nigger" ruling', appeared an excellent article written by journalist, Nicola McDougall, a New Zealander with progressive views.

For the first time favourable articles about my stand started to appear. 'A good man, and a very bad word' ran the editorial in the *Weekend Australian* of 26–27 April. 'Colourful term past its prime' headed Terry Sweetman's 'Friday View' in the *Courier Mail* on 25 April. 'Only a niggard would take offence at a nickname' wrote Peter Wear in his article in the *Courier Mail* on 26 April. And perhaps best of all, '"Nigger" should go, say most' turned up in the *Toowoomba Chronicle* on 25 April after the paper had conducted a street poll.

There was also a cartoon by Leahy in the *Courier Mail* on 26 April depicting an Aboriginal fronting angry white people under a sign 'ER "White Honky" Jones Stand' with the caption 'It wasn't offensive

the N word

at the time'. There are two people in the background. 'Who's that sitting on the fence?' '... oh that's Peter Beattie.'

On 26 April Australian Associated Press (AAP) ran a story on their wires, which helped to explain the cartoon in the *Courier Mail*.

> The Queensland Government has been accused of hypocrisy over its handling of racist place names, in the wake of a United Nations committee's call for the removal of the word 'nigger' from the controversial ES 'Nigger' Brown stand at the Toowoomba Sports Ground, west of Brisbane.
>
> The Government came under fire for refusing to act on the controversial grandstand, after the UN committee, Queensland Ant-Discrimination Commission and Aborigines called for the removal of the 'Nigger' reference.
>
> Queensland Natural Resources Minister Stephen Robertson recently approved name changes to Nigger and North Nigger creeks near the north Queensland town of Herberton.
>
> The move followed a submission by the Girringun Aboriginal Corporation on behalf of the Jiddabul people, who claimed that the creek names were racially offensive.
>
> Herberton Shire Council objected to the change on the grounds the creek names referred to a 19th century mining industry term for debris cleared out of a hole after blasting.
>
> After receiving 21 submissions, 12 of which supported a name change, Mr Robertson found there was clear evidence and public support for a change on the basis the creek names were racist. The creeks have been renamed Wondecia and North Wondecia creeks.
>
> Aboriginal activist Stephen Hagan, who secured the UN recommendation over the Toowoomba grandstand name, said the approval of the creek names was 'total hypocrisy'.
>
> "I think it's great to know that the Government has made a decision (on the creek names)," Mr Hagan said.

"All I'm asking now is to be consistent with their legislation and take the sign down, pronto."

A week later Stephen Gordon, manager of the *Koori Mail*, rang and asked me to write 1000 words on my campaign. In addition to my comments, they ran a full-page article under the banner 'Grandstand name "insulting"'. The story carried a photograph of Rhonda, Stephen and Jayde and another photograph of Russ Brown and myself. A third page was allocated for comments in the letters to the editor section.

I was delighted. The *Koori Mail* is viewed as a must-read for Indigenous people across the country and such prominent coverage felt like an endorsement of my stand by my people. This was gratifying in light of the enormous amount of negative public criticism I had received over the years.

Unfortunately, not all media were supportive of my UN win. Alan Jones, one of the most prominent political commentator in Australia, watched by over a million viewers every morning on Channel Nine's *Today Show*, launched a scathing attack. On 24 April 2003 he made the following comments on his show:

> Well, can you believe this?
> It's hard to imagine anything more stupid than this, but there is a grandstand at the Toowoomba Athletic Oval in Toowoomba, Queensland.
> It's called the Nigger Brown Stand, with Nigger in inverted commas.
> It was built four decades ago, named after Edward Stanley "Nigger" Brown, a Queensland and Australian Rugby League centre who toured Great Britain with the 1921-22 Kangaroos, before becoming a major figure in the Darling Downs trucking industry and a very well regarded civic leader.
> Nigger Brown died in 1972.
> He was known all his life as Nigger Brown.

the N word

Well, some dunce who calls himself an Aboriginal activist has been petitioning the United Nations Committee on the Elimination of Racial Discrimination, thank you very much, to have the word "nigger" removed.

And, are you sitting down?

An 11-page judgment by this same outfit, most probably made up of freedom loving people from Cuba, the Middle East and the darkest and despotic parts of Africa, has said the term was offensive and insulting.

A bit like their 11-page report.

Mr. Brown's son has said in the past that he's staggered that they were trying to change the name of the stand.

And as Mr. Brown Junior says, there was never any racial connotation in his father's nickname.

He said he was given the nickname by the mate of one of his elder brothers because he had snowy blond hair and a fair complexion.

And he said when his father was President of the Toowoomba Rugby League he was first to help indigenous players.

And quite rightly, the son says he would rather see the whole name go than have the word "Nigger" dropped.

Now this Aboriginal activist has already lost actions in the Federal and High Courts to have the word "nigger" removed from the sign.

So he has trotted off to the United Nations, most probably with our money.

They have delivered their usual nonsense and now this bloke is asking Premier Beattie in Queensland to order the sign's removal.

There is something desperately wrong with society when we have to fall over ourselves almost at every turn to accommodate buzzwords like reconciliation.

Reconciliation involves a bit of give and take on both sides.

There is no reason whatsoever why the grandstand should be renamed.

the N word

It's the activist who needs to change his ways, not those who named the stand nearly 50 years ago.

Soon after the screening of Jones' comments I filed a complaint to the Anti-Discrimination Commission Queensland (ADCQ). I'd received literally hundreds of calls asking if I had seen the show and whether I was going to do anything about it. Although I received a response from the ADCQ saying the matter was being investigated and they would get back to me if they thought it met with their criteria, I have heard nothing since.

※

After the initial positive coverage from the media, television stations began conducting polls which produced a different slant. Most indicated a response of around eighty-five percent against the name change and fifteen percent in support. However, despite the polls and comments from the likes of Alan Jones, there were a lot of positives that came from the victory in Geneva.

Even more significant than the results of the polls was the fact that people across Australia were discussing the issue. It became very evident that the UN decision had ruffled a lot of feathers—especially among the conservatives but also at various levels of government around the country.

At long last too, published letters to the editor were starting to gain some balance with authors writing to criticise as well as support me. It got to the stage in Toowoomba where people were buying the *Toowoomba Chronicle* and going straight to the letters page to see if someone had countered a letter printed the day before. After the first three court cases there'd been many more letters to the editor attacking me and my supporters and suggesting I should abide by the umpire's decision. However, the handing down of the UN decision changed the environment completely. It enabled those sitting on the fence to come forward and voice their support for me.

Even so, many critics on the other side still ran the line that the Toowoomba Sports Ground Trust had the full support of the Aboriginal community. But within a week of the UN decision I received word that a prominent Aboriginal activist had come forward to say that he had attended the community meeting and had voted against the resolution.

A few days later he rang me at home and confirmed that he had a ten-minute argument with the mayor, Di Thorley, over the retention of the name. He also said that a number of people were so offended by the resolution they abstained from voting at the meeting and added he was very disappointed that the minutes did not accurately reflect the heated debate or the votes against and the number of those abstentions. He signed a statutory declaration to this effect.

I was excited about the news and delighted that this person had chosen to come forward. However, I was also a little disappointed that the information wasn't available to my legal team at the time of the first court case. I believe it would have impacted on the judge's decision even if it didn't change his opinion.

※

Whether I liked it or not, in the wake of the 'Nigger' Brown case I was viewed as a can-do man. People began to get in touch with me about a number of civil matters that affected either them personally or their family. I took up the challenge of being an advocate for a number of Indigenous as well as non-Indigenous people who had grievances and were unable to get pro bono legal support.

I'm not entirely sure why I threw myself into these cases and I guess Rhonda would be just as perplexed as anyone, if not more so, that I would even consider putting myself and the family through even more sleepless nights and further rounds of public vilification. But I guess I felt a strong conviction to assist others who were experiencing discrimination, and with input and assistance from Peter Black, several cases were successfully settled.

Not only did I have the satisfaction of helping others in legal and other matters, but I was pleased that in the meantime both Rhonda and I had managed to complete our studies. Rhonda was the first to graduate.

On 7 April 2001 she was awarded a Bachelor of Arts Degree in Journalism. Her graduation ceremony with family members and friends was truly a remarkable day for us all—but especially for Rhonda as this was her first degree. She looked radiant as she posed for photographs with fellow graduates, family and friends. That evening we celebrated into the early hours, such was our delight at seeing that official USQ award certifying the reward for the long, hard hours she'd put into her studies.

After Rhonda's graduation ceremony I made a private commitment to myself to knuckle down and tackle my studies with renewed vigour. I thought how wonderful it would be to walk the long line in a flowing black gown to be handed my award to cheers of a packed house on graduation day. After the many frustrating years of my campaign it was therefore with enormous relief that I woke up on the Monday morning following my graduation ceremony in 2002, to read the front-page article in the *Toowoomba Chronicle* of 16 April:

> New business Master says hard work has been a habit.
> For Stephen Hagan, achievement has always been accompanied by hard work.
> From his early days in fringe camp outside Cunnamulla, through high school to boarding at Marist Brother College, Ashgrove, to university, to the Department of Foreign Affairs in Canberra.
> Mr Hagan has always had to work hard, often against the odds, to reach his goals.

"Making the First XV at rugby mad Ashgrove made life a little easier for me," he smiled.

"I was never a smart student but I was very determined to prove people wrong by succeeding.'

On Saturday, Mr Hagan took his place alongside hundreds of other University of Southern Queensland students at a graduation ceremony at the Empire Theatre.

... Mr Hagan is not the only member of his family to achieve through study.

"My wife Rhonda graduated from the USQ last year with a Bachelor of Arts in Journalism," he said.

"In recent weeks my brother-in-law Dennis graduated from the University of Queensland with a PhD and my father Jim enrolled for the first time at the USQ at the age of 70, after leaving school in Grade 5."

Dad and Mum had both been there when I was awarded my Bachelor of Arts Degree in Further Education from the Canberra College of Advanced Education (now the University of Canberra) back in May 1986. Unfortunately Mum could not be with us on the day of my MBA award but my proud dad sat in a top-tier seat with Rhonda, Stephen, Jayde and other family members and supporters.

I remembered going out to dinner with my parents on the night of my graduation in Canberra and although there wasn't a lot of back-slapping, I could tell they were very proud that their eldest son had finally achieved a tertiary qualification. I'm sure Mum would have been smiling down on me from above on the day I received my postgraduate award, no doubt chuckling as she reflected how I struggled and almost ripped her dress when she tried to hand me over to my teacher in Cunnamulla on my first day at school.

I was proud too. Even throughout the worst moments of my journey when assignments and exams were due I would still put in the study hours, after I completed my household chores and the children had gone to bed. I would not allow my political adversaries to sabotage my goal of successfully finishing my studies.

With all my newfound success and joy, there was one unfinished assignment that was proving more cumbersome by the day—the enforcement of the UN resolution to remove the E.S. 'Nigger' Brown Stand sign from the Athletic Oval grandstand. I thought a new controversy—over identical wording—would help to speed up a positive resolution.

The issue that put the whole public debate into perspective and into the public eye once again was a personal vendetta waged by a local resident about the dismissal by Council of his plans for extensions on his house in Godsall Street, no further than 200 metres from the E.S. 'Nigger' Brown Stand sign. The owner of the property in question, had written in bold, one-metre lettering THE NIGGER BROWN STAND on the front of his house on busy Godsall Street, adjacent to Queens Park.

In her article 'Move to block out "pig house"', the *Toowoomba Chronicle* journalist Sarah Vogler wrote on Thursday 22 May 2003:

> In an act of "desperation" yesterday, deputy Mayor Cr Peter Wood proposed council erect a barrier fence around the house to block it from the view of neighbours and passing motorists.
> The house is also believed to have sparked a rethink of the Carnival of flowers parade route.
> "Would it be possible to erect a screen along the footpath so offensive wording is screened from the public's gaze?" Cr Wood asked council officers during a Planning Committee meeting yesterday.
> "Council considers signage at the property to be grossly offensive and illegal."

the N word

> "This (the Nigger Brown sign) is of course, according to council, not an offensive name in Toowoomba and a name that I believe reflects the 'culture' prevalent in Toowoomba," Mr Hendicott (owner) said. Several councillors at the committee meeting agreed the offensive signs and slogans on and around the house had angered residents and visitors about what was otherwise a "beautiful street".

I received many calls from friends who thought that I should cash in on the campaign Hendicott was waging with the Toowoomba City Council. But although the thought did cross my mind I chose not to engage. The slinging match was receiving ample media coverage and ridicule without my help.

As the weeks passed the story developed into a bit of a soap opera, very much the same as my case had. It was good to sit back and laugh at the absurdity of the whole debate. But if I thought it was going to help bring about a softening of the Mayor's position on the 'Nigger' Brown Stand I was sadly mistaken. As far as Mayor Di Thorley was concerned there was absolutely no similarity between the E.S. 'Nigger' Brown sign written on the house of a private resident and the sign boldly illuminated on the grandstand at the Athletic Oval.

the N word

Self Belief

The morning of Monday 21 July 2003 ushered in a vital day in my life. A District Court judge was finally going to sit in judgment on my application over an unfair dismissal charge against my former employer, the Toowoomba Aboriginal Corporation for CDEP.

My old employers had convinced themselves—and everyone else who cared to listen—that I was a crook who, in addition to not adequately performing my job, had swindled thousands of dollars from them and deserved to be sacked. Now they were about to have their accusations tested in a court of law.

The day didn't start well for their legal team and the District Court judge was looking perplexed as no clear evidence to warrant the sacking was coming forward in their introductory briefs. Still, several impressively large boxes of official documents continued to be wheeled into the courtroom by junior lawyers, as a way of letting the judge know how well researched their case had been. Finally the judge remarked to the defence barrister, 'You've been scratching around for several hours and I'm still to hear anything of substance to warrant this case coming before me.'

About mid-afternoon, the case was adjourned, before time, and my legal team, barrister Michael Jarrett and solicitor Peter Black, said

the N word

they detected signs of a chink in the defence's armour. They thought the case wouldn't run the scheduled four days.

I arrived early the next morning to be told that the CDEP defence barrister had asked for a delay in the court proceedings to allow for an out-of-court settlement to be considered. Two hours later the case was settled, on our terms, without me contributing a single word in the witness box.

※

Just when I thought I would receive my compensation for being out of pocket for the breach of contract, I got another rude awakening. The date for the payment of the terms of the settlement came and went without a single dollar exchanging hands. I contacted Peter again to issue a writ for the case to be heard in the District Court.

As the matter wasn't concluded in court I had to go back before a judge to get his ruling. The whole process sounded complicated and messy but I was determined this time to see out the four-day trial and have a judge rule on the level of compensation I should receive.

With a day to run before we were due in court I answered a knock on my door and standing before me were two CDEP directors. They politely asked if they could have a talk with me. They showed me the figures so I knew what financial predicament the CDEP was in. They made it very clear that a payment of the size agreed on as the out-of-court settlement would force the CDEP into insolvent trading. I told them I would seek Peter's advice and be in touch.

I immediately rang Peter and after a short conversation we agreed to a new settlement to avoid the situation of having won the court case but gaining no financial compensation. It was always our biggest legal concern that the CDEP would be bankrupted by the suspect management practices of its senior staff and directors.

the N word

A fortnight after Peter received the final payment from the CDEP, the ATSIC Regional Manager in Roma suspended the board of directors and the operation was handed over to the Murrumba Housing Company in Dalby to administer. I felt sorry for the people of Toowoomba and especially the workers, most of whom had enjoyed working under my leadership. I had a business plan and strategies in place that I believed would have made it one of the most productive and respected CDEPs in the nation.

Unfortunately that was not to be and the consequence of three years of poor management resulted in the loss of a multi-million dollar project from Toowoomba to another community.

During my long wait for the CDEP court case I had to endure tortuous months of not earning any income to supplement Rhonda's wage. I was back where I was when I left Cairns for a better life in Toowoomba—broke. The payment of many bills, including school fees, was negotiated, and then renegotiated as a result of failed promises from potential employers.

With diminished employment opportunities in a regional town with a little over 100,000 residents, I was forced to work for eleven dollars an hour for a local agricultural company. Using a measuring stick, my job was to pull uneven corn plants from literally thousands of rows of the crop. I also accepted work on the night shift at the local pork abattoir doing industrial cleaning and packaging smallgoods for the domestic market and international export for eighteen dollars an hour.

As I worked those long hours I conjectured what the future held for an Aboriginal activist in an ultra-conservative town. Many co-workers, black and white, in those jobs recognised me from the media and I could sense they were a little uncomfortable working

the N word

with me. I'm not sure if this was because they were uneasy on account of my profile in the media or because they thought I was a stirrer who they had ridiculed over dinner during the height of my campaign.

In spite of the antagonism from so many Indigenous people during my long battle for social justice there was always support to keep me going. Apart from my family, friends and Indigenous colleagues, I also enjoyed sharing the journey with many non-Indigenous supporters. These special people brought to my struggle a range of skills and life experiences that assisted me immensely. Without their tireless and voluntary contributions I would still be on first base; without their help I would not have managed to succeed in my case before the UN. People of the calibre of David Curtis, Peter Black, Ernst Willheim and Dr Libby Connors all played a significant role in my victory. They never once wavered under the avalanche of public condemnation and were the untold reasons for the success of my astonishing campaign.

These days, many of my friends stop me on the street and ask about the status of the UN resolution directing the state—Australia—to remove the offending word. The answer is simple. I have won the legal battle at the highest court in the world, the United Nations, but still the sign remains unaltered.

It was a sad day for Rhonda and me when we had to sit down with Stephen and explain to him why he couldn't join his friends from school in a rugby league game at the oval. He told me the school would be short of players but he understood why the decision was made and would respect our position. Jayde sat in on the meeting and she also understood the predicament as much as any young child could under the circumstances.

the N word

Stephen sat beside the computer while I typed a letter to the school principal explaining our objection to our son's attendance at the Toowoomba Athletic Oval.

> ...I refer to a letter received from our son Stephen (Grade 6) to participate in the Foundation Cup commencing 13th May 2003.
> As you would be aware I have been actively campaigning against the E.S. 'Nigger' Brown Stand sign at the Athletic Oval for the past four years.
> My campaign has resulted in the matter being heard in the Federal Court and High Court of Australia and recently the United Nations in Geneva.
> As the sign, containing the offensive word, has not been removed it is my request that Stephen and Jayde (Grade 3) not participate in activities at the Athletic Oval or enter the ground as spectators.
> Please contact me at the above address if you wish to discuss the matter further...

I had tears in my eyes when I typed that letter and decided to make one final attempt at getting the offending sign removed. I would write to the man who I knew could issue an executive order to the Toowoomba Sports Ground Trust to have the sign taken down immediately—the Premier of Queensland, Peter Beattie, Member for Brisbane Central.

'Dear Premier Beattie' I began, then wrote the following first paragraph of what turned out to be quite a long letter:

> In the spirit of reconciliation I write to you requesting that you use your power to direct the Toowoomba Sports Ground Trust to remove the offending word 'Nigger' from the E.S. 'Nigger' Brown Stand emblazon on the public sign at the Athletic Oval in Toowoomba.

On 12 August 2003 I received a letter from the Premier's chief of staff, Rob Whiddon in which he stated that although the Premier believed

the N word

it would be inappropriate for the word 'nigger' to used today in the naming of a public building, in the E.S. "Nigger" Brown instance it had been used in a different era. He also stated that the use of the nickname was never intended to be racially motivated or intended as a racial slur.

I was so frustrated with the buck-passing that I decided to test the powers of the Anti Discrimination Commission Queensland office by complaining about the Premier:

> I wish to lodge a complaint against Peter Beattie, Queensland Premier, on the ground that he has racially discriminated against me by his refusal to direct the Toowoomba Sports Ground Trust to abide by the United Nations recommendation to remove the offending word 'Nigger' from the E.S. 'Nigger' Brown Stand at the Athletic Oval in Toowoomba.

The following Sunday, 17 August 2003, I read an article in the Sunday Mail by political editor Darrell Giles under the headlines: '"Beattie racist" charge'. Giles addressed issues raised in my letter to the Premier and in the closing paragraph quoted Beattie saying that Brown was a football legend from years ago and it was now time to move on.

※

On 5 February 2004 I received an official response to the UN decision from the Australian Government. The letter came from the Attorney-General's Department, Office of International Law, and stated that having regard to the context in which the word was used on the sign and after carefully considering the view of the UN Committee, which did not find any violation of the Convention, the Australian Government did not propose to remove the 'term in question' from the sign.

the N word

It was almost impossible to believe that the Australian Government would not abide by the direction of the UN but instead came up with some fancy legal talk and postulation on the fact that no breach was found. I immediately contacted Peter and Ernst to ask their responses. Unfortunately they doubted the government would shift from its position. Ernst added that the only hope I had was to have the Australian government's decision tested by the biggest court of all—the court of world opinion.

The Federal and High Court judges, as well as State and Federal government ministers and officials, had formed their judgment on my case based on the so-called 'community meeting' that allegedly voted to retain the word 'nigger' on the offending sign at the Athletic Oval Stand.

What remains of those organisations run by the majority of participants at that meeting in Bowen Street who reacted so strongly to my call for public accountability and transparency? The legal service, the child care agency, the housing company and the land council, all recipients of millions of dollars of taxpayers' money, have been closed, placed under administration or issued with notice to show cause why they shouldn't be shut down by the government. Today no Indigenous organisation operates out of Bowen Street.

※

As I prepared dinner one night I heard the doorbell ring and asked Jayde to look through the curtain to see who it was. (Rhonda and I have strict rules about the children opening doors since the mail threats from the KKK.) After peering through the curtain Jayde returned to the kitchen to inform me that it was a large white man in a white shirt. As I went to open the door I saw a car drive away.

Two hours later the doorbell rang again and this time I went to answer the door. Standing before me was the same man Jayde had

the N word

described earlier. I asked the gentleman what I could do for him and as soon as he handed me the open letter I knew I was being issued with a summons. And I knew what it was for. Strangely enough, the issuing officer said he had watched with interest my case unfold over the years and apologised for the fact he had the unenviable job of serving me with the papers. He wished me well and told me to keep up the good work. I thanked him for his comments.

By this time Rhonda had come to the front door to see who I was talking to. I informed her that I had just been served with a summons over the 'Nigger' Brown court costs and went into my room to read the fine print.

I read the instructions at the bottom of the summons and knew that there was no way of avoiding the court appearance. 'If you fail to attend a warrant may be issued to arrest you and have you brought before court. You may be liable to a penalty for being in contempt of Court.'

As I prepared myself to comply with the summons, it dawned on me that this process could ultimately render me bankrupt. In effect, I wouldn't be able to be a director of a company or enjoy the other benefits of being a private citizen in control of his or her finances. To think at the very beginning of my campaign I thought the most it would cost would be the price of a forty-five cent stamp to post my complaint to the Human Rights and Equal Opportunity Commission.

Conclusion

Would I have gone down the same path again if I knew the campaign would be so costly? Would I have continued if I had foreseen the great emotional rollercoaster ride that it would become for myself and my family?

I would—and I believe my father and his father before him would have done the same thing. Essentially, this long journey I've been on came about because of my inherited genes.

I still talk daily to Dad about the family and the state of the nation. He likes to keep his mind active and now in his seventies is studying at USQ. He enjoys trips away as Chairman of our Kullilli Native Title group, debating customary law and boundaries, mineral exploration and so on with our people, the government and mining corporations wishing to pursue interests on Kullilli land.

Dad also takes great pride in his elected role as Chairman of the Toowoomba Indigenous Elders Committee and likes to encourage young people, black and white, to gain an appreciation of the history of European and traditional owners' contact in their communities.

Other local Indigenous people are attempting to form another elders' group. Nonetheless it saddens me that, unlike Dad's group where members must be sixty-five years of age or older to qualify, this new group wants to lower the age for elders to forty-five years.

the N word

Dad likes to keep active by walking every morning and playing lawn bowls. He is one of only four Aboriginals in a club with many hundreds of members. His rise to the position of President of the largest bowling club in town, the Toowoomba West Bowls Club in Taylor Street is testimony to his standing in the community and the respect in which he is held by the club's predominantly white membership. It is to his great credit that he was elected unopposed when, as a young man, he wouldn't have made it past the front door of the Cunnamulla Bowling Club.

I still miss my mother deeply even though she passed away several years ago after a spirited fight against a heart condition. Mum held our family together, especially nurturing us children when Dad was away working on stations and later when meeting his commitments with the NAC. The last message I received from her was through Dad on the day before she passed on. 'Tell Stephen not to ring the hospital to put pressure on the doctors about my operation.'

I took comfort in knowing that Mum knew I wouldn't throw in the towel for her. However she went through so much pain towards the end that I realised she wanted to go on her terms. Still, she went to her grave with a broken heart knowing that her eldest son spent time in jail. I would like to think that she also gained strength in the knowledge that I was a fighter and that her entire family stood together throughout our ordeals.

On one front, it feels like the struggles go on. Nevertheless I will not give up on the promise I made to my family to have the 'n word' removed from the E.S. 'Nigger' Brown stand. I still have that vision of my children playing on the oval, free in the knowledge that they will not have to confront a relic of a racist past.

On the occasions I find my spirits flagging, I think of the fighting spirit of my great-grandmother Trella and her son Albert and the inspirational words of his son, my father Jim, 'A winner is not a quitter and a quitter is not a winner.'

the N word

Acknowledgements

Many of the photographs that appear in the photo section are from the private collection of the author. However, kind permission to reproduce has been received for the following :

p.2	photo 4:	Marist College Ashgrove, Ashgrove
p.3	photos 3&4:	Moral Re-Armament Group, Melbourne
p.6	photo 2:	*Courier Mail*, Queensland Newspapers
p.7	image 1:	Sean Leahy
p.7	photo 1:	Toowoomba Newspapers
p.8	photo 1:	Scott Fletcher, Toowoomba Newspapers

Thanks also to Alan Jones, Frank Manthey, Narelle Renn and staff of the University of Queensland Press, Australian Associated Press, the *Courier Mail*, the *Toowoomba Chronicle*, the *Sunday Mail*, Queensland Newspapers and Marist College Ashgrove for their assistance and permission to reproduce text.

Language Words

The Kullilli language words that appear in the text have been spelt phonetically.

the N word

Abbreviations

ABC	Australian Broadcasting Commission
ADC	Aboriginal Development Commission
ADCQ	Anti-Discrimination Commission Queensland
AEC	Australian Electoral Commission
AECG	Aboriginal Education Consultative Group
AEDP	Aboriginal Employment Development Programme
AIF	Australian Imperial Forces
ALP	Australian Labor Party
ALS	Aboriginal Legal Service
ANU	Australian National University
ATSIC	Aboriginal and Torres Strait Islander Commission
ATSIS	Aboriginal and Torres Strait Islander Services
AWU	Australian Worker's Union
CDEP	Community Development Employment Programme
CERD	Committee on the Elimination of Racial Discrimination
CJC	Criminal Justice Commission
DAA	Department of Aboriginal Affairs
DEET	Department of Employment, Education and Training
FAIRA	Foundation for Aboriginal and Islander Research Action
HREOC	Human Rights and Equal Opportunity Commission
MRA	Moral Re-Armament
NACC	National Aboriginal Consultative Committee
NAC	National Aboriginal Conference
NAIDOC	National Aboriginal and Islander Day of Observance Committee
PM&C	Prime Minister and Cabinet
RSL	Returned Servicemen's League
STF	State Tripartite Forum
TAFE	Technical and Further Education
TSI	Torres Strait Islander
QATSILSS	Queensland Aboriginal & Torres Strait Islander Legal Service Secretariat
USQ	University of Southern Queensland
UN	United Nations
WTC	Woden Town Club

the N word

References

1. McMahon, Thos J, 'A Flourishing Pastoral Town', *Brisbane Courier*, Brisbane, 5 January 1924.
2. Johnston W Ross, *A Documentary History of Queensland*, University of Queensland Press, Brisbane, pp.138-39, 1988.
3. ibid. pp.69-71.
4. ibid. p.160.
5. Renn, Narelle, *Anything's Possible! The Bilby Fence and Beyond*, Save the Bilby Fund, Brisbane, pp.68-69, 2003.
6. *National Aboriginal Conference Newsletter*, 1;3, NAC, Woden, p.37, 1981.
7. *Blue & Gold*, Magazine of Marist College, Ashgrove, 1977.
8. ibid.
9. Matthews, Gordon, *An Australian Son*, William Heinemann Australia, Melbourne, 1996.
10. R v Hagan [1996] QCA No. 447.
11. Hagan v Trustees of the Toowoomba Sporting Ground [2000] FCA 1615.
12. Hagan v Trustees of the Toowoomba Sports Ground Trust FCA [2001] 123.
13. Hagan v Trustees of the Toowoomba Sports Ground Trust B17/2001 (High Court of Australia transcript, 19 March 2002).
14. ibid.
15. Communication No. 26/2002 : Australia. 14/04/2003. Committee on the Elimination of Racial Discrimination, Sixty-second session, 3–21 March 2003.

Bibliography

Horton, David Dr, *The Encyclopaedia of Aboriginal Australia*, Australian Institute of Aboriginal and Torres Strait Islander Studies, Canberra, 1994.

Johnston W Ross, *A Documentary History of Queensland*, University of Queensland Press, Brisbane, 1988.

McKellar, H, *Matya Mundu*, Cunnamulla Australian Native Welfare Association, Cunnamulla, 1984.

May, Dawn, *Aboriginal Labour and the Cattle Industry*, Cambridge University Press, Melbourne, 1994.

Reynolds, Henry, *Frontier*, Allen & Unwin, 1987.

Roberts, Janine, *From Massacres to Mining*, War on Want, London, 1978.